JIMMY CARTER ON PROPOSITION 13:

"...has sent a shock wave through the consciousness of every public servant."

TIME MAGAZINE ON PROPOSITION 13:

"One of the most important political and sociological events of the year...transforming Jarvis into a national symbol of middle-class Americans' mounting anger."

HOWARD JARVIS ON PROPOSITION 13:

"In plain English, what we were trying to accomplish was to put a fence between the hogs and the swill bucket."

I'M MAD AS HELL

The story of the great American tax revolt

HOWARD JARVIS

with ROBERT PACK

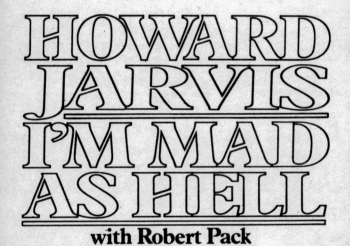

HOWARD JARVIS
I'M MAD AS HELL

with Robert Pack

BERKLEY BOOKS, NEW YORK

This Berkley book contains the complete
text of the original hardcover edition.
It has been completely reset in a type face
designed for easy reading, and was printed
from new film.

I'M MAD AS HELL

A Berkley Book / published by arrangement with
Times Books

PRINTING HISTORY
Times Books edition / October 1979
Berkley edition / July 1980

ISBN: 0-425-04705-9

A BERKLEY BOOK ® TM 757,375
Berkley Books are published by Berkley Publishing Corporation,
200 Madison Avenue, New York, New York 10016.
PRINTED IN THE UNITED STATES OF AMERICA

ACKNOWLEDGMENTS

We cannot begin to name all of the people who helped us produce this book. However, there are a few whose extraordinary contributions cannot go unmentioned.

First, no one played as important a role as Mel Berger, our agent at the William Morris Agency, who conceived this book; sold it to all of the parties involved, including us; and shepherded it from start to finish.

In addition, we want to express our utmost gratitude to Joe Micciche, the publicist for the Proposition 13 campaign, who had the presence of mind to subscribe to and retain the products of a clipping service during the hectic months before the election. The files he provided were invaluable.

Finally, in spite of past differences between one of the authors of this book and those who set the editorial policies of the *Los Angeles Times*, Mark Murphy, the paper's metropolitan editor, and Ken Hayes, the librarian of the *Times*, showed real class by granting us access to their files. Glenn Potter of the *Times* library also assisted us. Our thanks to all of them and everyone else who helped us.

Los Angeles   May, 1979

Howard Jarvis,
Robert Pack

This book is dedicated to the two lovely ladies with whom I live: Estelle, my wife, and her sister, Dolores Tuttle. And to the thousands and thousands of other people who labored during the sixteen years we turned the elusive dream of tax reduction into the reality of Proposition 13.

CONTENTS

★★★★★★★★★★★★★★★★★★★★★★★★★★★★★★★★

Can America Be Saved?
Yes—And Here's How

All of us are concerned about the budget levels, about unnecessary spending, about more efficient operation of government and about lower taxation.

> —President Jimmy Carter
> at a press conference soon after
> Proposition 13 passed

I think there are lessons to be learned from Proposition 13. I think the passage of Proposition 13 has sent a shock wave through the consciousness of every public servant—presidents, governors, mayors, state legislators, members of Congress. . . . I do believe that Proposition 13 is an accurate expression of, first of all, the distrust of government. I'd like to restore that trust.

> —President Jimmy Carter
> in a July 28, 1978 interview
> with editors and broadcast news
> directors at the White House

ABOUT 12 YEARS AGO, at the time I was becoming totally absorbed in the fight to reduce taxes, I saw a middle-aged woman drop dead at the Los Angeles County Hall of Administration in the very act of pleading about the prohibitive level of the property taxes on her home. She was a woman I had come to know during the tax movement. I had been over at her house in the San Fernando Valley to talk to her about her tax problems. By then I had been involved in the crusade against taxes for nearly five years, and I was already fired up. You can bet that seeing this lady die suddenly fired me up even more. That event was the inspiration for a slogan I used to sum up the situation for my audiences during the campaign for Proposition 13 in 1978: "Death and taxes may be inevitable, but being taxed to death is not!"

As many people are aware, "I'm mad as hell" was a phrase coined by the television anchorman played by Peter Finch in the movie *Network* several years ago. The character played by Finch was as angry with the problems he saw as those of us in the tax fight were with property taxes, and he urged his followers to yell, "I'm mad as hell, and I'm not going to take it anymore."

For me, the words "I'm mad as hell" are more than a national saying, more than the title of this book; they express exactly how I feel and exactly how I felt about the woman who died at the County building, as well as countless other victims of exorbitant taxes. I can tell you, there have been thousands of people who've had heart attacks—some fatal—or suffered severe emotional distress as they saw their lives drastically worsened by intolerable, unproductive, and unfair taxes made all the worse by inflation and an energy crisis that the politicians and bureaucrats have not been willing to face up to.

Since Proposition 13 passed on June 6, 1978, many people have told me that I must be a master of timing, that I had this tax-reduction thing ready just when people wanted it. I have to laugh at that. Actually, I started working on this campaign to reduce taxes in California in 1962. In fact, I've been a life-long activist for lowering taxes. Way back in 1932, when I was a young newspaper publisher in Utah, where I originally came from, Governor George H. Dern, knowing of my concern about high taxes, appointed me as a member of the State Tax Commission and as a delegate to the tenth annual conference of the Western States

Taxpayers' Association, which met in Colorado Springs. My basic feeling hasn't changed a bit over all those years: money is much better off in the hands of the average citizen than it is in the greedy hands of those who live off the public payroll. Dern knew how I felt because I ran many stories and editorials about the problems caused by excessive taxation in the chain of newspapers I owned.

I was on the State Tax Commission for about five years. There were five members, and we must have had about fifty meetings while I was on it. Among our significant actions were:

—We helped create a Public Utilities Commission, which ordered lower power and light rates in the state.

—We overhauled the State Highway Commission so that it had fewer employees on the public payroll, but worked efficiently.

—We increased the tax for extracting copper on the mining companies operating in the state, thereby reducing taxes for the average taxpayer.

When I served as a delegate to the Western States Taxpayers' Association meeting in 1932, I exchanged ideas on cutting taxes with other delegates from about ten states. After that convention, each of us returned home with better ideas for lowering taxes in our own states. This experience may well have planted the seed that later grew into Proposition 13. Of course, I had no way of knowing then that nearly a half century later I would lead the campaign.

In 1935 I sold my newspapers in Utah and moved to California, where I was involved in a number of manufacturing firms until 1962. Meanwhile, starting in Utah in the mid-1920s and continuing after I relocated in Los Angeles, I was active in politics for almost forty years. In 1962, when I was nearly sixty, I decided to retire from both business and politics and enjoy what remaining years I had left.

It was at that point that I was invited to my first meeting on taxes. The meeting took place at a neighbor's home in Los Angeles, with about twenty ordinary people who were concerned about how fast property taxes were rising in California. Ever since World War II, land prices have been booming in California, particularly in the Los Angeles, Orange County and San Diego areas. The land boom had resulted in spiraling assessed valuations placed on land creating the monumental increases in property taxes, which the politicians were unwilling or unable to do anything about before Proposition 13.

Although I have been financially independent for half a century and I never had any problems paying my own taxes, I was deeply worried about the tens of thousands of people who were being forced out of their own homes because, through no fault of theirs, the taxes on their homes were rising to a point beyond their ability to pay them. Love for this country was instilled in me when I was growing up outside of Salt Lake City, and I have always believed that private ownership of property and the idea that a man's home was his castle made the United States the greatest and freest country the world has ever known. If you destroy the residential property base, you destroy the country—and that was exactly what I could see taking place.

Many people don't understand that property taxes have absolutely no relation to a property owner's ability to pay—unlike the two other major forms of taxation, income taxes and sales taxes. From that very first meeting back in 1962, those of us in the tax movement decided that our efforts must be directed toward bringing all taxes—but especially property taxes—down to a level where most people could pay them without undue hardship.

None of us who gathered around a living-room table in that modest California house seventeen years ago foresaw back then that one day there would be a proposition called 13 which would shake up the entire country. At that point, none of us even knew very much about the details of property taxes or other taxes, except that we were unified by the belief that they were too high and counterproductive.

We did know that the American dream of home ownership for everyone was being sabotaged by exploding property taxes. The entire basis of free government in America was being destroyed by virtually unlimited taxation, which can only lead first to bankruptcy and then to dictatorship. A French Controller General of Finance had expressed the way most politicians and bureaucrats think when he declared, around 1700, "The art of taxation consists of so plucking the goose as to obtain the largest amount of feathers with the least amount of hissing."

We made up our minds, back in 1962, that government officials might continue plucking our feathers, but that we were not going to allow them to do it without a lot of hissing on our part. Most of all, we determined that we were never going to quit until we won. Since Proposition 13 won, those of us who stuck it out all those years have received a lot of glory and a huge share of the limelight. But believe me: there wasn't any glory during those fifteen years when every time I walked across the street, someone shot me in the rear, when most people either ignored us or called us a bunch of kooks, just because we wanted to reduce taxes to a reasonable level.

A year or two after that first meeting, several dozen of us formed a California group called the United Organizations of Taxpayers, of which I was elected state chairman. As the years went by, we affiliated with hundreds of tax organizations and thousands of people all over the state. Volunteer organizations are hard to hold together, but we fought very hard and managed to sell the idea of loyalty and unity among ourselves. We told our tax fighters to hang tight because we knew that numbers gave us some political clout. We knew which side we were on and who our enemies were. We knew we were in a political war; one that was not fought with guns, clubs or bullets. Our weapons were fountain pens, and we had to prove again that the pen is mightier than the sword. We took a credo from former Secretary of State James E. Byrnes, who said, "I discovered at an early age that most of the difference between average people and great people can be explained in three words: 'And then some.'" The top people in our group did what was expected of them—and then some. They met their obligations and responsibilities fairly and squarely—and then some. They could be counted on in emergencies, of which there were many over the years—and then some.

We adopted a phrase used by Winston Churchill in answer to Hitler's demand that Britain surrender to the Nazis, who were just 27 miles across the English Channel. In refusing to surrender, Churchill said, "What kind of people do you think we are?" We believed that although every American is different from every other American, no American has the right to be indifferent or apathetic when liberty and freedom for all Americans are on the auction block. We knew we had to prove again that the American system of freedom and liberty is the greatest in the world.

We experienced a number of defeats before we got the sweet

taste of victory. During our fifteen-year struggle against property taxes, we were never even able to gather enough signatures to qualify our tax initiatives for the ballot, until the end of 1977, when we succeeded in collecting 1.5 million signatures of registered California voters—the most in the state's history. In thousands of appearances all over the state during the Proposition 13 campaign, Paul Gann, other people, and I hammered home the message: "You have a chance to vote for yourselves just this once. The people of California are the government. The people we elect are not the bosses; we are. The elected officials are just temporary employees, and this is your chance to tell them you're fed up with their record of 'Tax, tax, tax, spend, spend, spend, reelect, reelect, reelect.' " It was the truth; it was exciting; it triumphed.

Finally on D-day, June 6, 1978, we won an overwhelming victory, with 65% of California voters opting for 13. Proposition 13 cut California property taxes in half, but, in spite of politicians' dire predictions about the effect 13 would have, it seems to have been beneficial. For instance, a UCLA study that was widely cited during the campaign by Governor Jerry Brown and other opponents of 13 predicted that 451,000 employees of state and local governments would lose their jobs if 13 passed. Nearly a year after 13's victory, only 20,000 public workers had been laid off. Some 91,000 people had found jobs in the private sector as a result of 13, according to studies by the state Employment Development Department. In short, just as we had anticipated, 13 not only cut taxes, it stimulated the state's economy by giving the consumers more money to spend. Proposition 13 was intended to benefit the people, not the government, and that's the way it worked out. Isn't that the way it should be? Shouldn't government serve the people, instead of vice versa? Who lost on 13? Certainly not the people.

Proposition 13 is described as the most significant tax cut in our nation's history. A successful campaign by citizen action of this magnitude should be described in detail and analyzed, and this book does. In this book I will explain how and why we succeeded, and tell you something about me and who I am as instigator and implementer of this movement.

Proposition 13 is not the end of the movement to lower taxes; it is just the beginning. In the months and years ahead you'll be hearing more from me. I'll probably be visiting your state, and possibly even meeting you, as I have met tens of thousands of other concerned citizens during and since the 13 campaign. In fact, since 13 passed, I have visited forty-eight of the fifty states— so far every one but North Dakota and Alaska. And every place I go, people say to me, "I want my taxes cut, and I don't care what else happens." These sentiments are borne out by polls which show that 13 is even more popular in California now than it was when we won by a margin of almost 2 to 1, and that the idea of 13-type reductions is very popular all across the land. In fact, in November 1978, five months after 13 passed in California, voters in Idaho and Nevada approved similar amendments. Voters in nine other states from coast to coast and from the Dakotas to Texas came out in favor of measures to reduce government taxes, spending, or both.

Proposition 13 also has turned out to have appeal across all income brackets, contradicting the criticisms that it was intended to benefit the middle class and the wealthy at the expense of the poor. According to the March 26, 1979, issue of *Fortune*, Americans were polled on the question: "Would you welcome lowering property taxes in the spirit of California's Proposition 13?" The results: 70% of those who earned less than $7,000 a year said yes; 70% of those who made between $7,000 and $14,999 a year said yes; 69% of those in the $15,000 to $24,999 said yes, and 65% of the people who earned $25,000 a year or more said yes. Proposition 13 was more popular in the lower income brackets than it was with the middle class and the wealthy!

The tax-reduction movement is continuing on several fronts, and is stronger than ever since 13 passed. On April 16, 1979, the day federal and California income taxes were due, I announced the launching of a drive to reduce personal income taxes in California by 50%. I hope to gather enough signatures to qualify this proposal for the state ballot in June 1980.

Proposition 13 could never have been achieved without the initiative process. In California we have the right to place amendments to the state constitution on the ballot through the initiative process: circulating petitions and collecting signatures from registered voters. About half the states do not now permit the right of initiative—which I consider more important than the right to vote, as I will explain in this book—and I am lending my support to secure these rights in all fifty states.

In addition, I am trying to help angry taxpayers all over the country gain approval of tax-reduction measures, either through the ballot process, as we were able to do in California, or through action of their state legislatures.

Finally, and perhaps most important, the Los Angeles-based American Tax Reduction Movement, of which I am national chairman, has had H.R. 1000 introduced into Congress. Our aim in this campaign is to reduce federal taxes by $50 billion over a four-year period, cut federal spending by $100 billion during the same period, and lower the federal capital-gains tax from its current level of up to 40% to a flat 15%.

I am convinced that inflation is the most serious problem now facing this country. I am equally convinced that this monumental problem of inflation is caused by excess government taxation and spending. Many people attribute our problems to the ever-rising cost of oil, and certainly our dependence on foreign oil is a major cause of our difficulties. Nevertheless, Japan, which, unlike the United States, was nearly destroyed by war a generation ago, and which, again, in contrast to this nation, must import virtually all of its oil, finds itself with less inflation than we do. The yen is much stronger than the dollar, and Japan's balance of foreign trade is a huge surplus instead of a huge deficit. I believe that near the heart of our problems is the insistence by state and federal officials to attempt to solve problems by raising taxes and spending more money, which only pours fuel on the fire of inflation. In addition, when government officials find resistance to tax increases, they resort to the simplistic and wrongheaded solution of printing more money, which further weakens the dollar and our purchasing power. A stark example of this practice: it took twenty-seven years, from 1944 to 1971, for the national debt to double from $200 billion to $400 billion, but just eight years later, by April 9, 1979, the national debt had redoubled. This cycle must be stopped!

I urge every American who is concerned about the rising cost of government and the inflationary spiral to write or call his or her senator or congressman and ask them to support H.R. 1000, and to call on their state and local officials for reductions in taxation and government spending.

The message of Proposition 13 and its aftermath is clear: People *can* collectively effect change in the public interest, if only they get mad enough, and if their anger is rational and justified. People who want to do something don't have to wait for somebody else to lead them. I hope that's one message that will come loud and clear out of 13: Americans can do things for themselves. Everyone knows ten or twenty or thirty people who will work with them. You don't need a campaign manager to lead you; you can be your own campaign manager and lead yourself. If there is something about government you don't like, get together and do something about it. Get as many people as you know to put their names on a petition. Even if the petition has no legal effect, it will impress and scare the hell out of the elected officials. That's all you have to do to get action, whether you're trying to reach a member of the city council or the President of the United States.

I hope that the success of Proposition 13 and this book will help reinstill in the American people the knowledge that ours is a government of the people, by the people, and for the people—instead of of, by, and for the politicians. The brains and capacities of the citizens of the United States are invariably greater than the brains and the capacities of the bureaucracy—now misnamed government.

The last lines in our national anthem, "The Star Spangled Banner," are: "The land of the free and the home of the brave." These words mean that the people cannot be free if they are not brave. Our small group of taxpayers in California consisted of brave souls who eventually slew the giant. They had the will, the persistence, and the guts to fight and win against great political odds. They re-established the definition of what freedom is, what it is worth and what it takes to keep it. Proposition 13 proved beyond any reasonable doubt that the people can achieve the kind of government structure they want if they are willing to fight for it. In an important sense this realization is more significant than the actual victory of 13.

The people can make democracy work, if they want to. I hope my book, *I'm Mad as Hell*, inspires every reader to join the fight for tax reduction and inspires ten others to carry the new American tax message to Washington and to every state capital.

You, too, can get mad as hell, along with us Californians. We won, and so can you. Get going now!

CHAPTER 1

A Second
American Revolution—
The Americans Win Again

Howard Jarvis, 76, a retired home-appliance manufacturer, is an unlikely prophet. Yet in 1978, after 16 years of trying, he caught the crest of a national wave of discontent and succeeded spectacularly in selling his tax-slashing ideas.... On Election Day, voters by 2 to 1 approved Proposition 13, making it one of the most important political and sociological events of the year, and transforming Jarvis into a national symbol of middle-class Americans' mounting anger with expensive government programs that yield too few benefits, big budget deficits and intrusive government regulations.

> —*Time,* January 1, 1979,
> in naming Howard Jarvis one of
> four runners-up for Man of the Year

WHEN I WAS A youngster back in Utah, I used to fish. The only way to catch a fish was to put the worm on your hook, throw it in the water, and leave it there until a fish came along and took it. If you took the worm out of the water, you weren't going to get a bite. We didn't know it at the time we started this tax movement in 1962, but we were going to have to leave our worm in the water for fifteen years before we would get a bite. But when we got it, it was a big one. If somebody wants to call that timing, it's all right with me, but I don't think that's what it was at all. We didn't have some kind of omniscient genius that told us when the time would be right for 13. It was guts and persistence that did it: nothing less and nothing more.

Our first tax meeting in 1962 was held at the home of a guy who lived on Los Feliz Boulevard in Los Angeles, not far from where I live on North Crescent Heights Boulevard. There's a little story in the name of that street where we met for the first time. The English translation of Los Feliz is "The Happy Ones." Paul Gann—whom I didn't meet until many years later—lives in Carmichael, outside of Sacramento. Believe it or not, Gann lives on Los Feliz Way!

This was just a little meeting of about twenty ordinary people who were concerned about how fast property taxes were going up. They wanted to try to do something about it. There were no big wheels there. (Mike Rubino, one member, later became a city councilman in Alhambra.) Many people there were in their late fifties and sixties, just like me, and they were worried about something that has since become a lot more common: Elderly people on fixed incomes were being forced to give up the homes where they had lived for many years because they couldn't make the property-tax payments.

Up until then, I had always been on the political end of things. I knew something about taxes, but I had never had a chance to specialize in them. The people at this meeting asked me to write their bylaws, which I did. Then they wanted me to be their chairman. Originally they had wanted Mike Rubino to be chairman, but he had founded a homeowners' group in the San Gabriel Valley and was too involved in other things, so they asked me. I said I would do it just long enough to help them get on their feet.

The more I got my nose into taxes, the more it interested me.

And the first thing you know, it was a full-time deal. I'm not a guy to sit around on my butt. It was either go or don't go, and I decided to go.

There were two people from that original group in addition to me who stayed in this from then all the way until now, through all the attempts and failures, through Proposition 13 and everything. The other two were Leona Magidson, our secretary-treasurer, and Jimmy Christo, our president, who deserves much of the credit. Leona's house on West Fifth Street in West Los Angeles has been our headquarters over the years. That's where everything got done, where hundreds of thousands of pieces of mail were sent out from, where we made our calls from, where we received our mail. And many nights when I would be on Ray Briem's or other talk shows from midnight until dawn, I would say over the air that if people couldn't get through to me at the radio station, they could call Leona for the answers to their questions. I would give out her phone number, and people would be calling her all night. Then she would spend all day addressing envelopes, stamping them, and stuffing them and sealing them. Leona has really been at the center of our operation.

This is how Leona remembers those early days: "My husband had just died and about the same time my property taxes went up $500 in one year—$500 in one year! And this was fifteen years ago, when that was even more money than it is now.

"I was upset about that huge increase, so I went to my first tax meeting. I didn't know anything about politics; I'd been a housewife and mother all my life. The most I had ever done was go to PTA meetings.

"When I first met Howard at my first meeting, the thing that came to my mind was: 'God, he's smart.' I didn't know anybody like that. He seemed to know everything about taxes, although we all learned a lot more as we went along.

"All of a sudden, we had a leader. Howard knew what to say and how to say it and when to say it. He always knew what he was talking about.

"Howard Jarvis is the reason I stayed with it all these years. I just believed in him. I felt that any man who could do what he was doing for nothing, I could believe in. He was the first human being I had come across politically whom I thought cared.

"How do I feel now that we've won?—I smile, because Howard has proven to me that if you stick with something long enough and you know you're right, you will succeed."

After we had gotten on our feet, the other people in the group asked me to stay on as permanent chairman. I'll take credit for this much: I made everybody take sort of a blood oath that we would never quit until we had won. I said to them, "If you want me to be the chairman of this organization, I want to tell you something: I'm not a quitter. If I come in here, we're never going to quit. If you have any idea that you're ever going to walk away, say so now. But don't vote for me unless you intend to keep at this until we win."

It was awfully hard to get people to stay together on a job like this one which took such a long time. People don't understand that it took almost two hundred years for the government to plant this tax yoke on our necks. People were impatient. They thought it could be fixed in twenty minutes. Lots of people thought that. I never thought it would be a short-term thing, but I didn't think it would take fifteen years. I thought we could accomplish something in maybe five years.

We decided on a set of principles to begin with. We still believe in the same principles, and everything we've ever done has been directed toward them:

First: property taxes in California should be fair and should be applied to all the property in California that should be taxed. We're not talking about church buildings or private schools furnishing a service that would otherwise have to be paid for by the state. Health facilities are in the same category. Nor do we think the public buildings and schools should be on the tax rolls; all you're doing is taking money out of one pocket and putting it in another.

The property owners built all the schools. They built the whole educational system. They have to pay off all the bonds because a bond issue is a first mortgage on their houses. People were getting first mortgages on their homes that they didn't know were there because the politicians passed bond issue after bond issue after bond issue, far beyond any degree of common sense in operating government. The public never approved any bond issue that I know of—unless you want to say that when we have a 30% vote and 70% stay home and 15.1% vote yes and 14.9% vote no, that that constitutes a majority to impose a forty- or fifty-year mortgage on anybody who owns residential or business property in that district.

No, I don't believe that the people vote for these things. A great many people are too lazy to vote, too affable, too trusting in government. They say, "The government won't do this to us." Well, they found out a darned sight different.

In California thousands of acres are off the tax rolls because they are owned on the face by something like 64,000 tax-exempt corporations and 18,000 charitable trusts. It's an unfair system. A pays taxes, but B doesn't pay on the same type of property. Much of this property belongs to organizations that are listed as religions, but they're not really religions. They're just a fake to get a tax break. It's nothing less and nothing more than revenue racketeering.* There are also a great many corporations retaining a tax-exempt status in California that have become multi-billion dollar, multi-layer businesses, but they never pay any tax at all. It has been a swindle for years and years.

So we wanted taxes to be fair.

Second: we wanted taxes to be equal for everybody. Of course, there's no way to create equality in life, or in taxes, or in death, or in anything else. But we wanted to do our best. We felt that if two people had houses just alike, like tract houses, and the owner on the right side of the street paid $3,000 a year in taxes and the owner on the left side of the street paid $1,000 a year in taxes, they weren't being treated equally. If someone on one side of the street sold his house, all the other houses on that side went up in assessed valuation and had to pay higher property taxes, but the people across the street didn't have their taxes go up. Or, the assessor would come in and re-assess—which means raise—the houses on one side of the street one year, but he wouldn't hit the people on the other side until one, two, or three years later. We didn't think that was right.

Each year they would assess only one-fifth of the properties in each county, which meant that taxes for 20% of the property owners would go up, while taxes for the other 80% would generally remain the same. As far as we were concerned, that meant

*This statement was made three months before the People's Temple massacre in Jonestown, Guyana.

the county assessors were constantly violating the equal-protection clause of the state and federal constitutions. Nobody but us said anything, nobody did anything, and as the value of California real estate rose the situation got progressively worse.

We felt the solution was to take one year as an arbitrary base year and then say that all property—except what was voluntarily re-assessed because it was sold—could be increased only an equal amount in assessed valuation each year. We decided that a fair annual increase would be 2%, which is what we tried to get over those fifteen years and what we finally got in Proposition 13. (In Proposition 13 we used 1975–76 as the base year, because our lawyers said we had to have a base year before we started the campaign. And 1975 and 1976 were the highest years in the state's history for assessed valuations—until 1977 and 1978 came along. We did this on sound legal advice.)

Third, and the most important thing in any American tax system: we were determined that the tax system be within the ability of the people who were taxed to pay it. In California some three or four million elderly people who years ago had bought and paid for their homes—the only asset they had—were being forced out because they couldn't pay their taxes.

We also found that the middle-class guy with a wife and two kids who takes home $1,000 a month had to pay $65,000 for a house. His taxes, insurance, and upkeep are already more than he makes. So he can't buy the house. And when he can't buy it, nobody builds it. Then we have unemployment.

And we had in mind the young people who, because of the incredible increases in property values and taxes during the years we were trying to get taxes reduced, could not afford to buy a home. For all intents and purposes, the enormous increases in property taxes, along with the need for a down payment and the credit checking and all, priced the young couples out of the market.

All of these factors added together raised the very serious point which the politicians weren't smart enough to recognize: More and more of the residential property was in the hands of people in their fifties and older. Most of these people's incomes are going down. A great many of them are retiring on incomes of $307 a month Social Security. Others who were executives are retiring. Instead of making $35,000 or $50,000 or $100,000 a year, they're on pensions of $9,000 or $15,000 or $20,000.

So the residential-property tax base was contracting rapidly. Taxes were going up, but the incomes of many of the owners were going down. These people couldn't possibly pay more taxes.

I hope that Proposition 13 will signal the entire country so that the politicians will wake up and see what's happening. If they don't, one of these days they're going to find out that the best residential-property tax base is gone. And then we'll have a catastrophe. But politicians never think about things like this until three months after the catastrophe occurs. Then it will be too late. If too many people don't have enough money to pay their taxes, the cities and counties will all be out of money overnight—unless they foreclose on most of the property, and that won't produce very much revenue for the state for very long. If the state were to foreclose, it would take all these people out of the tax base altogether, which would be a disaster. Of course, the state or the federal government could confiscate everyone's money. They could do that anytime. But that would destroy the country, the same as if they confiscated all the property through taxes.

An oppressive legislature could drive the people to refuse to pay their taxes and to revolt with guns. We didn't want that, so we were trying to create a revolution with fountain pens, rather than with rifles, clubs, or a confrontation between the people and the government.

We tried originally to be a tax leader for the state of California, to encourage the reduction of taxes—particularly property taxes. We wanted to be a source of information for other tax organizations from various parts of California. Of course, if an organization from Santa Ana joined us, we did not go to Santa Ana and tell them what they should do—unless they had a problem and asked our advice. Then, and only then, would we actually go in there. Otherwise, we just acted as a clearinghouse of information for them and for all the other tax groups in California.

We had two kinds of memberships: $5 a year for individuals and $25 a year for organizations. Even if they had 700 or 800 members, they still paid only $25 a year. We were not in business to make money out of this. We were in business to do something about high taxes. Period. I never got a nickel, Leona never got a nickel, Christo never got a nickel; nor did any other officer or

director. Neither did anyone else who was associated with us. I
have always felt that if somebody sent us $25 to fight taxes, they
were entitled to have their $25 spent on fighting taxes, not on
ripoffs for the people in the organization.

Not only did I never receive a nickel for my work, I spent
about $100,000 out of my own pocket over the fifteen years. I
wore out two cars driving around the state and spent thousands
of dollars on motels and meals while I was traveling around and
leading the drive to lower taxes. And I bought typewriters, a press
to print news releases on, stamps—you name it. My wife Estelle,
the loveliest lady I know, whom I met in Los Angeles in the early
1960s and married in 1965, used to say to me during the lonely
years when I was working on tax reduction and most people were
either ignoring me or laughing at me, "Why don't you spend our
money on us? You're going out there and working yourself to
death and spending our money—and most people don't appreciate
it. If anything happened to you they'd walk away, just like flies
from a carcass." But Estelle worked as hard as anyone, and she
never meant it when she said we should quit. And when Proposition 13 came along, she organized a crew of women to gather
signatures. She would pick them up in her car every day, make
their lunch, and take them to a supermarket where they stood
outside and got people to sign our petitions. Her crew turned in
about a thousand signatures a day from September to November
1977.

I think people in most political campaigns squander 90% of
their money. They throw it up in the air and hope to God it comes
down in the right place. They don't know what they're doing.
I've always thought the best name for politics is "organized chaos."
But we watched every cent we spent. We saved our money, so
we could keep trying over and over again. To give just one example: when we finally qualified for the ballot in 1977, we spent
only $28,500 to get 1.5 million signatures. That is phenomenally
low for an initiative campaign.

The campaign against taxes literally started with a bang for me.
I was giving one of my first speeches at a high school gymnasium
in San Jose when a heavy pole that held up the curtain fell down

and hit my right shoulder. It broke all the bones and tore all the cartilage in my shoulder. It hurt like hell, and I was in a cast for about eight weeks. My shoulder never healed entirely. That didn't help my golf game.

From the earliest days I started writing arguments against tax increase proposals that were on the ballot. These arguments were carried in the voting pamphlet over my signature. The politicians in California have made it very difficult for an ordinary citizen to write a ballot argument. The law says a public official has the first priority to write the argument. The school board official who puts a bond issue on the ballot has the first chance to write the ballot argument against it. Naturally, he's not going to write a very strong argument against it.

The second priority for writing a ballot argument goes to a properly organized group. We didn't qualify under that provision in the first few years because we were a very loose-knit organization.

Last of all comes the citizen. When the politicians used to try to stop me, I would say, "If you do, I will file a writ in court tomorrow asking that the court order that I be allowed to write an argument. Here is the writ, all made out." Usually that would cause them to back down and let me write the argument. Nine times out of ten, if they had gone to court, they would have won. But they didn't have the brains to know it or the guts to do it. For the last ten or twelve years, I haven't had any trouble getting one of my ballot arguments accepted. I've had my name on several dozen ballot arguments, and almost all of them have resulted in the defeat of some type of tax increase.

We had meetings once a month at Leona's house on West Fifth Street in Los Angeles, starting in 1962. And we still meet often. In 1965 we decided to incorporate as the United Organizations of Taxpayers. We had tax organizations all over the state and some from outside the state affiliate with us. At one time we had a peak membership of about 120,000, but other times it would be down to 50,000 as people got discouraged and quit the tax movement.

By 1965 I was starting to be recognized as the number-one leader in the tax movement. An article in the *Los Angeles Times* on June 7, 1970, stated: "Jarvis in the past five years has become the chief spokesman for a large group of disgruntled California property owners who are convinced, simply, that they pay too much of the cost of government."

That same story said that my "name has become well known in the past five years before legislative committees, boards of supervisors, city councils and school boards all over California." On dozens of occasions I testified before these committees, even though I knew most of the members weren't paying any attention to me. But I knew that anytime my remarks got reported in the press, it would give a little publicity to our cause.

I used to testify every year at the budget hearing of the Los Angeles Board of Supervisors. The Los Angeles county budget is a big, thick book. I wasn't getting $50,000 a year from the city or the county to study the budget; I wasn't getting any money at all. Of course, it was *my* money they were talking about spending. Most of the elected officials don't bother to read the budget themselves. They have the department heads read each section, and they take their word for what's in it.

Each year I would go down there and pick out one or two items in the budget that I thought had too much fat. But the political operation is so rotten and has been for so long that the supervisors and the school boards don't want any testimony from the public on the budget. The law requires them to hold public hearings, but they don't want anybody to testify on the budget. They especially don't want anybody knowledgeable to testify because they never read the budget. And they don't want to sit up there and look like fools. So when I testified, they walked around and talked to each other, or they accepted phone calls. Then the chairman would say, "Your five minutes are up." The last time I was before one of those committees I said, "Well, gentlemen, budget time is here again. You've seen me here many times, much to your discomfort. Today you're not going to have to listen to me for very long (that got their attention), because all I want to say is that I think your budget hearings are just like a striptease dancer in a massage parlor. That's what the budget hearings amount to. They're a fake and a fraud, and you know it, and I know it, so good day, gentleman." They gave a few sheepish smiles.

One year I was invited to testify before the Assembly Revenue and Taxation Committee, which holds the hearings on the state budget. I was allotted forty-five minutes, so I worked my head off to prepare myself. I went up to Sacramento and the whole committee was there, sitting up on these high chairs so that you were sitting down there like a mole. I gave my testimony, and when I got through, I said I'd be very glad to answer any questions. There wasn't a sound. Not a single one of them had a question for me. I said, "Well, gentlemen, I'm not so presumptuous as to think you all agree with everything I said. There ought to be some questions." There was a guy by the name of Vincent Thomas, a Democrat from San Pedro, sitting way down on the end. He'd been in the Assembly for about thirty years—since 1941. He said, "I'll tell you, Mr. Jarvis, if you want to know the truth about it. There isn't anybody on this committee who knows anything about taxes. So how are they going to ask you a question?" Just imagine. This was the committee that is responsible for studying every line in the budget. And I believe what Thomas said. I absolutely believe it.

Because I was so active in the tax movement, I became interested in the fact that a woman named Dorothy Healey was running for Los Angeles County Tax Assessor in 1966. The reason for my interest was that Dorothy Healey was one of the best-known Communists in the United States. She had been arrested in 1951 on charges of violating the Smith Act, and had been indicted that same year for conspiring to teach and advocate the overthrow of the U.S. government by force and violence. She was convicted on the Smith Act charge and sentenced to five years in prison and a $10,000 fine, but the case was appealed to the Supreme Court, which granted her a new trial. Then the government dismissed the case against her. A 1959 report by the House Un-American Activities Committee described her as "chairman of the Communist Party's new Southern California District" and listed her occupation as "professional Communist."

The county assessor has access to aircraft companies and their top-secret records for purposes of assessing their property, and there are a number of large aircraft companies in Los Angeles County. It worried me very much that a well-known, admitted member of the Communist Party would have access to records like those. I didn't think Communists should be allowed to hold office for the same reason that I don't think you should give Al Capone the key to your safe-deposit box. I thought they were a dirty bunch of lousy traitors and thieves who would steal everything they could and would work against the United States, and I haven't changed my mind. They were enemies of the United States, and therefore they were *my* enemies.

So I filed suit in Superior Court to keep Dorothy Healey off the ballot, or at least to force her to list herself on the ballot as "Communist Party organizer" instead of just as "organizer," which was the way she had it. I was handling my own case. She was represented by a lawyer from the American Civil Liberties Union. The judge who was presiding over the case ruled in her favor every chance he got. Finally I made a few remarks, and he threatened to hold me in contempt of court. The truth is, I did have contempt for his court, but he would have had a hell of a time proving it. He and I got in a big row, and I persuaded the judge in charge to take this judge off the case. I got another judge, who was a hell of a lot worse. And he ruled in favor of Dorothy Healey. That case got an awful lot of publicity. In any event, Mrs. Healey was allowed to remain on the ballot, and she got 86,149 votes. Phil Watson got reelected with 1,131,160.

Every year the members of the legislature promised the public they were going to do something about taxes next year. And when next year—the off-election year—came, the politicians *did* do something about taxes. They raised them.

There are two factors that determine how much property tax people pay in California: the assessed valuation of the property is multiplied by the tax rate that is set by the city councils, the county boards of supervisors, the school districts, the water districts, the hospital districts, and the other tax jurisdictions. The assessed valuation is supposed to be equal to 25% of the market value of the property. The politicians and the bureaucrats had a little game they liked to play with the poor boobs who paid the taxes: raise the appraised value one year, raise the tax rate the next. There was always the same loser in this game: the taxpayer. Then the politicians came up with a plan to give tax money back to the people who didn't pay it. It was called the circuit-breaker formula. Fancy name for a swindle, isn't it?

Finally, in 1968 we got to the point where we thought we were ready to circulate petitions to get a property-tax initiative on the ballot. California had become the tenth state in the country to permit initiative and referendum, on October 10, 1911. The right of initiative and referendum originated in California with Hiram Johnson, who was governor from 1911 to 1917. He was probably the most progressive governor the state ever had. In fact, he ran for reelection in 1914 as a member of the Progressive Party, after he was originally elected as a Republican in 1910. Hiram Johnson had found out that the state legislature was pretty much a wholly-owned subsidiary of the Southern Pacific and the other railroads, which at the time had a monopoly on the state of California. They ran the state—not the people or the elected officials. The railroads bought all the candidates; they got legislation that they wanted passed and got legislation that they didn't want defeated. So Governor Johnson had succeeded in getting written into the state constitution the right of the people to petition—a legal right, not a fictitious right. Now if the people of California don't like what the politicians are doing, they can write a law that they want enacted, and they can place it on the ballot.

That is not to say that getting an initiative on the ballot and getting it approved is an easy process. Between 1960 and 1978, there were 148 initiatives proposed in the state, but only 26 got on the ballot and only 7 were approved by a majority of the voters. So only about 5% of the initiatives that started out actually became law.

Nevertheless, if we did not have the right to petition in California, the shot that was heard around the world on June 6, 1978, never would have happened. And the people of California would still be mucked under the heels of irresponsible, unaccountable politicians. But today the shoe is on the other foot. The worm has turned.

The people in the United States—or at least some of the states*—have two basic rights, the right to vote and the right to legally petition. I think the right to petition is more important than

---

*At present, 25 states permit referenda, 22 allow initiatives, and 14 permit the recall of state officers. The right of initiative and referendum is not included in the U.S. Constitution, although there is a move to adopt an amendment granting that right.

the right to vote because the right to petition means that people can group together to stand up to the politicians and the bureaucrats. But when you vote, you go in there in solitary and vote in the booth, and that's it. I think every state and the federal government should provide the right to petition. Of course, even in the states that have the right to petition, the legislatures are making tremendous efforts to make it more difficult.

They say that it's a negation of representative government. That would be true if the politicians represented us. But they don't. What we have is the facade of a representative government. Most of the legislators, state and federal, have special vested voting blocs that they pass legislation for and appropriate money for, for the simple purpose of getting themselves reelected. That's true, regardless of party. In California, for instance, 117 out of 120 state legislators received major campaign contributions from public employee unions. As far as I'm concerned, that is a cancer on free government. If the public employee unions can elect their bosses to office, the general public is screwed, blewed, and tattooed.

Don't misunderstand me: the politicians don't mind petitions, as long as they have no legal effect. As long as they mean as much as writing a letter to Santa Claus. They don't read the mail, anyway. They don't want the people to have the legal authority to take control of their government. Government controls people by putting up barriers that reduce the people's right to participate in government, so legislators generally don't like the right to petition. It frightens them, as it should, and they fight it every step of the way. As long as the people don't have the right to petition, the politicians can sit up on their thrones and say, "We don't give a damn what the people say." They can do that because they know the people have no way of fighting back.

It's only natural that the legislature resents the initiative process, because it limits their function. It takes some of the power out of their hands. But we believe that we have a government of the people, not of elected politicians and unelected bureaucrats. They are supposed to do what the people want, not the other way around.

Over the years one of the main ploys by our politicians has been to make government so complicated that people can't understand it. What the people can't understand, they're afraid of and walk away from. That leaves the politicians with a free hand.

The politicians certainly wanted to make the initiative process as complicated as possible in order to discourage people from trying to place initiatives on the ballot. When we first started circulating petitions, there was a requirement that in addition to the name and address of each person who signed, the petition had to have the number of the precinct they lived in. Now, how many people know their precinct number? Hardly anyone, including me. That meant that after our volunteers collected signatures, someone had to sit down with a list of precincts and fill them in. And if the precinct number was wrong, whether it was because the volunteers had put a signer in the wrong precinct or because they just made a mistake when they copied the precinct number onto the petition, the signature would be disqualified. That made it mighty difficult. I finally got the precinct requirement repealed.

On top of that, it was true back in 1968—and it still is today— that you had to obtain the signatures of 8% as many voters as the total vote for governor in the last election. In the last few elections, the turnout has generally been 6 million votes or so, which means getting about 500,000 *valid* signatures in order to qualify for the ballot. That's a hell of a lot of signatures. I think it's too many. I don't think you should have to get more than 5%, which would be about 300,000 valid signatures, in order to put a measure on the ballot so the people can simply vote yes or no. But I haven't been able to get that changed. Yet.

Our first petition had only 100,000 signatures or so. We didn't even come close to qualifying. You have to figure that about one-third of the signatures you gather will be invalidated for one reason or another, so you have to collect half again as many signatures as you really need to qualify. Using that rule of thumb, if you need 500,000 valid signatures to get on the ballot, you have to gather 750,000 to be sure you will wind up with enough valid ones.

After our first attempt failed, we supported a 1968 initiative that Phil Watson, the Los Angeles County Tax Assessor, succeeded in qualifying for the ballot that year. The 1968 Watson initiative, which was Proposition 9 on the ballot in November, called for property taxes to be limited to 1% of full market value:

the same as what we tried to qualify and pass for ten years and
what we ultimately used in Proposition 13.

We arrived at that 1% figure because we thought that property-
related services were all that property should have to pay for.
Property-related services include police, fire, garbage, streets,
lights, and sewers. The 1% limit would provide about one-third
more than enough money to pay for those services. We felt that
property owners should not be made the goat for school, food
stamps, welfare, libraries, and all the rest. Those programs should
be paid for by everybody, not just by property owners.

The politicians used scare tactics. They said that Watson's
Proposition 9 would cause huge cuts in vital services, the same
tactic they used successfully against another Watson initiative in
1972, an initiative by Governor Ronald Reagan in 1973 and our
attempts to qualify other initiatives for the ballot. In 1968 the
politicians also used a second ploy that they came up with again
to attack Proposition 13 in 1978. They put another measure on
the ballot that offered a much smaller reduction in taxes: only
$90 for the owner of a home worth $22,500.

Those politicians' tactics worked in 1968. We did all we could
to help pass Proposition 9, but it received only 2,146,010 yes
votes (32%) to 4,570,097 no votes (68%). And the measly measure
the politicians put on the ballot passed. Big deal!

The following year I led the campaign against Propositions A,
B, and C on the Los Angeles ballot. We managed to defeat all
three measures, which would have cost the taxpayers $600 million
if they had passed. Then in March 1970, we defeated a school tax
override in Los Angeles that would have cost the taxpayers $358
million. On that campaign we spent the most we ever had during
a single campaign up until then: $10,800. But we started that
campaign with $500 in the bank, and we finished it with $1,000.
So not only were the United Organizations of Taxpayers solvent
to the tune of a few hundred dollars, we took on the politicians
and defeated $1 billion worth of tax increases in 1969 and 1970.
The politicians had no need for all that money, and we proved it
to the taxpayers.

Later on that same year, 1970, after I'd been involved in tax
reduction for eight years, some of Reagan's friends urged me to
run for the State Board of Equalization. I didn't particularly want

the job. But it is important because the five members of the board have the responsibility of overseeing all the tax assessments and all the tax collections in the state.

At that time, Richard Nevins, a Democrat, was the representative on the board of equalization from our district, which included Los Angeles, Orange, San Diego, Riverside, Imperial, San Bernardino, Santa Barbara and Ventura counties. That area was the stronghold of the United Organizations of Taxpayers.

In the primary in June, Nevins got 1 million votes, I got 400,000, the third highest candidate got 150,000 votes, and five others split another 400,000 votes among them. That meant that Nevins and I had to have a runoff in November.

I was listed on the ballot as a "tax reduction expert," and my campaign really got rolling. For a while, I was afraid I was going to win. I didn't want the job at all. I felt and still feel that being in office would hamstring me and keep me from speaking out against taxes the way I want to. I wound up spending something like $8,000 on that campaign, and I got 1.5 million votes. But Nevins got 2 million, which was fine with me. After I was sure I had lost, Estelle and I had a little celebration. And that was my last fling in Republican politics; after that election, I dropped out.

I agreed to run for that office only so that I could have a forum to campaign for tax reduction and for Reagan, who was up for his second term. I actually used my campaign to campaign for Reagan all over the state. I would spend about six minutes talking about tax reduction and about two minutes talking about Reagan. I never campaigned for myself at all.

While I was campaigning in Santa Barbara that year I discovered the most fantastic political gimmick. I had given my speech about tax reduction and Reagan, and then I sat down. A guy in the crowd got up and said, "Mr. Jarvis, aren't you on the ballot?"

I said, "Yes, I am."

He said, "Well, you didn't say anything about it."

I answered, "The reason I didn't mention it is because I'm interested number one in taxes and number two in Reagan. If anybody wants to vote for me for this office, they can look on the ballot and find my name, but I'm not here to ask for any votes for myself."

The entire audience stood up and cheered.

Well, from then on, I took a guy with me, and he'd go sit in the back of the hall. I'd make the same speech as the one in Santa Barbara. Then the guy I had brought with me would get up and ask the question the guy in Santa Barbara had asked me. He was a nondescript guy from Los Angeles. Anybody can go to a political meeting, you know. I paid him a few bucks and coached him a little on how to do it. It helped make my speeches more effective.

During that campaign for the board of equalization, the news media and the television stations made a big thing about how all the candidates ought to publish their financial statements. I thought it was foolish, but I published mine anyway. I even printed it on my brochures. My assets were my home in Los Angeles, which was then worth $30,000, some land in Wyoming worth $21,000, trust deeds (loans I had made that were secured by real estate)— valued at $117,250, and $54,000 in other liquid assets, such as bank accounts. I had no liabilities, so my net worth was $222,250; not a huge amount, but ten years ago, before today's ruinous inflation, the equivalent of about $500,000 today.

None of the other candidates issued their financial statements— and the hypocritical press never mentioned it. I even took particular pains to mail my financial statement and a letter to the news media explaining that I was the only candidate who had made my financial statement public. And I never got one word out of any newspaper or radio or television station. They were just hoodwinking the public, as usual.

In our fight against taxation, we became involved against *any* program in the state of California that would raise taxes on property or anything else. For example, in March 1971, I filed suit against the Los Angeles County Board of Supervisors to prevent them from paying $100,000 to underwrite the cost of a visit to Los Angeles by the New York City Opera the previous year. I saw no reason why the taxpayers should have to bear the burden of something like that, when maybe one-tenth of one percent of the taxpayers were interested in opera. But the courts didn't see it that way. My suit was dismissed on the ground that I hadn't shown that the board of supervisors didn't have the power to contribute the $100,000. Still, I was in there fighting.

In May 1971 we launched our second attempt to get a property-tax initiative on the ballot. This one was aimed at limiting taxes to 1% of the market value of the property, the same as Proposition 13 and the others we tried. There were two other important provisions in the initiative:

—It would have prohibited special assessments on real property. The politicians were putting so many special levies on the taxpayers that the bonded indebtedness of property was getting to be more than the property was worth. That was potentially catastrophic.

—It provided that all real property would be subject to taxes unless the two houses of the legislature voted for exemptions for particular categories. The vote for exemptions would have had to be by a two-thirds majority of each house. That part of the initiative reflected our growing concern about all the property belonging to phony churches and charitable institutions that was being exempted from taxes, which put a bigger burden on the homeowners.

We had no intention of denying property tax-exemption to legitimate churches, private schools, and charities. We felt confident that the legislature would grant exemptions to them, but the outfits that had no right to an exemption wouldn't be able to get a two-thirds vote in the legislature.

However, the Catholic church didn't understand that we were not trying to eliminate their tax exemption. We had until January 3, 1972 to come up with 520,806 valid signatures. Right around Christmas, just as we were coming down the home stretch, the Catholic church put out a bulletin which called our initiative "nefarious" and said it "totally disregards the benefits derived by the community from religious and private educational programs and their great contributions to the welfare of all." They didn't get our message at all, which I suppose was partly our fault.

During the campaign for that initiative I said in my speeches essentially the same thing I said later:

The government has never been helpless in getting revenue. What we are trying to do is have them get it from the most reasonable source.

In Los Angeles County alone, 400,000 people did not pay their property tax this year because they didn't have the money. They run the risk of being forced out of their homes, which I personally believe is un-American, indecent, and criminal. There is nothing more sacred than the place where a man lives.

We must have a new system—one which gets the property that ought to pay taxes back on the tax rolls.

I don't think there's any one perfect tax law, but I think generally speaking that our amendment will help about 90% of the people in California.

Many people didn't believe us when we forecast in our literature that

within the next two to three years property taxes can be expected to triple, and residential foreclosures are expected to reach levels of from 300,000 to 450,000 per year in California.

This will be inevitable without realistic property-tax relief. And if the trends of welfare and school expenditures and other ill-conceived and maladministered public programs are permitted to expand under union and giveaway political pressures, as they have been at such an accelerating pace these last few years, we are headed for disaster.

It is obvious that our legislature is not capable of coming up with an intelligent property-tax-reduction bill.

One of the interesting things about that campaign was that Assemblyman Joseph Gonsalves—a Democrat who sponsored an attempt to have the legislature put a property-tax-relief measure on the ballot—was one of the leaders of the campaign against our initiative. In other words, if the politicians write a sham amendment, it's good law; but if the people write one that offers real tax relief, it's no good.

We fell about 100,000 signatures short of the number we needed to qualify for the ballot. At least that's what the politicians said. Among those politicians was Jerry Brown, who was then Secretary of State and was responsible for certifying our petitions.

Actually, the politicians had to bend the law to keep us off the ballot that time. I don't know if they did it on purpose or through sheer incompetence. We filed more than 650,000 signatures before the deadline, but then more than 200,000 of them were arbitrarily discarded by temporary help: boobs who were hired off the streets by county registrars' offices throughout the state. More than 100,000 signatures were thrown out in Los Angeles County alone, and about three-quarters of them should have been allowed. But these temporary employees who went through the petitions didn't know what they were doing. And after they refused to accept a lot of valid signatures, Brown wouldn't extend our deadline and give us a chance to submit more signatures. Another thing that hurt us that year was the requirement for precinct numbers on the petitions.

Nevertheless, we made a great showing that year and came close to getting on the ballot. And we had our moments. One time we set up a table to get signatures at the Los Angeles County Hall of Administration, where people had to go to pay their taxes. A security guard threw us out. So we went to the county counsel and got authorization to have our tables there in the Hall of Administration. And that same guard who had thrown us out before signed one of our petitions!

When we fell short with our 1% initiative in 1972, we teamed up with Phil Watson. This time he was circulating petitions calling for a ceiling of 1.75%. At the time, most property owners in the cities were paying about 3.25%. That meant that a property owner was paying over $900 a year in taxes on a house assessed at $30,000. Watson's initiative would have cut that to $540; ours would have cut it to $300.

Watson learned his lesson from 1968, when one of the arguments against him was that his initiative failed to explain how the money that Proposition 9 cut would have been made up. Now he told the voters that his initiative would cut property taxes by $2 billion a year and would require increases in sales taxes, higher taxes on liquor and tobacco, and increases in some business taxes. He made it onto the ballot again. And lost again, although he did slightly better than he had in 1968. Watson's 1972 Proposition 14 received 2,700,095 yes votes (34%), and 5,213,485 no votes (66%).

The following year, Ronald Reagan placed Proposition 1 on the ballot. Proposition 1, which Milton Friedman helped write, proposed that state spending be limited to 8.3% of personal income in the state, and that spending would then be required to decrease by 0.1% a year until it reached 7%. Neil Jacoby, who later joined with Friedman to support Proposition 13, campaigned against Proposition 1.

I was for Proposition 1; but, unfortunately, it had some very serious defects. It contained about 5,700 words, and you had to be a genius to figure out whether a yes vote or a no vote was a vote to reduce taxes. (A yes vote on Proposition 1 would have reduced taxes.) Proposition 1 lost, but it still came a lot closer than either of the Watson initiatives. The vote was 1,945,123 yes (46%), and 2,284,705 no (54%).

The outcome of the Proposition 1 election encouraged us because it did so much better than the Watson initiatives. But it was also encouraging to the politicians. They evidently felt that the defeat of three straight constitutional amendments to limit property taxes gave them carte blanche to raise the cost of state government. State spending, which had been increasing at the rate of 3.1% per year from 1967 to 1973, climbed at the rate of 6.5% a year during the next five years—until June 6, 1978.

Jerry Brown was elected governor in November 1974. The total number of votes cast in that election was 6,248,075. Eight percent of 6,248,075 is 499,846. I'm not reciting these figures in hopes of winning a trivia contest. The magic number for us became 499,846—the number of valid signatures we needed in order to qualify a petition for the ballot.

We circulated our third petition during the first six months of 1976. This time we really came close; we got 489,348 signatures— just 10,000 less than what we needed. Watson tried again, this time with a limit of 1.5% of market value (ours was 1%). But he didn't qualify, either.

We received official notice that we had fallen short on our signature drive on August 5, 1976. On October 18, 1976, we started all over again. In order to attract publicity for that campaign, I announced in December 1976, just before the December 10 deadline for paying property taxes, that I was not going to pay my taxes. In the past I had been opposed to people's withholding their property taxes, but I finally came to the conclusion that this was the only means of bringing pressure on the legislature. As I said at the time, "The only way the people can control government is not to give the government so much of their earnings in taxes. The only way to reduce government spending is to not give the government so much money in the first place."

In California, if you refuse to pay your property taxes, the state can't do much about it for five years, except charge you a 6% penalty and interest. The tax collector stamps "Sold to the State" on your property record, but the state can't foreclose your property until five years have passed. Anytime within those five years, you can pay your taxes, penalty, and interest, and get your record cleared. After five years, however, the state does auction off the property to satisfy the tax claim. I have until December 10, 1981, to pay the first installment for 1976–77. I fully intend to pay it instead of allowing the state to take my house, but this way I have a legal right to sue them whenever I want to. I have paid each of the two annual tax installments that have come due since then, so I skipped only one payment.

Meanwhile, I was also running for mayor of Los Angeles. A lot of stories have been written about how I was a "perennial losing candidate for office," but whoever writes those stories just doesn't understand that I didn't expect to be elected mayor, or to the U.S. Senate, or to any other office. All I was doing was using my campaign as a platform for tax reduction.

I'm not mayor of Los Angeles, so I guess that means I lost again. But I made a pretty damn good showing. Tom Bradley, the incumbent, was reelected with 287,927 votes, or 59%; Alan Robbins, a conservative Democratic member of the State Senate who, like Bradley, was very well known, was second with 136,180 votes, or 28%; and I finished third with 47,665 votes, or 10%. So Bradley got six times as many votes as I did, but Bradley outspent me by about 100 to 1, and Robbins spent about ten times as much as I did.

There was one unfortunate incident in that campaign for mayor against Bradley, who is black. My campaign manager, Fred Gage, invited Louise Day Hicks, the segregationist member of the Boston City Council, to come to Los Angeles and campaign for me. However, Gage invited Mrs. Hicks without my knowledge or consent, and I took over as my own campaign manager because of that. Gage thought she would be a ten-strike and I thought having her come in would be a disaster. I didn't want to bring in an outsider and make a racial issue out of it. I called Mrs. Hicks and told her that I didn't want her to come; and that if she came anyway, I wouldn't have anything to do with her. She never came. And the truth is that Tom Bradley and I are friends to this day, and I think he's a hell of a nice guy. I think he's a marinated politician and a big spender, and I disagree with him over that. But there are quite a few other politicians I disagree with, too.

During that campaign for mayor, a congressional committee held some hearings in Los Angeles on ways to improve the postal service. I had written them some letters about the postal service, and they invited me to testify. The hearing was out near the airport. I prepared a paper on what I thought ought to be done. I told them that to begin with, the shortest distance between two points was a straight line, and if they applied that principle to the postal service, instead of shipping mail from Los Angeles to Chicago and then back to Riverside, they might be able to save a little money. I told them that people should be required to have mailboxes out at the street, so the postman wouldn't have to walk all the way up to the door, which would save maybe 50% of their time. I also told them I had found out there was $13 million a day in theft from the post office by postal employees, and that I thought they ought to have a strict clearance procedure before they hired them, like most businesses do these days. And I told them that Saturday deliveries should be eliminated because most businesses are closed and the ones that are open and the residents can wait for mail until Monday without much inconvenience.

When I got through testifying, the head of the committee told me he thought mine was the most impressive and objective testimony they had heard in hearings all over the country. He asked me if I would like to go to Washington right away and help them with their investigation. I said, "Well, I have an application in for a job here right now. I'm running for mayor."

He said, "Anytime you want to come to Washington, we'd love to have you."

I never went, but I appreciated his invitation; and I think if they took my advice, they could go a long way toward cutting down all the waste and inefficiency in the post office and every other department of government.

The election for mayor of Los Angeles took place in April 1977. Right after that was over I started making frequent appearances on George Putnam's talk show on radio station KIEV in Los Angeles. Putnam is a conservative who was looking for a way to boost his ratings. Here is how *Los Angeles Magazine* described what happened in its April 1978 issue:

> Jarvis became one of the show's regular guests about a year ago. And anyone who either listened to KIEV then or wandered by to watch the show unfold through the plate-glass windows at KIEV's subterranean studios in the Arco Plaza would not be surprised, as some folks obviously are, at Jarvis' most recent success. One thing was clear even then: Crazy Howard Jarvis had his finger on the pulse of the audience's discontent. . . . The first hint that Jarvis and his "mad as hell" message were having an impact came on the Putnam show and arrived in the form of better ratings, obviously a solid indicator of political trends, among other things. Soon Jarvis was guesting at least once a week, and the crowd outside the KIEV fishbowl studio swelled with noonday shoppers when Howard was on.

The petitions we had been circulating while I was running for mayor, and when I first started appearing regularly on the George Putnam show, came about as close as you can come without qualifying for the ballot. We got 498,500 signatures, just 1,400 shy of what we needed.

We were so discouraged that we didn't start another petition drive until the next day.

Over the years we had been criticized severely and frequently because we were in the petition business. So was Governor Reagan, and so was Phil Watson, and so were several others, but we had never been able to work together. That campaign that just barely failed in the first part of 1977 was a good example: in addition to the United Organizations of Taxpayers, three other groups were each circulating a tax relief petition of their own. Not only did we not qualify for the ballot, none of the other groups did either. For that matter, none of the others even came close. But it was obvious that if we had teamed up, we would have been able to qualify one of our petitions.

People would constantly be criticizing us for this. They would say, "Why don't all of you get together? Why can't you put all your eggs in one basket, for God's sake? Instead of being fragmented, you could give people a chance to decide on one petition."

I thought the criticism of me and the United Organizations was unjustified because I had tried several times to work out an agreement with Phil Watson. I went to see him a number of times and reach an agreement where we would both circulate the same petitions. But we had always had a very serious barrier to our agreement. I was convinced—and still am—that you cannot have a tax petition that works unless you limit both the tax rate *and* the arbitrary power of the assessor to increase the market value. That difference kept me and Watson apart for several years. He was a tax assessor, and no tax assessor wants to limit the market value raises because, really, the market value raise becomes the major raise. In fact, in many areas, tax rates were actually going down, but taxes were increasing rapidly because of the huge paper increases in the value of property. And, of course, if a tax assessor can't reappraise property, what does that leave for him to do?

Finally, in 1972, Watson gave up the stand he had taken, and it looked like we would get together. We made an agreement and Phil was going to have his lawyers draft our petition. Then he and I were going to get together and file the petition with the State Attorney General's office, as the law requires. For some reason or other, his attorneys were unable to get this petition written. I called him and called him and called him, but he was very hard to get. Finally I reached him in Acapulco. I had to get in touch with him while he was down there because at that point we only had five days left to file the petition if we were going to meet the deadline for getting on the ballot that year. Otherwise, we would have had to wait until the next year.

When I finally got Watson in Acapulco, he said, "Why don't we let it go for a year?"

I said, "We can't do that." So we filed our own petition. We didn't make the ballot, but Watson turned around and filed one of his own, qualified for the ballot, and lost with his Proposition 14.

That created a tremendous hue and cry for us to get together, but it was four more years before we finally did. When we met to write that petition, Phil Watson had gotten hold of Paul Gann up in Carmichael and invited him to participate. Gann was head of People's Advocate, a much smaller group than the United

Organizations of Taxpayers. Up until then, Gann had never been in the picture.

By then, Watson had gotten into a lot of trouble in his office, which eventually wound up with him resigning as assessor. Watson, Gann, and I worked out an agreement on every point except one—who would sign the petition. The three of us had even appeared together on Hilly Rose's talk show on KFI radio in Los Angeles and stated publicly that we had reached an agreement.

Watson suggested that he and Gann sign the petition, but I said, "No soap." I wasn't going to participate in a petition drive where the United Organizations had no authority whatsoever. They could have used our name, they could have gone out and collected money; but if my name wasn't on the petition, we wouldn't have had any say in what they were doing. Finally, I said, "My stipulation is that Watson can't sign it because his office is under serious investigation and he may be indicted. The only way in the world I will agree to it is if Watson's signature isn't on it. I will sign it and I will accept Gann's signature." That was finally agreed on.

We signed all the papers. Gann said he was going back to Sacramento—Carmichael is a suburb of Sacramento—and he would file the petition. I said, "Let's mail it," and he said, "No, I'll file it." I agreed and gave them my personal check for the $200 filing fee. The next day I left for Wyoming, where I fish every year with my only child, Elaine (who lives in Phoenix and in addition to being great at fishing is a former champion skeet shooter).

I'd been up in Wyoming about a week when Estelle called me from Los Angeles and said, "There's some hanky panky going on."

I said, "What do you mean?"

She said, "There are rumors going around that your name is not on the petition." I called the Secretary of State and found out that they had left my name off the petition. Gann's was the only name on it. I flew back to California and filed our own petition, which we had already written. So we had a horse race. And neither Gann nor I was able to qualify a petition.

I later found out that Watson had ordered Gann to take my name off the petition. Gann admitted to me that Watson had offered to raise money for him if my name wasn't on the petition. Watson was unhappy that I was on the petition and he wasn't, because he and I had had our disagreements in the past and he blamed me for keeping him off the petition.

I had a good reason for keeping him off. I couldn't afford to have one of the signers indicted in the middle of the petition drive. I had no grudge against Gann for what had happened. I felt that Watson had taken advantage of him. Gann is susceptible to being taken advantage of; he listens to the last person who talks to him.

We received word in late April or early May of 1977 that we had missed qualifying for the ballot by 1,400 signatures. As I said before, I figured we actually needed 750,000 signatures in order to make sure we had the 499,846 valid ones we had to have to get on the ballot. We had always concentrated our efforts on the eight counties from Santa Barbara to San Diego, where two-thirds of the state's population lives. I figured we could get 600,000 signatures in those eight counties. We had never had the manpower to cover the fifty counties north of Santa Barbara. I thought if we could find an organization that was based up north and they could get 150,000 signatures in that part of the state and we could get 600,000 in our part of the state, we could make the ballot. So, as soon as we found out that we had missed with the first 1977 petition, I called Gann.

I said, "I'll make a deal with you. You want to go in with me on this petition? You and I will sign it. I'll write it. Your job is to get 150,000 signatures in the fifty northern counties, and ours is to get 600,000 in Southern California." He agreed, and we were in business together.

We filed our petition with the Attorney General's office. Then we had to wait about sixty days for them to write a title and a summary of twelve lines or so. That takes them two months. And the petition was virtually identical to the ones we had circulated before. They could have copied the title and summary off the earlier ones, except for maybe a word here and there. Talk about efficiency in government!

On July 6, 1977, Vance W. Raye, Deputy Attorney General, notified us that we could begin circulating petitions for "PROPERTY TAX LIMITATION. INITIATIVE CONSTITUTIONAL AMENDMENT. Limits ad valorem taxes on real property to 1%

of value," and so forth. We had until December 2, 1977, to file the signatures of 499,846 registered voters with the registrars of voters in the various counties. We were off and running.

It took a lot of years to get ready for this—fifteen, to be exact—but this time we were ready. We had made a lot of mistakes during those years, but we had learned from them. When we started circulating petitions, we carried them from door to door; but we soon found out it was much more efficient to have our people at shopping centers and office buildings, where they could reach large numbers of people in a relatively short time. We learned the best approach to use on someone when you want to get their signature on a petition: "Sign this—it will help lower your taxes." That usually worked.

At the start, we really had no idea how to organize the entire state. We took it for granted that things would happen, that people knew what to do without being trained. We found out it didn't work that way. So we trained them and we organized them.

We learned to send out three press releases a week to every tax organization in the state so that there would be a coordinated effort and everybody would know what was going on. We didn't want one group saying one thing to the press and the group in the next town saying the opposite. And all of these newsletters made our people around the state feel they were a part of something, which was very important. They had a sense of identity.

There were a thousand little things. We learned what day to mail, when was the best time to hold a press conference, who you had to contact at every newspaper and every radio and television station if you wanted to get good coverage, where you could get good printing done at a reasonable price.

For instance, we learned in the early days that the best time and place to hold a press conference is right after somebody important held one, and in the same location. If someone very prominent is going to hold a press conference at 10:00 Monday morning, you go there and hold one at 10:30. That was very successful for me. For a long time, I would wait until a senator or a governor was having a press conference and then have one right after him. If there wasn't a press conference with someone big that week, I wouldn't have a press conference that week. I would wait until there was somebody. If the big guy had twenty reporters, I would have five. But five was four more than we would get if we held one on our own.

We learned what kind of mail was effective. The best piece of mail we sent out in the entire sixteen years was one during the 13 campaign that told every property owner how much his tax bill was, how much he would save on 13 in one year, and how much he'd save in five years. We'd say, "You're going to save $4,000 in five years, send us twenty-five bucks." And they did.

We learned to print enough petitions so that everybody could have one to read before they signed it. We had 700,000 petitions printed with room on each one for ten people to sign it, even though it only took 500,000 to qualify.

We learned that if you have space for ten names on a petition, your petition bearers will take five petitions, but if there is room for twenty names, they'll only take one.

Most of all, we learned more about taxes and more about the people of the state of California than the politicians or anyone else knew. In fifteen years we learned 10% about taxes, which was 9% more than anyone else knew.

By July 1977, when we started circulating the petitions for what was to become Proposition 13, several things had happened. Number one: in fifteen years we educated a lot of people around the state so that they knew something about taxes. I made hundreds and hundreds of radio and television appearances and held hundreds of press conferences during those fifteen years. I used to go on the Ray Briem show on radio station KABC in Los Angeles from midnight until dawn. About 1,200 calls would come in and Ray and I would answer about 60 questions on taxes each night. Ray said I was the hottest thing on the air for him; when I was on his show, he got the most calls. I don't know if he meant that or not. But I do know that he has twenty-four phone lines and when I make my first statement on the air all twenty-four lines light up, and when I go home at five o'clock in the morning there are still those twenty-four lights. The Briem Show was the biggest thing we had going for us over the years, and Ray Briem is the most knowledgeable broadcaster about taxes on the air. And we printed stuff by the bale and shipped it all over the state. For many years I wrote a weekly column called "The People Must Know," and sent it out to 140 publications. Many newspapers would take my stuff and use it without using my name. But that was okay with me because all I wanted to do was get my message across.

Second: all the predictions that I was making came true in spades. The people found out that what I was saying around the state all those years was true. But of course, when you're blessed with the power of foresight, some people say you're crazy. Then when your foresight comes true, some people are mad at you because they didn't think of it themselves. Along about 1972 I began to predict that we were going to have increases of 100% or more a year in the market value of property, which really controls the amount of taxes you pay. Few people believed me. And then about 1975 we started to get 100% and 200% and 300% raises in one year. All those years few believed a word I told them—most people laughed at me—and then it all came true.

The third thing: since Watergate, I suppose, the people don't believe a Goddamned word a politician says. No matter what he says, they don't believe it. And they had good reason not to believe it.

Soon after Gann and I got together and started circulating petitions, Gann told me his little organization, People's Advocate, didn't have any money. So we had to finance People's Advocate, which we did until the petitions were turned in. We voluntarily paid People's Advocate $1,000 a week during the petition drive for three reasons: I knew they didn't have a very large organization, I knew they didn't have any money, and I knew that if he was going to go around Northern California he had to have money to buy gas and food and hotel rooms and airplane tickets and whatever. A thousand dollars a week is not really a lot of money when you think of the distances he had to travel and the phone bills and the hotel bills and the traveling 50 counties for 150 days. He earned it. He got signatures in every one of those counties. To do that he had to plow through the snow to get ten signatures in Sierra County and twenty in Alpine County. We wound up with signatures from every county in the state, all 58 of them, for the first time in history. We couldn't have done that without Paul Gann. As far as I'm concerned, we had a good relationship throughout the campaign. He did exactly what he said he would, and so did I. He said he would get 150,000 signatures, and he got about 158,000. I had no way of knowing that we would get 1.2 million in Southern California. But even if I had known that, I would have joined up with Gann anyway. It was important to have signatures from every county so that it didn't appear that this was something all those crazies and Birchers who, some think, make up 100% of the population of Southern California, were trying to put over on the rest of the state.

We immediately started getting good results with the signature drive. But a lot of people were skeptical, and they certainly had a right to be. The politicians, in particular, didn't take us seriously. After all, we'd had four petitions before, and none of them had gotten on the ballot. The amendments that had made the ballot— the two by Watson and the one by Reagan—had all lost. So there was nothing to worry about this time—right?

As the deadline for filing all the signatures approached, we went all out to get all the people who had been collecting signatures to be sure to turn them in. I said in my newspaper column:

> I urge all of the people who have the Jarvis-Gann petitions to limit property taxes to send them to our main office or our county chairmen so that we have them in our hands by December 2, 1977. We have several hundred thousand petitions out and they are useless if we do not get them returned to us in time to file them on the due date, so that the people will be able to vote on how much taxes they will have to pay.

And I bought thirty days of radio time statewide and went on the air and said:

> We have sent 700,000 petitions out. There are a great many of you who have gotten petitions signed and they are lying on your desk or in your dresser drawer, where they are no good. If you don't send them to us by December second, we're going to lose. We need them as soon as possible so that we have time to process them.

Some of the people who wanted to reduce taxes had turned to gimmicks, without my approval. One group collected signatures from a million people who favored tax relief, put them in a brown bag, and dropped them on Governor Brown's desk. A gal out in the Valley came up with the idea of using a tea bag as a symbol, to remind everyone of the Boston Tea Party. I thought both of those ideas were strictly one-day news items. Our job was to get people to sign petitions that had legal authority; regardless of what Governor Brown might have thought and regardless of whether we had any cliché symbols or not. We had to have the signatures. The signatures were the only thing that would wake up the politicians and the public. All this jumping up and down and picketing this and picketing that and passing out tea bags was a waste of time and effort. I never gave much credence to it. What had merit was that I was able to cross the state and get twenty women in San Jose and twenty-three in Oakland and eighteen in Pasadena and thirty in Palm Springs and eleven in Santa Monica and twelve in Culver City to go out and collect signatures every day.

The people who circulated the petitions and the ones who put their names on those 13 petitions are the ones who had the guts. They put their names on the line for the politicians and anyone else to see. The people who voted for it had a little bit of guts. But they knew that nobody would ever know how they voted. At least they had the guts to throw a silent punch against the politicians, which is more punch than they'd ever shown before. But what they did didn't compare to what the people did who circulated and signed the petitions.

You must be brave in order to be free. And our little band of ordinary, run-of-the-mill taxpayers was brave. We tackled the giant with honesty and decency and sweat and blood and tears, and we cut his head off.

Back at headquarters, many volunteers—most of them women— had been working every day since July checking every name on every petition to make sure it was valid. We didn't want to come close the way we had before and lose out because signers made a mistake when they wrote down their addresses.

About two weeks before the December 2 deadline, everything came together in a big way. All of a sudden, the signatures started pouring in. It was an avalanche. They started coming in by the truckload. We still didn't have any paid help. These volunteers were sorting through all these sacks of mail. By the deadline, 1,200,000 signatures had been counted, and there were 300,000 more that we didn't have time to count until later. Altogether, it was a total of 1,500,000: twice as many as anyone had ever collected before.

And the whole campaign had cost us only about $28,500 for printing the petitions, postage, telephones, office space, our ads, and Paul's expense money. Our success was a tribute to a supreme, dedicated effort by thousands of volunteer workers. Not a penny was paid to professional petition circulators.

All of a sudden, something else had happened, too:

The politicians weren't laughing anymore.

CHAPTER TWO

Know Your Enemy:
Blackmail and Brown-mail

If I were a Communist and wanted to destroy this country, I would support the Jarvis amendment.

> —Pat Brown, former Governor
> of California, before Proposition
> 13 passed

Proposition 13 would replace "one monster with another."

> —Jerry Brown, Governor of California,
> before Proposition 13 passed

Proposition 13 creates challenges, it creates problems, but it creates an opportunity to make government in California a model for people all over the country. . . . A great opportunity, although it's going to be a painful and difficult process. . . . We have our marching

orders from the people. This is the strongest expression of the
democratic process in a decade. . . . Things will never be the same.

—Jerry Brown, Governor of California,
after Proposition 13 passed

No, THE POLITICIANS WEREN'T laughing at us any longer. They
started running scared once they saw how the signatures were
rolling in. They showed what they were really like: vindictive,
and usually with a yellow streak a mile wide down their backs.

I've been in politics a long time; over half a century, to be
exact. And the campaign against 13 was the most hypocritical
one—filled with monumental lies told by monumental liars—that
I've ever seen.

The *Los Angeles Herald-Examiner*, which I believe was the
only major newspaper in the state to support us, said in a May
24, 1978 editorial that opponents of Proposition 13 had "stooped
so low on a number of occasions that some of them need a hook-
and-ladder to see over the curb." And Jack L. Loether, president
and publisher of the *Glendora Press*, wrote on May 18, 1978:

Holier-than-thou Democrats and bureaucrats are making
Richard Nixon's Watergate scandal look like child's games,
when compared with dirty tricks being pulled against Prop.
13 on the June 6 ballot.

The thought that the common folks will approve Prop.
13, and put a stop to big-spending politicians, is scaring
the hell out of the gold bricks on the public payroll. In an
effort to defeat the tax reform measure the dead-beats in
government are sparing no cost to fight the initiative.

How low did the opposition go? For openers, they stooped to
using young children against us. One night about nine o'clock
when I went to give a speech at the Long Beach Hyatt House, I
encountered a group of youngsters between ten and fourteen years

old picketing against Proposition 13. Having children out picketing in the dark along a busy road like Pacific Coast Highway is what I call underhanded. That was about the most ruthless, coercive method I had ever seen used in politics. The school administrators and teachers had frightened the children into believing that classrooms would be eliminated and even recess would be cut because of a lack of playground equipment if Proposition 13 passed. Those children shouldn't have been used to picket. It was a disgrace. The school personnel were instigating this cruel exploitation of children for political purposes. That really infuriated me.

A similar thing happened up in Burlingame, outside of San Francisco. A note signed by the sixth-grade class at Crocker School in Hillsborough urging a vote against 13 was shoved under the windshield wipers of parked cars. That incident resulted in the *Antioch Ledger* running an editorial on May 10, 1978 that is one of my favorites. It said in part:

> While it is understandable that people are worried about losing jobs because of cutbacks, it is deplorable that children should be dragged into the controversy.
>
> If the students in the 6th grade class at Crocker wrote the note and then made the parking lot rounds, it is obvious the thrust to do so came not from the students but from their teachers or even the school administration. . . .
>
> But the tone of the note and the way it was written leads this newspaper to think the note was written by teachers who wanted to make the public think it was written by the students.
>
> This type of action should not be tolerated, especially from a profession that is supposed to teach children the differences between right and wrong and to have strong moral fiber.
>
> How can the students possibly learn this lesson when the people teaching it haven't learned?

And in Hayward, classes were shortened by one hour one day so that teachers and the administration could discuss Proposition 13. You might ask why they couldn't have a meeting and talk about 13 on their own time, instead of refusing to provide the services they're paid for. That, in fact, is exactly what the *Fremont Argus* did ask in a May 2, 1978 editorial which referred to the meeting as an "obvious anti-Prop. 13 rally."

Of course I can understand why school-district employees were worried that Proposition 13 might cost them their jobs. They were having pressure put on them by the school boards. On February 20 the Los Angeles School Board sent out notices to 21,000 teachers and administrators warning them that their contract might not be renewed for the 1978–79 school year. Superintendent of Schools William Johnston said the district faced a deficit as high as $780 million in 1978–79 if 13 passed.

Johnston didn't bother to add that at the same time the school board was trying to scare all these people into thinking they were going to lose their jobs, the district was recruiting for teachers—not only in California, but all over the Southwest. Imagine the stir we created when we distributed thousands of reprints of advertisements with the words "TEACHERS WANTED, Los Angeles City Schools" in huge letters that appeared in the *Houston Chronicle* on January 29, the *Phoenix Gazette* on February 2, and the *Dallas Morning News* and the *Albuquerque Journal* on February 26.

On February 26 I mentioned these advertisements during a debate I had with Howard Miller, president of the Los Angeles School Board, on KNBC, Channel 4. Miller didn't comment during the show, which was taped at 2:00 P.M. on February 24. Then, on February 27, the day after the show was on the air, Miller told the press that the recruiting of new teachers had been called off before he and I taped our debate. But then the district's head of personnel said the decision to stop recruiting was made in a meeting that was held several hours *after* Miller and I taped our debate at KNBC. If this wasn't like the Watergate cover-up, nothing ever was. On top of that, the school officials changed their minds two weeks later and started looking for bilingual teachers again, even though the first teachers they would have had to lay off—if they had to lay any off, which they didn't—would have been minority and bilingual teachers, because they were low on the totem pole in seniority. (In March 1979, nine months after Proposition 13 won, the Los Angeles School District was again advertising in out of town papers for a wide variety of teachers in math, science, English and bilingual studies.)

And then the Browns—Jerry, Willie, and Pat got into the act. Jerry—our governor—signed a law that provided for the phase-out of California's annual tax on business inventory. Every March businesses in the state have to pay a tax on all the inventory they have in stock, which amounts to hundreds of millions of dollars a year, and deprives the state of much business. Many companies locate their warehouses in Nevada or Oregon, just outside the California border, so they don't have to pay our business inventory tax. There's no question that eliminating the tax is a good idea, because it will help business, and in turn will benefit the state. The only problem with the bill Brown signed was that it provided for an end to the business inventory tax *only if* Proposition 13 was defeated. Talk about trying to buy votes!

Still, this ploy by Jerry Brown wasn't much compared to the stunts pulled by his father and by the other Brown, Willie. In a letter dated February 16, 1978, Pat Brown, our esteemed former governor, wrote to Republicans:

"If I were a Communist and wanted to destroy this country, I would support the Jarvis amendment. Your fellow Republicans who waffle on it should be impeached."

Just in case anyone thinks I'm quoting what Pat Brown said out of context, those two sentences were the entire text of his letters, which was sent out over his signature on the stationery of his law firm, Ball, Hunt, Hart, Brown and Baerwitz, in Beverly Hills.

Pat Brown's intemperate remarks were an insult to the 1.5 million Californians who signed the tax-reform initiatives, and to the 4.3 million who voted for it in June. All of these people are loyal Americans. What Pat Brown said was a slur on the integrity and Americanism of everybody who supported the amendment, including 800,000 members of his own Democratic party who signed our petitions.

Of course, nothing Pat Brown did would surprise me. But that "Communist" statement showed just how dumb and just how far off his rocker he is. You've gotta be awful goddamned stupid to make remarks like that one—and like the one he made when he was running against Ronald Reagan for governor in 1966. In that campaign Pat Brown was shown on television telling a group of schoolchildren, "Remember that it was an actor who shot Lincoln." I guess that's his idea of humor. That also explains why Reagan beat Brown by a million votes, even though Brown had been governor for eight years and was the favorite.

Paul Ziffren, a brilliant guy who was a leader of the Democratic party and was a national committeeman, once told me that Pat Brown was the dumbest guy he'd ever seen in politics who got to hold as high an office as governor. As far as I'm concerned, Pat Brown was, is, and always will be nothing more than an opportunistic politician. And he's a pretty unattractive person to boot—which is another reason Reagan was able to beat him, because he got his puss on the tube too much. He should have lain low. The Reagan people like to think they beat Pat Brown. But the truth of it is that, for the most part, Pat Brown beat himself. And of course, as I've said many times, Pat Brown never would have gotten anywhere in politics had it not been for Earl Warren's refusal to campaign for Republicans.

What Pat Brown said was so outrageous that even the *Los Angeles Times*, which has always greatly preferred him to me, editorialized on March 26, 1978 that his remarks were "nonsense, and the senior Brown must know it. . . . To suggest that Red legions are waiting to take advantage of it [Proposition 13] is plain silly."

Ironically, even the Communist Party in California was opposed to Proposition 13. When I found out the Communists were campaigning against 13, I put out a statement saying, "If Communists are against our 1% property tax reduction initiative, then it must be good for the people of California." After all, the Communists were out to destroy our free-enterprise system and our democratic form of government, and would resort to every means at their disposal to accomplish their mission.

Willie Brown is a Democratic Assemblyman from San Francisco. He is chairman of the Assembly Revenue and Taxation Committee. He's supposed to be a real bright guy, so I'll have to assume that what he did was malicious instead of just stupid. During the campaign, Willie Brown suggested that the legislature should "punish" and "reward" California cities, depending on how residents of each city voted on Proposition 13. In other words, cities where people voted against 13 would get more state money than cities where they voted for it. That was pure and simple blackmail. He made it sound like the tax money belongs to the politicians, not to the taxpayers.

As the *Berkeley Gazette* said in a May 23, 1978 editorial headlined "An Asinine Idea From Willie Brown":

> Brown's proposal amounts to a veiled—or perhaps not so veiled—threat against the voters: Either they vote his way or they pay the penalty. Such a precedent would be dangerous as well as foolish. It is also arrogant, since state funds are provided in large part by the taxpayer and do not "belong" to Willie Brown and the legislature.

Some of the politicians never did catch on. In January 1979 it was revealed that twenty-four municipal court judges in Los Angeles had contracted with a private law firm to help them find ways to get around Proposition 13. And these judges tried to get the county to pay the legal fees by pretending that the money was spent for travel, testimony by witnesses and stationery. The county actually issued checks for $53,000 to the law firm, Gibson, Dunn and Crutcher, but before the law firm got around to cashing the checks, the county found out what had happened and stopped payment. Robert Bush, who is assistant to Kenneth Hahn, the chairman of the board of supervisors, said that either the law firm "is going to donate this service to the judges or the judges are going to pay for it out of their own pocket." It was my news release that exposed this ripoff.

Probably the cruelest trick played on the public during the 13 campaign was a notice that was sent out by the senior citizens' division of the Franchise Tax Board about a month before the election. The Franchise Tax Board collects state taxes. The notice read:

> Senior Citizens Property Tax and Rent Assistance Claim forms and instructions for 1978 will not be mailed until after the June 6, 1978 statewide election. The filing period for such claims will begin on June 16, 1978 rather than May 16, 1978. The reason for the delay is that the specific benefits available to senior citizen claimants will not be

determined until the election results are known, inasmuch
as the new table of benefits provided by Chapter 24 of the
Statutues of 1978 will not be in effect unless Proposition
8 is approved and Proposition 13 is rejected at the June 6,
1978 election.

Proposition 8 was a competing tax relief measure placed on
the ballot by the politicians in an attempt to defeat Proposition 13.
It would have provided only one-fifth as much relief as Proposition
13 and for one year only.

The obvious implication of the notice was that senior citizens
might lose some tax benefits if 13 passed. In fact, 13 didn't affect
tax exemptions and assistance for the elderly at all. But these
notices were sent to 460,000 senior citizens, many of whom didn't
understand very much about taxes and as a result were scared half
to death by the notice. As Mrs. K. V. Chase of Laguna Hills told
the *Santa Ana Register* on May 12, 1978, the notice "sure sounds
like manipulation to me. It sort of brings it down to 'if you don't
do this, we're going to do this to you.' It gives me the impression
I won't get anything if (Prop.) 13 passes. It's like a big stick being
held over our heads."

In the same article, Stan Williams, a spokesman for the Tax
Board, admitted that his office had received many calls from senior
citizens who thought the notice meant they would have to pay
higher taxes if 13 passed. "In hindsight, we could have added that
the current program would remain in effect" whether 13 passed
or not, said Williams.

In a May 18, 1978 editorial about the notice from the Franchise
Tax Board, the *Costa Mesa Daily Pilot* said:

> Its wording gave the very clear impression that benefits
> would not be "in effect" unless Prop. 8 is approved and
> Prop. 13 rejected June 6. This is not true.
>
>   It is hard to believe that the wording was not a deliberate
> attempt to rally opposition to Prop. 13. If not deliberate,
> it was so inexcusably stupid and shortsighed that those re-
> sponsible should be promptly removed from positions in-
> volving communication with the public.

As I said, the trick the bureaucrats tried to play on the elderly, many of whom were helpless and uninformed, was no doubt the lowest blow of all.

The campaign against 13 was marked repeatedly by the technique of The Big Lie. The lies actually began about two weeks before the signatures had to be handed in, when the politicians put out the word that we already had more signatures than we needed, so we didn't need more people to sign the petitions. That, of course, was false.

Once we had qualified for the ballot, the politicians and bureaucrats turned to substantive issues and used lie after lie after lie after lie.

Lie Number One: They said the reason we had launched our campaign was because of the state surplus.

The fact is that we wanted to reduce taxes, property taxes, and all other taxes, whether the state had a surplus or not. That was our mission back in 1962, and it never changed. Back in those days, there was no surplus because Pat Brown spent every penny he could get his mitts on. As recently as 1975, when Jerry Brown succeeded Reagan, the surplus was "only" $500 million. The surplus mushroomed under Jerry Brown, who refused to spend the money, which was a pretty good idea, but who also wouldn't return the surplus to the people, where it belonged. For that matter, they even lied about the size of the surplus. The opposition said the surplus was $1 or $2 billion; I said it was $6 or $7 billion. It turned out I was right.

Lie Number Two: Proposition 13 was intended to benefit the owners of apartment buildings, based on the fact that I am executive director of the Apartment Association of Los Angeles County.

The fact is that I didn't join the apartment association until ten years after I first got involved in the tax movement in 1962. The United Organizations of Taxpayers and I had already tried to qualify two initiatives for the ballot before I went to work for the apartment association.

I never discussed 13 with anybody in the apartment business before I decided to try to reduce property taxes. While we were in the process of gathering signatures in 1977, the members of the apartment association asked me if I would like them to put some money in the campaign, and I said no. I told them that if they gave us money it would hurt us, because then people would truthfully be able to say that we were connected with the apartment owners in this. After we qualified for the ballot, they offered us money again, and we accepted.

The story that I represented the landlords and that they were the prime beneficiaries of Proposition 13 was a monumental lie. They were not the prime beneficiaries. Every business and every property owner in California got the same property-tax reduction that the apartment owners got. If the apartment owners reduced their rents because of 13, it was obligatory upon the May Company and the Bank of America and the title companies and the lawyers to reduce their charges, too.

The landlords are not solely responsible for high rents, and they should not be singled out for returning their 13 savings to the consumer. Apartment owners make less profit than the television industry. And, as in the television business and the newspaper business and the oil business and the shipping business, there are a certain number of lousy, no-good stinkers in the apartment business. But they're no worse than anybody else.

However, I've always thought that apartment owners were performing as great a service for the public as any other industry. There are 11.5 million tenants in California. If the apartment owners didn't build and maintain those buildings, where in the hell would those people live? They live in an apartment only because it's the cheapest place for them—the only place they can afford, in most cases. If we didn't have the guys who invest in apartments, Los Angeles would look like Tijuana. Except that Los Angeles is so big that you wouldn't be able to miss it.

I've felt for many years that rent raises are caused by politicians, not by landlords. The unnecessary, stupid laws they pass without any regard for common sense are forcing the rents up. The taxes are forcing the rents up. The minimum wage forces rents up. Having to pay workmen's compensation insurance forces rents up. The zoning ordinances force rents up. The high interest rates, which are largely the fault of the politicians, force the rents up. The high cost of the plumber and the carpenter and the brick-layer forces rents up.

What we're seeing is that the price of everything is being forced up by the politicians—food prices, clothing, gasoline, medical costs, everything. Dr. Michael DeBakey, the famous Houston heart specialist, told me that the cost of medical care is forced up 35% because of unnecessary government regulations that have to be followed and reports the government requires people in medicine to fill out.

I think the fact that so many people are forced to live in apartments is bad for the country. The solution is more building, but the politicians have made it impossible to build. People don't have as much interest in keeping an eye on government and politicians when they rent, instead of owning their own home.

It's rough out there. Whether you're a plumber or a lawyer or a petition gatherer, life is rough outside. I think one of the great strengths of the United States for many years was that when a guy got through with a rough day at work, he went home and, by God, his home was his castle. He could shut the door and thumb his nose at the whole damned world and have sixteen hours of saying, "Go to hell, buster." That makes him an independent American citizen. But if you're living under the threat of eviction, or raises in rent beyond your income, or in an apartment so noisy that you can hear the plumbing in the next apartment and the one on top, I don't think that's conducive to the most freedom.

I'd like to see everybody be able to own their own house. The country is a hell of a lot more important than the landlords. See, I'm head of the landlords' association. But I am the most different head of a landlords' association you will find. I'm the head of the landlords' association because they needed me and not because I needed them. And they know that.

When I agreed to go to work for the apartment association, they were floundering. They were losing $1,500 a month. They owed $40,000 in open accounts that were past due. They owed a $26,000 mortgage on their building. When they asked me to take the job, I didn't want it, and I told them I didn't want it. I finally agreed to take it on one condition: that I would make the decisions. I told them, "I know you have a corporation. I know you have a board of directors. But if I take this job, I'm going to make the decisions. Now, if you want me to take the job, you put that in writing." They did, and then I said, "Now that I've got that, I'm going to give you something in writing. It's my resignation. And anytime you don't like any decision I make, all you need to do is accept my resignation. Other than that, you can't do a damned thing. Until you decide to accept my resignation, I'm running the show."

They asked me how much salary I wanted, and I told them they couldn't afford to pay any. I told them that offering to pay me when they had no money and were deeply in debt was a dream. I said, "I'll decide on what salary I want when I'm ready, and if you don't like it, you accept my letter of resignation." I didn't take any salary at all for two years, and then I decided on $1,700 a month.

I also got them out of debt. I told them, "I'm not going to run any association that owes overdue bills. You might as well understand that. If I go in there, the day a bill comes in, we send out a check. Not the next day. And if you're not agreeable to that, I don't want any part of this."

When I went in there, they had 1,100 members. Now they have 5,000 out of about 64,000 apartment owners in Los Angeles. It's the biggest association of apartment owners in the United States. Each member has an average of 11 units, and the association represents the owners of more than 50,000 apartment units.

I started a new thing in the apartment industry called, "Tenants Are Customers." I used the illustration that if my wife spends $200 a month at Bullock's, they treat her like the Queen of the May. I told the landlords that if someone is paying them $200 a month, they ought to treat them good, too. It works. Unfortunately, some apartment owners don't know enough about running a business, and they're the ones that give the apartment industry a bad name. Most of them had no business experience, no public relations experience. They had been a machinist or a bricklayer or a carpenter or a farmer or a clerk, and they had no experience in selling or servicing a customer. So they don't know how to do it very well. It's a sad thing. I try to teach them. For about four years before Proposition 13, I held a meeting every Saturday morning and taught classes in business operations for landlords.

We had about 200 owners every months, and close to 10,000 over the course of four years.

During the time I've been working for apartment owners, I've persuaded the state legislature to kill a rent-control bill that would have doomed the California apartment industry like it did in New York, and I persuaded the Los Angeles City Council to kill a proposed earthquake ordinance that would have required the demolition of 14,000 brick buildings and put 100,000 tenants out of their apartments. I also got the city council to vote against an ordinance that would have required the installation of new locks whenever an apartment is rented to a new tenant, as well as an ordinance that would have ended free municipal rubbish collection for all apartment houses containing more than four units. The owners were already paying for rubbish collection in their property taxes.

So I think I've done a good job for the apartment business. But the apartment business in California is so rough that if somebody wanted to give me an apartment house, I wouldn't take it. And I think I know what I'm talking about, because I know as much about the apartment business as anyone in California. Out of all the guys I know in the apartment business, there's only one who makes big money. He owns about 250 units in the Wilshire district and makes about 18% on his cash flow. Most other owners would be better off if they just put their money in the bank.

I think the apartment business is just too tough. Most apartment owners work like dogs, around the clock, seven days a week, including Saturdays, Sundays, and holidays. And they don't get a nickel for their labor. The apartment-house owner is like a slave—the only guy left in the United States that is still in involuntary servitude. And if they decide to sell, the capital gains tax wipes out any legitimate profit they might have made. But the politicians have made the word "landlord" sound like the word "Mafia."

During the campaign for Proposition 13, I had several debates with Leo McCarthy, the Speaker of the Assembly. He is generally considered to be the most powerful politician in California, except for the governor. And McCarthy was not too bright. You see, all these politicians think they are so big, they're not used to having people come out and hit 'em on the nose. A few people feint with a left at 'em but they make sure they don't hit 'em. But I come out swinging. I hit McCarthy right on the beak every time we got together. Right off the bat I would hit him with a right cross.

One time he and I were having a televised debate—I think it was on Channel 4, the NBC station in San Francisco—when McCarthy said I was being paid by the Apartment Association of Los Angeles. He said it was obvious that I wrote this amendment for them and for me, and not for anybody else.

I said, "I'll tell you, the Speaker seems to think there's something tainted about my affiliation with the Apartment Association. I just want to tell the Speaker, because he doesn't seem to know, this is the fifth amendment I've proposed. I proposed two before I ever became affiliated with the apartment industry. I never discussed the present amendment with anybody in the apartment industry. It was none of their business. This is the United Organizations' amendment, not the Apartment Association's."

Then I said, "Now that we've got that straight, I'll tell you about some *real* dirty money. Every year McCarthy gets tens of thousands of dollars from the public employee unions, and this source of campaign money is a terminal cancer on this state." Then I held up a sheet of paper showing that 117 of the 120 members of the legislature take this money, and that McCarthy gets nearly half of his campaign funds—$50,000 or more every election—from the public employee unions. I said, "He got it before he was elected. They bought him and they own him. But I worked for my money, and nobody tells me how to spend it."

You know what he said? "I don't use any of the money myself. I give it to other candidates." Which is largely true. He gives it to other Democrats and buys their votes for himself. That's how he got them to elect him Speaker.

I said to him, "You mean you launder it, like Watergate?" That was one politician who was damn glad to get off the air that night.

Lie Number Three: The opposition tried to get people to believe that under Proposition 13 the market value of a piece of property that declined in value because of fire, flood, earthquake, or other disaster, or because the neighborhood deteriorated could not be reduced. It has always been the law of the state of California and it still is the law of the state of California that if something damages your property, the county assessor has the authority to reduce the market value. Proposition 13 made no change in that law whatsoever. All Proposition 13 says is that the assessor cannot raise the market value more than 2% in one year. And the assessor doesn't even have to raise the value 2%, assuming the value does not increase. The 2% is not a minimum, it's a maximum.

Lie Number Four: The politicians said that because business owns two thirds of the privately owned property in California, Proposition 13 would give a *new* windfall to business. The important word is *new*. That is a lie, because for more than fifty years the state constitution has required that residential and business property be appraised, assessed and taxed on exactly the same basis: the tax rate multiplied by the assessed value, which is equal to 25% of the fair market price.

Proposition 13 did not touch that formula, which is still in effect. So if Proposition 13 gave a windfall to business, it's the same old windfall the politicians have been giving to business for over half a century.

It was strictly a desperation tactic to try to inflame the majority of people who don't own businesses into voting against 13 by claiming it was intended to benefit business. Then the opposition had to swallow that stuff real hard when the Bank of America and a number of other big businesses came out against 13. This wasn't for business, this was for everybody. And business got the same benefits from 13 as everybody else.

Besides, the people who made that argument don't understand that business doesn't pay any taxes. All business does is collect the taxes from the consumer and pass them along to the government. Let me repeat: business doesn't pay a penny in such taxes. For instance, if the sales tax is five cents on the dollar, a store sells a $1 item for $1.05, and passes the nickel on to the state. When I tell people that, most of them give me a blank stare. But it happens to be true. Don't take my word for it; ask Milton Friedman, who is probably the most respected economist in the country.

This was really a contest between the maximum political con artists and the public. The maximum political hot air artists like to tell the public, "We'll raise the tax on business, but we won't raise your taxes." The only thing that happens when they raise taxes on business is that it raises all consumer prices. The guy who buys the stuff pays the taxes, but the politician points his finger at the May Company or the Ford Motor Company and says, "Look what they did—they robbed you!" It's a hell of a big scam. You know, I found out that on my Thunderbird, for which I paid $8,000, the total of all the taxes levied by all the different government agencies came to $4,500. Ford didn't get a penny of that. If it wasn't for the taxes, I would have paid $3,500 for the car.

Lie Number Five: Along the same lines, some critics said that if the intent of 13 was to lower the taxes on residential property, then 13 should have dealt only with residential property. We didn't try to do that because, based on the best legal advice available, we felt that such a law would be unconstitutional. You can't discriminate for or against one class of property. Besides, we wanted to give a tax break to business as well as to everybody else. The people in California who hire other people are in business. We were losing dozens of companies and thousands of jobs every year because business taxes were too high. And the property tax was one main reason.

Lie Number Six: According to its opponents, 13 gave a hidden benefit to business because residential property is sold more often than business property. When a parcel of property is sold, 13 permits the new market value to be the purchase price.

My response to that argument is that when they said business doesn't turn over as fast as residential property, they always used the illustration of the Telephone Company buildings and Bank of America buildings. But 90% of the business in California is small business in small buildings. It's the stores along Pico Boulevard and Market Street. They are small businesses, and they turn over as fast as residential property, if not faster.

Lie Number Seven: The politicians said 13 was unfair because it increased the taxes on properties that were sold, but not on properties that didn't change hands.

It is true under 13 that if you have two houses side by side that are appraised at $50,000 each and somebody comes along and decides to pay $80,000 for one of them, his market valuation goes from $50,000 to $80,000 and he pays 60% more in property taxes than the guy next door, whose house is still appraised at $50,000.

That may sound unfair, but it really isn't. The man who pays $80,000 for the house does so voluntarily. He sets his own price, and he sets his own taxes. Nobody else does. Take the same situation before 13 was passed. There are two $50,000 houses next to each other. Someone comes along and buys one of them for $80,000. That raises the taxes on similar properties for miles around to $80,000, whether they like it or not. And that is what is really unfair.

What we did cured 99 and 99/100% of this thieving system they had before. There's no way in God's green world that you can have a perfect system as long as you have a property tax at all. The constitution of the state of California says that property shall be taxed at its market value. The market value of a steak or a pair of shoes or an automobile or a house is what someone is willing to pay for it. The whole property tax system is tied to market value. Under 13, the guy that pays $80,000 for the house makes his own market value. He controls his own decision, he decides what the price of his house is going to be, and he decides what his taxes are going to be.

Lie Number Eight: One of the most outrageous tactics the opposition used against us was to claim that the entire state of California would virtually come to a halt if 13 passed. Here are a few examples of what they said:

—In February, when there was a lot of hysteria about the Hillside Strangler case, Assistant Los Angeles Police Chief Louis Sporrer said that if 13 won, the police department would have to eliminate the major-crimes unit, which had been in charge of investigating the Hillside Strangler. He was obviously implying that the police would give up the Hillside Strangler investigation if 13 passed. That was just as obviously false.

—The Los Angeles County employees distributed a newsletter with a great big headline: "Grim Outlook If Prop. 13 Passes."

Harry Hufford, the county's chief administrative officer and personnel director, was quoted as saying, "We would have to lay off 20,000 County employees from our work force of 76,500."

The newsletter also claimed that passage of Proposition 13 would result in an "end of all paramedic rescue service and the closing of at least half the district's fire stations"; the removal of "70% of street lights"; and the "closure of 45 of the 93 libraries."

On top of that, they said that if 13 passed, "Eventually the whole [sewer] system would fail and sewer service would not be available for approximately two million County residents."

You know what that argument amounted to? The stuff that flows in the sewers!

—San Francisco Mayor George Moscone proposed a budget that he said would not allow pay raises for most city employees. The head of his Social Services Department, Edwin Sarsfield, said that most of the 1,500 employees in the Social Services area would lose their jobs and "The mayor will declare a state of emergency" if 13 passes.

—The Milpitas City Council tried to scare residents of that town by adopting a budget that called for several new taxes to make up for the losses that 13 allegedly would have caused. They would not admit that 13 would leave them more than enough money to provide essential services, and that people who voted for 13 wanted lower taxes, not the same amount of taxes in different forms.

—One of the most callous tricks of all was the release of a "study" by the UCLA Graduate School of Management which claimed that passage of 13 would result in the loss of 451,300 jobs around the state, and that the state unemployment rate would nearly double to over 10%.

The truth was that the politicians have the power to use a public institution like UCLA for their own ends. They got a bunch of punk students that knew about as much about economics as a mud turtle and had them concoct a phony report. They thought that would have some effect on the electorate, over the knowledgeable word of such renowned economists as Neil Jacoby, Milton Friedman, and Arthur Laffer. That report fell flat on its butt. The only thing it did was bolster the politicians and the bureaucrats and the schoolteachers into the false impression that they were accomplishing something. I think it actually produced a backlash and won us many votes.

New West Magazine hit the nail right on the head when it wrote on July 17, 1978, shortly after 13 passed:

> Why, only last month, hundreds of thousands of state workers faced immediate termination in the event Proposition 13 passed. A UC economist determined that a full-scale depression would sweep the state once those state workers ran out of unemployment benefits. It turns out those dire predictions were contingent on Sacramento not voting any increased aid to local governments. Since there was virtually no chance of that happening, the citizenry is to be forgiven for concluding that, because of the surplus from our prior tax payments, those dire predictions were misleading.

—The opposition ran ads and cartoons that said things like, "If your house catches fire, call Howard Jarvis. If you need a cop to protect you, call Howard Jarvis."

Talk about cheap shots!

—Wilson Riles, the State Superintendent of Public Schools, said that Proposition 13 "would do nothing short of destroying education in California." He also said, "I have a headache occasionally, but you don't solve that by chopping off one's head, and that is the Jarvis approach."

In fact, the situation in California before 13 was a little more serious than a headache. And the "Jarvis approach" was a little less drastic than "chopping off one's head," although I can think of a lot of heads I'd like to chop, and Riles's is right at the top of my list.

—The opposition also referred to 13 as "the meat-ax approach." The real meat-ax approach was forcing elderly people to leave their homes because they couldn't pay the taxes.

—The worst offender, of course, was my good friend Leo T. McCarthy. From the time we qualified 13 for the ballot he was saying things like 13 would "strip cities of services such as police and parks" and would "destroy the school systems of the state." He also referred to Proposition 13 as "financial disaster." But in a debate he and I had on April 26, six weeks before the election, on television station KNXT in Los Angeles, I forced the Speaker to admit that 13 would not cause the schools to close or to curtail essential services, because the state constitution requires the legislature to provide funds for public schools.

In my debates with McCarthy and the other politicians around the state, I had the facts cold on taxes, and they didn't. I annihilated them. Maybe that's why, shortly after 13 won, the strain of fighting 13 and then having to find ways of getting by with less money caused McCarthy to have an allergic reaction to some almonds he had eaten. He wound up in the hospital. It was probably just nervous exhaustion. Since McCarthy was forty-eight and I was seventy-four and going strong, I took that as another omen that I was fighting for and winning the good fight.

McCarthy and the other politicians got what they deserved, considering the kind of campaign they ran against 13. If they could have laid off a paraplegic with one eye and half his nose gone, they would have done it and blamed it on 13, so the *Los Angeles Times* could put the guy's picture on the front page.

Lie Number Nine: When the politicians saw that people weren't buying their arguments against 13, they tried to snow people into believing that 13 would be struck down by the courts if it passed. Judge Bruce Sumner of Orange County even filed suit during the campaign. He alleged that 13 violated the state constitution because it dealt with more than one subject. What Sumner did was not a surprise to me—he used to be in the Assembly.

Sumner's argument was absolutely false, and he didn't get anywhere with it. Proposition 13 dealt with just one topic: property taxes. Besides, what Sumner and the others who pretended that 13 was unconstitutional overlooked was that we had gone through a long legal process to make certain that 13 did meet all the requirements of the law and the constitution. Every time we wrote an amendment, we submitted it to leading constitutional lawyers who were not affiliated with the United Organizations, and got their opinion. Next we would present it to the California Legislative Council, a group of lawyers whose principal job is writing laws for members of the legislature and who check the language and content of proposed amendments. They always said our amendments were valid, and we consider them to be the second highest legal authority in California, after the State Supreme Court. In addition, before an amendment can be offered to the people for their signatures on petitions, the Attorney General and the State Finance Director study it for its legality and financial effect, and the Attorney General writes the title and a brief description. So we had gone through each of those steps several times over the years, and we had no doubts about the constitutionality of 13.

In a February 15, 1978 editorial, the *Redlands Daily Facts* did an excellent job of pointing out what Sumner was trying to pull on us:

> The deeper reason for disapproving of the legalistic attempt to beat Jarvis is that it bespeaks scorn for the People. What going to the courts says is that the People of California are not to be trusted.
>
> On the contrary, the People of California have earned the right to be trusted by their consistently excellent judgment on ballot measures. In any case where there is a choice of who is to be trusted—the People or the Legislature—bet on the People every time.
>
> Suppose that the Jarvis amendment does pass in spite of the hysterical campaign that will surely be mounted against it.
>
> The People of California would not come to such a radical decision unless they were profoundly discontented with the present tax structure....
>
> The only way that the People can revolt is by approving Proposition 13.

There didn't seem to be any limit to which the tax gougers would not go in order to defeat any measure that would help the people who pay the taxes. When they realized they weren't scoring points with their attacks on 13, they started attacking me personally.

On March 14, 1978, less than three months before the vote on 13, I was arrested in Ventura County on a trumped-up charge of drunk driving. I had just left the home of my friends Al and Marcia Green.

There was a tax rally in Ventura, with about 1,500 people

there. Before the meeting, Estelle and I had dinner and one drink
with the Greens. After the meeting we went back to the Greens'
house. There were a lot of people there who wanted to meet me.
I had two or three cups of coffee, which I later found out contained
kahlua. I didn't know it at the time.

Finally, along about midnight, Estelle and I had to leave. We
didn't want to be rude, but I had to be in Oceanside at 8:00 the
next morning, and that meant we had to leave Los Angeles about
6:00.

I was driving on 101 toward Los Angeles. I had the car in
cruise at 55 miles an hour and we were listening to the radio and
talking. It was darker than hell. About twenty minutes after we
left Ventura, a car suddenly came up behind us. It seemed to be
going awfully fast. It didn't have any police lights on or anything.
Throughout the campaign, I had received threats on my life and
from time to time some off-duty Los Angeles police acted as
bodyguards for me. These police often drove me places because
they didn't think I should be out driving by myself. They told me
if I did have to be out without them and a car came up behind me
real fast, I should try changing lanes and speed to see if they were
following me. But in no event should I stop.

I tried changing lanes and going faster and slower that night,
but that car stayed right behind me. Finally it pulled up beside us
and put on the police light. We were glad it was the police—we
had really been frightened.

I got out of the car in the pitch-black. I have arteriosclerosis,
and after I've been sitting for a while, I don't walk so well for
a few minutes. I stumbled a bit on the side of the road and had
to grab onto the car door. The highway patrolman saw me do that
and said he wanted to see my driver's license. Estelle is always
afraid I'll lose my wallet, so she sews my back pocket to make
it smaller, and I had trouble getting my wallet out. Then I dropped
it. The cop said, "I think you're drunk."

I said, "I think you're nuts."

I volunteered to take a breath test, and the police decided to
take me to the station. They asked Estelle if she could drive and
told her to follow us. Then they took off at 100 miles an hour,
and there was no way Estelle could keep up. She had no idea

where the police station was, and she drove halfway to Los Angeles before she could find someone to give her directions. It took her an hour and a half before she got to the station.

When I got to the police station, the officers gave me the breath test. After a few minutes they told me I had passed it and they said I could go. But then one officer told me that maybe I should take a blood test, too, "for my own protection." I told him I saw no reason to take another test, since I had already passed the breath test and been told I could leave. But then I got to thinking that if I didn't play along, there would be newspaper headlines saying, "Jarvis picked up for drunk driving; refuses to take blood test." So I told them to go ahead and give me the blood test too. I told them I take an anticoagulant for my blood, but they said a doctor would administer the test and he would understand. They took me over to Los Robles Hospital in Thousand Oaks for the blood test, and it was immediately obvious to me that the guy administering it was not a doctor because he didn't even know how to get the needle into me.

Several weeks later, I was notified that they were going to prosecute me for drunk driving, based on the results of the blood test. The way I found out was interesting, too: some wire-service reporters called me and told me.

It wasn't until after 13 passed that we had the trial. When my attorney, Trevor Grimm, who also represents the apartment association, went in for a conference with the presiding judge, the judge said to the assistant D.A. who had been assigned to prosecute the case, "What in the hell are you guys prosecuting this case for? You have absolutely no case. All you're going to do is cost the county $25,000."

The assistant D.A. said, "I was ordered from up above to bring this case to trial."

The judge said, "Who is 'up above'?"

The D.A. said, "I'm not at liberty to say."

Ordinarily, a case like this takes about thirty minutes. This case took five days. And in the end I got acquitted, and all they did was cost the county $25,000, just like the judge had predicted.

I had good reason to be jumpy the night that highway patrol car followed me in such suspicious fashion before they pulled me over. I received several threats during the campaign. All of the threats were referred to the police and the FBI. One call that I remember in particular came one night when I was home. A young guy who sounded like he was on dope said, "You son of a bitch, we're going to cut your goddamned throat." And I got a few letters and cards that said, "We're going to blow up your home" or "We're going to blow up your car."

I'm a lot more worried about the guy that doesn't call than I am about the one who calls and says he's going to do this or that. But Estelle and some of my friends and the police who were guarding me got the jitters. And when everyone else around me got the jitters, I got the jitters a little bit myself. I had heavy steel mesh put over the windows of our house at a cost of $1,000 so no one could throw anything through the windows. I had an alarm put on my car so that if anyone opens the hood or touches it, a bell rings. There's nothing to stop someone from putting a plastic bomb under my car, but the police told me that for a bomb like that they have to make a connection to the ground somewhere so that when you move the car it kicks off the switch. So, instead of taking four pushups on the bedroom floor, I take my four push-ups next to the car every morning. I try my best to watch where I'm going. I don't get out of the car on a dark street anymore. I'm a whole lot more careful about locking the car. I won't stop for somebody unless I know him personally.

I try to be as careful as I can, but if somebody really wants to get you, there's not much you can do about it. If they couldn't protect Jack Kennedy and Bobby Kennedy and George Wallace and Martin Luther King, someone could get me, too. And I'm still in the phone book. I've had a listed number since I moved into the house in 1941 and I'm not going to change that now. I don't have anything to hide and I've never turned away anybody who wanted to talk to me. Besides, all they have to do is go down to the county recorder's office and they can get your address. And if anybody walks into my office and says they want to see me, I say, "Okay, come on in."

Still, ever since the campaign, my life has been curtailed some-what. I know that somebody might want to get me. I'm not fright-ened, it's not constantly on my mind, but I am aware of it. And for several weeks during the campaign I had to hire around-the-clock bodyguards, which cost about $5,000. I'm not accusing the opposition of any of these tactics, but I think my arrest was politically motivated, and if I was driving in an unusual way before the police stopped me, it's because I was afraid of who they might be, and because I was following the instructions my security people had given me.

THE ANTI-13 POLITICIANS

Fortunately for us, the politicians who were against 13 were not a very bright lot. They could have lowered taxes voluntarily and returned the $7 billion surplus to the taxpayers, which would have avoided the need for 13. But they were too dumb to do that. Dumb is not exactly the right word—because they're not dumb at all. They play dumb when it comes to looking out for the people, but they're wise when it comes to looking out for themselves. They were willing to sacrifice the country to feather their own nests. Their big objective is to keep people's noses out of government. They don't want any interference. That goes for everyone from the board of supervisors and the city council all the way up to president. They want Joe Doakes to stay over on his side of the fence—they don't want to hear from him at all. Proposition 13 has not changed that yet, but every day that goes by is going to change it more.

The other side could have argued, had they had the courage, that property should pay for other than property-related services. I think they would have lost anyway. But at least it would have been a legitimate argument, instead of all the phony ones they used. And the tactics they used backfired on them.

Almost everything they did played right into our hands. The San Diego City Council voted to raise their own salaries by 53%, from $17,000 to $26,000 a year, and to raise the salary of Mayor Pete Wilson by 20%, from $25,000 to $30,000. This occurred about three months before the election, and you can imagine the effect it had on the voters. The council couldn't have done a better job for us if we had asked them to help us. Even the *San Diego*

Union, which was crusading against us, pointed out on March 6, 1978:

> The City Council could not have given the advocates of Jarvis-Gann a better symbol of the excesses of local government with which to campaign.... The incredible percentage—53 percent—...so constantly and disgustingly keeps coming to mind.

In fairness to Pete Wilson, I should say that he didn't ask for the raise; in fact, he was opposed to it. He was one of the few astute politicians, even though he wasn't for 13. Way back in January, five months before the 13 election, Wilson predicted that the public employee unions would wage an extensive campaign against us, but that the voters, who were fed up with high taxes, would approve 13 anyway. Wilson has done a hell of a job as mayor of San Diego. It's too bad he didn't get on 13. He might have been the strongest candidate for governor the Republicans could have fielded.

Similarly, two months before the June election, the Conejo School Board up in Ventura County voted to extend the contract of the district superintendent for two years, at $45,000 a year. This was at a time when his current contract still had more than a year and a half to run. When some taxpayers asked the board if the extension was legal, the board said of course it was, so why should the taxpayers question their judgment? When the taxpayers asked the board's attorney for a legal opinion, he said that he was attorney for the board, not for the public, and any ruling he might make would be given to the school board, not to the public. All of this prompted the *Thousand Oaks Chronicle* to write in an April 3, 1978 editorial:

> The board has obviously forgotten that the $90,000 it chose to spend will be paid by the taxpayers.
>
> The county counsel has obviously forgotten that the taxpayers pay the salary, rent, law library, secretarial staff, and own the desk, rug and chair on which the counsel sits. The public is the client here, not the school board—or should be.

And the voters have long memories, and the taxpayers are getting short tempers.

Faced with that kind of a situation, is it any wonder that the voters are looking at the Jarvis-Gann initiative as a way of getting control of a system that now appears to be totally out of their control?

Our campaign was rolling along, and then Alexander Pope and Kenneth Hahn got into the act. The L.A. County Board of Supervisors had forced Phil Watson to retire from his job as Los Angeles County Assessor in October 1977. I was never satisfied that the charges were proven against Phil, but the board members made life so difficult for him that his only choice was to resign.

I applied for his job, although I knew there wasn't a chance in a million that the supervisors would appoint me. I just wanted to stir things up, although if they had named me I think my knowledge of taxes would have enabled me to do a good job. Actually, I was supporting Frank Hill, an old friend of mine.

The board of supervisors finally narrowed it down to Hill and Alexander Pope. Then Hill said he was for 13, and that decided the supervisors. They wanted a puppet assessor who they could control, in spite of the California law and constitution. So they picked Pope, who was totally unqualified for the job and knew absolutely nothing about assessment practices, which are very complicated.

Pope took office in February and immediately got in trouble when he said that many parcels of property were going to have assessed valuations 50% or 100% higher than they'd had the previous year. But he refused to send out the new tax notices as soon as they were prepared so that people could find out who was getting hit with the huge increases, even though many other counties were sending them out early. Then the board of supervisors ordered Pope to send out the assessment notices by June 1, five days before the election on 13, and a month earlier than they had to be sent out under state law.

When the public wasn't appeased by the prospect of receiving assessment notices on June 1, Kenneth Hahn, the most powerful member of the board of supervisors, took matters into his own hands. He railroaded the board into pressuring Pope to rescind the increases on 500,000 homes and 200,000 commercial properties and to restore their assessed valuations to the 1977 level. That's when the public caught on that the politicians were playing politics with their taxes. You see, first the politicians said they couldn't live with the assessment rollbacks that Proposition 13 would force. But when the pols realized that 13 was going to pass anyway, they rolled back the assessments themselves, in hopes that that would defuse the support for 13. Of course, if they had succeeded in defeating 13, they could have put the increased assessments back into effect as soon as June 6 passed.

Our friends at the *Los Angeles Herald Examiner* noted on May 26, 1978:

> Why can they [the politicians] now do what only a few days ago they were denouncing as irresponsible? . . . The people of Los Angeles are nowhere near as easily duped as the politicians believe. Those who were planning to vote for Proposition 13 will now do so even if they have to wait in line for hours like teens at a rock-concert ticket office. . . . Hahn and Co. have not killed 13's chances; they have rekindled all the voter cynicism and frustration which lie beneath the political surface like an underground stream. . . .
>
> We have faith in your intelligence. The politicians don't.

Pope, a bumbler at best, put some water on the 13 wheel and helped make it turn. I don't think his action was decisive, because we had 60% of the vote anyway, but it didn't hurt. I think it was very helpful to 13 to have a totally inept guy in the Los Angeles assessor's office. Of course, there are 57 other counties in the state, but in Los Angeles County, partly because of Pope's incompetence, we got better than a 2-to-1 yes vote and a 700,000-vote plurality on 13.

The bigwigs in labor and business went all out to defeat 13. They all tried to outdo one another in issuing doomsday prophecies about what passage of 13 would mean. Maybe they believed what they were saying, but the people they were trying to influence sure as hell didn't.

In view of all the scare stories about how 13 would cause huge cuts in public services such as fire departments and result in layoffs of most of the firefighters and other public workers, you would expect the firefighters to have been adamantly opposed to 13, wouldn't you? But that wasn't the case at all. Shortly before the election, leaders of Local 112 of the United Fire Fighters of Los Angeles, AFL-CIO, polled the membership. The result was 353 in favor of Proposition 13 and 184 opposed. And yet all the stories said these would be the first people to lose their jobs if 13 passed.

Similarly, the rank-and-file membership of a union in the private sector, UAW Local 216, put out a newsletter stating: "Prop. 13 will reduce your property tax by 60%" and urging all the members to "Save Your Home—Vote Yes on Prop. 13 June 6th!!"

And the state board of the California Chamber of Commerce took a stand against 13. But a majority of the 8,000 members—most of whom owned small businesses, unlike the members of the board—announced in May that they were supporting 13.

On election day itself, according to *Newsweek* (June 26, 1978), "One analysis showed that 43% of government workers in California voted for Proposition 13—even though some of them were bound to lose their jobs."

According to my information, about 30% of the state public employees voted for 13, even though they knew that if it passed, some of them might lose their jobs. I think that's a very striking example of how concerned people had become about what's happening to this country. They understood that if they had a job but couldn't afford to pay their property taxes, they would lose their home anyway. I think they were very bright to understand that. For many people, their only real asset is their home. And to have the government levy an absolutely confiscatory tax on their house, and for them then to foreclose people's homes for taxes, I think, is a high crime and misdemeanor on the part of government. I'd like to impeach them all for that. We have impeached people for less.

So the fat-cats mounted a very tough campaign against us. Unfortunately for them, they didn't understand what people were thinking at all. The average guy—a plumber or a carpenter—he's had it pretty good in the United States and he's got himself a $60,000 home. Now he could see the taxes killing him.

When you stop to consider what we were up against, it's a miracle that 13 won at all, much less by a margin of almost 2 to 1. Here are some of the organizations that came out against 13:

Labor: The AFL-CIO, the California Teachers Association, the American Federation of Teachers, the California State Employees Association, the Los Angeles City Employees Union—Local 347, the Los Angeles County Employees Association, the California Fire Services Coalition, and the American Federation of State, County and Municipal Employees.

Business: Bank of America, Atlantic Richfield, the Southern Pacific Railroad, Standard Oil of California, the Irvine Company, the Title Insurance Corporation, and several large brokerage houses.

Political groups: Common Cause, the League of Women Voters, the California PTA, the Commission on Aging, the League of California Cities, and—oh, yes—the Democratic Party leaders.

The press: Every major newspaper in California except the *Los Angeles Herald Examiner*, and most of the smaller newspapers in the state.

The politicians: About 90% of the members of the legislature, the county boards of supervisors, city councils, school boards, water districts, and hospital districts. Also, every present or former governor named Edmund G. Brown.

All we had against that lineup were the people.

The fact that we had hardly any endorsements from large groups like the other side had was partly by design. To the best of my knowledge, the only organization of a comparable size that supported 13 was the State Farm Bureau. The Republican Party didn't take a stand on 13, but I told them I didn't want their endorsement. I'm not saying they would have endorsed us anyway. Proposition 13 was such a popular cause that, given their past performance, they probably would have been too stupid to support 13 even if we had asked them to. I also asked the real estate associations and the landlords not to endorse 13, although I do know that individually, most of them were for it.

When I told these groups I didn't want their endorsements, they couldn't believe it. Everyone had been kowtowing to them for years to get endorsements. Well, not me. If we had had their official endorsements we could have lost. If the Republicans had endorsed it, for example, we might have lost most of the Democratic vote. And we couldn't have won without the Democrats. In California, 56% of the registered voters are Democrats, 35% are Republicans, 8% decline to state a party, and the other 1% belong to the minor parties. If the Republicans, who make up only one third of the state's voters, had endorsed 13, it would have become a Republican issue. That would have been the kiss of death. And if the realtors or the landlords had endorsed 13, it would have been even worse. That would have given validity to the claim that those groups were intended to be the beneficiaries.

The heavy hitters didn't just come out against 13; they put up a lot of money to beat us, too. Some of the larger donations that were pumped into the "no on 13" campaign were $100,000 from the California Teachers Association; $30,000 from the Los Angeles County Employees Association; $25,000 each from the California State Employees Association, the Association of California School Administrators, Bank of America, Atlantic Richfield, Southern California Edison and the Pacific Lighting Corporation; $20,000 each from the Los Angeles City and County School Employees and California Federated Teachers, and $15,000 each from the Southern Pacific and Standard Oil of California.

Our largest donation was $16,000 from the apartment association. Unlike the opposition, we had thousands and thousands of individuals, many of them retired, who gave us $100 or $50 or $20 or $10. We filled up a couple of telephone-book-sized reports listing all of our donors.

It was a case of David against Goliath and David won.

Actually, a number of people in a position to know told me that the Bank of America and the other big corporations that came out against 13 wanted to support it. But Assembly Speaker Leo McCarthy let them know that if they didn't oppose 13, the legislature would find a way to punish them. I think he meant it, and I think the giant companies believed him too, and they knuckled under.

CHAPTER THREE

The Media Be Damned—I'd Rather Be Right

The citizenry thumbed its nose at government because of burdensome taxes, and Howard Jarvis and his Posposition 13 were prophetic.

> —Anthony Lewis in *The New York Times*,
> after Proposition 13 passed

Anybody who was in the U.S. on the day when California passed Proposition 13 last June and at the time of the November elections had to notice a new spirit in the excited air.

> —Norman Macrae, deputy editor of the
> *Economist* of London

Defying the counsel of politicians, labor leaders and economists, a damn-it-all 65 per cent of the voters backed a proposal to slash their own property taxes—and made tax revolt the new gut issue

in American politics. . . . The California tax revolt had raced the
middle-class pulse of the country as feverishly as anything since
the invention of the station wagon.

—*Newsweek*, June 19, 1978

FOUR WEEKS BEFORE THE 13 election, on May 9, 1978, the *Los
Angeles Herald Examiner*—which, as I said, was the only major
newspaper on our side editorially—accused its crosstown rival,
the *Los Angeles Times*, of shifting from "animosity to hysteria"
in its campaign against 13. I think the *Herald Examiner* editorial
was, if anything, too charitable toward the *Times*.

In some ways, the press campaign against 13 was ludicrous.
On May 11, 1978, the *Chula Vista Star News* called 13 a "con
game" that "was generated by apartment house landlords, who
saw a way to save themselves a bundle by capitalizing on dissat-
isfaction of homeowners over property tax increases." Just to show
how well that newspaper understood what was going on, they said
in the same editorial, "Paul Jarvis, co-author of this abomination,
makes his money by running an association of apartment house
landlords." This was less than four weeks before the election,
when I had become one of the more famous people in the country.
I wonder what Howard Gann did for a living.

In an editorial a week later, on May 17, the *Monterey Peninsula
Herald* said the public had "been so outrageously deluded by a
pair of slick Southern California real estate operators." They were
0-for-2 in their description of Paul and me. First, neither one of
us owned any California real estate except for our own homes,
so that hardly qualifies us as "slick real estate operators." Second,
Paul lives in a suburb of Sacramento, which the *Monterey Peninsula Herald* might want to know is *not* in Southern California.

In April the student newspaper, the *Clarion*, at Granite Hills
High School in San Diego wrote that Paul and I owned huge
amounts of real estate in California, and that each one of us would
make millions of dollars if 13 passed. Gann and I responded by
slapping the kid who wrote the story and the school district with

a libel suit for $800,000. Some people criticized us for making such a big deal over something as insignificant as a high school paper. But we were tired of the teachers and school administrators using the students as a front for their own campaign against 13. And the father of the student who wrote that story happened to be the principal of another high school in San Diego. After the *Clarion* printed a retraction of the story, we dropped our suit.

New West wrote on February 27, 1978: "All you really need to know about the property tax initiative on the June ballot is that Howard Jarvis, the 75-year-old [sic] sponsor of the proposition, is also the paid director of an association of apartment house owners in Los Angeles." And all you have to know about the guy who wrote that story, Ed Salzman, is that he's a hack journalist who is editor of a rag called *California Journal*, which, like Salzman, is based in Sacramento and is written by the political establishment about the political establishment and for the political establishment.

Some of the publications in California were so ignorant about taxes, politics, and the law that they should have been banned from writing about 13—if for no other reason than to protect themselves from being laughed at. The *San Jose Mercury* was against 13 very vigorously, and, I thought, improperly. They were misrepresenting fact after fact after fact. I was concerned because I had a lot of support in the San Jose area, and I didn't want people who were in favor of 13 to believe any inaccuracies the *Mercury* editors might print because of a lack of understanding of the facts, and change their votes.

I got an appointment with the paper's editorial board. There was a long table with a bunch of "journalists" around it. I laid out the whole picture and went through it from soup to nuts. The publisher, a young fellow named Tony Ridder, who got to where he is on the basis of inheritance rather than brains or ability, was disagreeing with every word I said. He even questioned the legality of the amendment.

I told them 13 had originally been presented for its legality to the California Legislative Council, which had approved it. Someone at the table asked, "What is the California Legislative Council?" I said, "Does anybody here know who the California

Legislative Council is?" No one did. So I explained that it's a group of lawyers who write all the legislation in Sacramento. Assemblymen don't write the bills, the governor doesn't write the bills—the Legislative Council writes the bills. And I explained how you can submit a proposed constitutional amendment to the Legislative Council for an opinion as to its legality, and that it is the most authoritative group in the state except for the Supreme Court.

A little later in the meeting, I got into a discussion of the California tax system. I told them it was based on a mythical formula called the comparable sales ratio formula. Somebody asked, "What's that?" Nobody knew what it was.

I leaned back in my chair and I said, "Gentlemen, you've got this big building and this well-established newspaper. But I might as well tell you now, if no one here knows what the California Legislative Council is and if nobody here knows what the comparable sales ratio formula is, this paper doesn't have the right to print one damned word about my amendment or about taxation. Not a word. My advice to you is before you print anything else, you hire somebody who knows something, because obviously none of you do."

Sometimes the newspaper criticism of 13 was so heavy-handed that I think it helped us more than it hurt us. The *San Diego Union* ran an editorial on March 31, 1978 saying things like:

> Proposition 13 is the difference between putting a mechanic to work on an engine that's out of tune, and giving a chimpanzee a hammer to beat on it until it falls apart.... Proposition 13 is an unvarnished piece of demogoguery.... The amendment would require a massive increase in state taxes to prevent a disastrous collapse.... [The] crude amendment [is] as poorly thought-out as something one might draft on the back of an envelope.

The most important thing to know about the *San Diego Union* is that they also have a young guy as publisher, and he was just as ignorant and uninformed about taxes as Ridder at the *San Jose Mercury*. Also, I guess nobody at the *Union* ever heard that Abraham Lincoln supposedly drafted the Gettysburg Address on the back of an envelope and on scraps of paper.

In terms of bias on the part of the press against 13, the *Los Angeles Times* was in a category of its own. I think "hysterical" is too soft a word to describe the editorials by the *Times* on 13. Here are some examples:

On April 30 the *Times* had a long editorial in which it repeated as fact the claims by the opposition that

Los Angeles County would eliminate all of the Fire Department's paramedic units, and would close half of the 129 fire stations. It would also close half of the county's 93 libraries. . . . More than 30,000 county employees would be laid off. The city of Los Angeles is considering the dismissal of 2,152 police officers and the closing of six stations. More than 1,000 firefighters would be cut, and 56 stations would be shut down. . . . The prospect for Los Angeles schools is even darker. More than 18,000 teachers would be laid off. Class sizes would increase, and many pupils would be on half-day sessions.

I repeat: the *Times* reprinted those lies as if they were fact. There was no disclaimer, no introductory words, such as: "Foes of Proposition 13 say that 'Los Angeles County would eliminate all of the Fire Department's paramedic units,'" and so forth.

That same editorial from which I just quoted had the following statement in italics:

"Vote Yes on Proposition 13 and send a message to tens of thousands of teachers, librarians, firefighters, paramedics, police officers, sanitation workers and public-health specialists that you can safely dispense with their services."

That is what I call an inflammatory lie. And that is why I meant it when I said that if the *Times* could have dug up a crippled government worker who was going to be laid off because of 13, they would have printed his picture on the front page, along with a bold-faced caption like "JARVIS VICTIM!!!" Bold-faced print for bold-faced lies, italicized print for italicized lies.

A *Times* editorial on May 28, just nine days before the election, stated that "The destructive effect that Jarvis-Gann would have on the public and social institutions of California is not [justified]. . . . We oppose Proposition 13, with its elusive promise of even greater tax relief, because it would do violence to the spirit and quality of life in California and to our prospects for enriching it."

At one point during its savage crusade against 13, the *Times* switched from reprinting lies by other people to purposely making distortions on its own. In an editorial on May 7 headlined "Deceit on the Schools," the *Times* quoted from the state constitution as follows: "'There shall be apportioned to each school district in each fiscal year . . . $120 per pupil in average daily attendance in the district during the next preceding fiscal year.'"

Take a close look at those three dots between the words "year" and "$120." Those dots are very important.

The *Times* went on to say: "That limit is the state's *only* (italics theirs) constitutional obligation to the districts. . . . Nothing in the Constitution requires the state to enlarge its present contribution of $120 per pupil if there is a decline in *local* (italics theirs) revenues for the schools, as there would be under Proposition 13."

The *Times* was trying to accuse Proposition 13 of potentially crippling the schools. They were attempting to make the point that we were lying when we cited the constitutional requirement that the state provide funds to the school districts as proof that 13 would not have such drastic effects on the needed school programs.

Let's talk about lies. Let's provide the three words between "year" and "$120" in the state constitution that the *Times* chose to leave out and replace with three dots. The three missing words are "not less than"!

What the constitution actually says is: "There shall be apportioned to each school district in each fiscal year *not less than* (italics added) $120 per pupil."

The *Times'* premeditated omission changed the meaning of the constitutional provision it cited so that it sounded as if $120 was the *maximum* the state had to provide to the schools, when in fact $120 is the *minimum*.

April 30, May 7, and May 28, 1978, when those three editorials ran in the *Los Angeles Times*, have something in common: they all fell on Sunday. That's when the *Times* has 30% more readership than it does on weekdays. Don't think for a minute it's a coincidence that the *Times* picked Sundays to print its harshest criticism of 13. They wanted to make sure their lies would get the widest possible dissemination.

I want to emphasize one thing in my discussion of the *Times* and the way it handled Proposition 13: I'm talking about the paper's editorials, not the news coverage. The *Times* reporters who wrote about 13 generally wrote accurate and balanced stories. It's the same thing as what we ran into with big labor and big business: The average working guy gave us a much fairer shake than the fat-cats did. Fortunately for us, the little guys had a thousand times as many votes as the fat-cats did.

The people who run the *Times* have good reason not to like me. Back in 1962 I filed suit to keep the city and county from using public funds to build the Music Center and the Performing Arts Center, which were the pet projects of Buffy Chandler, the wife of the publisher of the *Times*. The Music Center was put on the ballot and the people rejected it, but the board of supervisors voted to provide funds anyway, because of the Chandler family influence. Finally we dropped our suit and let them build those buildings. But they cost the taxpayers thousands of dollars a day, and only ½ of 1% of the people of Los Angeles ever go to the Music Center. We never should have let it be built. Why should the general public have to pay through their noses to maintain it instead of the people who actually use the center?

The suit we filed did delay construction of the two buildings. That really put a pinprick in the *Times'* bubble. I think they've resented it ever since. And they've opposed me ever since on everything I wanted to do in the way of tax reform or anything else, like running for office.

Then when Proposition 13 came along, the *Times* knew its effect would be to kill the redevelopment of downtown, which would have cost the property taxpayers of Los Angeles County $6 billion. The *Times* wanted to have downtown rehabilitated because that's where they're located. Not only is their plant down there, but they own dozens of parking lots in the downtown area. If downtown were fixed up and real estate prices skyrocketed, how do you think it would affect the value of all the property the *Times* owns? You guessed it.

I decided there is no way to justify rehabilitating the downtown area of Los Angeles at the expense of the average taxpayer for a very simple reason: Most people won't go there. The hassle is too great, the parking prices are too high—most notably in the lots the *Times* owns—and if they didn't have the courthouses and all the county buildings downtown, nobody would ever go there. Which wouldn't please the *Times* at all. If private industry can't find a way to pay for the rehabilitation of downtown Los Angeles, I think they ought to raze it and turn it into a park. Why should the homeowners in Long Beach or Santa Monica or the San Fernando Valley have their property taxes raised to pay for the rehabilitation of downtown Los Angeles?

The *Times* couldn't tolerate me or anybody else who disagreed with them or got in the way of their schemes. It is true, though, that since the election the *Times* has been nicer to me. They know that when they're beat, they're beat. I think they're just like the politicians, they go with the wind. I respect them even less now that they're a little less hostile just because we won. I've never thought much of that newspaper, and I don't think much of it now. But you have to read it to see what the enemy of the people is doing. I think the *Los Angeles Times* is the enemy of the people.

I think the *Los Angeles Times*, because its major interests are not in the newspaper business, slants the news to benefit its major investments. Of course, the same is true of many other large newspapers and the television networks. And then in addition, television news is mainly show business, it has little to do with the facts.

It was very tough to have 90% of the media against us. But 90% of the media had been taken in by the phony politicians. They had swallowed these great, monumental lies that had been handed out in press releases. The press didn't know anything about taxes to begin with, and didn't know much more after the campaign was over.

I don't think the press would have paid any attention to me if I hadn't finally won. God knows they ignored me for all those years. The media sort of laughed me off as a kook. They called me irresponsible, a demogogue, every ridiculous thing they could dream up. They dismissed me as a right-wing extremist. Of course, they were 100% wrong. A doctor buries his mistakes, but the *Times* covers up its mistakes, as does television. And because they have the chance to publish a paper or go on the air every day, they are able to crush almost anybody, just by the sheer weight of repetition.

I think it was a miracle I was able to overcome the attacks that were made on me hundreds of times over the years by the press. But I never asked any newspaper or radio or TV station to use a story. I'd issue a press release and it was wholly up to them whether they used it or not. I contrast that with a lot of people in the United States who spend a fortune to get their names in the paper or their faces on the tube. I never spent a nickel, except for postage and running off copies of the releases, which amounted to almost nothing. I had enough people who believed in what I did and were interested in it to make it worthwhile for the press to cover me without my having to pay for it.

I also think the press finally began giving me more coverage because I never knowingly told a lie and because I answered the questions, no matter how embarrassing they were to me. I've had top reporters tell me they like to interview me although they don't agree with a lot I say, because when they leave an interview with me they get answers, and when they talk to a politician they get runarounds. One time before 1962, when I was still active in politics, Carl Greenberg and Dick Bergholz of the *L.A. Times* took me to lunch because I was the only guy in the Republican Party who would tell them the truth. I think that's quite a badge of honor. And Dick Bergholz and I have always disagreed politically.

I tell off the reporters when I think they're asking me a stupid question or an irrevelant one. I compare their business to everyone else's. I say they're not a privileged class. They have no right to ask me what color toilet paper I use any more than I have a right to ask them how many times they had sex last week. And when they suggest that the apartment business should be under rent control, I say, "How would you like it if you were under censorship?" That always stops them. There's this one girl, Heidi Schulman, who works for Channel 4 in Los Angeles, and she knows less about taxes than a good reporter should. But the station insisted on sending her out to cover me. So finally I told her I just wasn't going to answer any more of her questions until she went and read up and prepared herself properly. Just being pretty isn't enough for me. But I like her personally just fine, even if she doesn't know much about taxes.

There is one interesting footnote to my ongoing feud with the Chandlers and the *Los Angeles Times:* In 1963 the Apartment House Owners Association of Los Angeles, as it was then known, presented its first annual award for Southern California's most distinguished citizen to Buffy Chandler. She was honored "for her efforts in spearheading the drive for the new Music Center and for other cultural activities"! Of course, that was ten years before I became affiliated with the association.

Not all of the newspapers were as hostile in their attitude toward Proposition 13 as the *Times* and its fellow travelers. Here is a sampling of what some of the more enlightened publications had to say:

> It has become an almost daily event for some municipality or school district to issue the news that it will have to all but close its doors should the Jarvis-Gann property tax limitation initiative pass this June.... This newspaper doubts the scare tactics being used by [opponents of 13] are proper. (*Pasadena Star News*, February 27, 1978)

> The recent behavior of politicians and bureaucrats throughout California has erased any doubt whether the Jarvis-Gann Initiative (Proposition 13) should be passed on June 6.
> It should be passed—by an overwhelming margin. (*San Francisco Progress*, April 26, 1978)

> We are growing a bit impatient with the Jarvis-Gann calamity howlers: Firemen who scream that we'll have to go back to volunteers and bucket brigades, park administrators who see themselves pushing lawnmowers in parks with no recreation programs and county people wringing their hands at the prospect of cutting 2,000 people off their payrolls.
> It should be noted that the Jarvis-Gann initiative says absolutely nothing about park districts, or schools, or fire districts, or laying off county employees. All it does is say—"This is the end on property taxes." (*East Yolo Record*, May 3, 1978)

> Bureaucrats, many of them prominent, and so-called businessmen who do most of their business with the government, have come out with misleading statements against Prop. 13....

Not only are the protests against Prop. 13 untrue, but Prop. 13 will do a great deal to make men freer by cutting out non-essential and control-happy agencies. (*Anaheim Bulletin*, May 25, 1978)

Even the *Fresno Bee*, which along with its sister *Bee* papers in Sacramento and Modesto, was certainly no friend of 13, had this to say (May 17, 1978) about the campaign against 13:

Given all the real drawbacks and dangers in Proposition 13, the Jarvis-Gann property tax initiative, it's hardly necessary for state and local agencies to conjure up half-baked objections not justified by the facts. . . .

Local library systems in a number of cities have been posting notices that libraries will be closed if Jarvis-Gann passes. That . . . is a scare tactic not yet supported by the facts.

. . . For state and local agencies to predict reductions in services or benefits not warranted by the provisions of the initiative is not merely unethical and irresponsible; it is also to undermine confidence in legitimate, factually based criticism of the measure.

Two friends of 13 used their columns to come to our support. Ronald Reagan, who signed one of our petitions, wrote in his nationally syndicated newspaper column in March, "Predictably, free spending legislators (backed by a chorus of special interests who depend on a brimful public trough) have proclaimed that the sky is falling."

After the election, Milton Friedman said in his June 19, 1978 column in *Newsweek:*

Despite the use of scare tactics including notices to teachers of automatic dismissal on passage of Jarvis-Gann, advance local budgets threatening drastic cuts in police and fire protection, and whatever other portents of catastrophe desperate feeders at the public trough could devise, the public refused to be bamboozled this time, as they had been so often before while watching taxes mount and governmental services deteriorate. This time, the scare tactics simply produced a backlash.

CHAPTER FOUR

The Campaign for 13:
The Impossible Dream

Government does not know how to cut. All Congress knows is how to add. The art of subtraction seems to be beyond its intellectual capacities. And the same applies, as we all know from experience, to state and local governments.

—S. I. Hayakawa, Senator, R-California

Any candidate who underestimates the potential of the tax revolt "is a political idiot."

—Howard Baker, R-Tennessee, Senate Minority Leader, after Proposition 13 passed

A warning signal to those in Washington that taxpayers are tired of being overburdened.

—David Boren, Governor of Oklahoma, after Proposition 13 passed

A valid expression of taxpayer rage and frustration.

—Blair Lee III, Acting Governor of
Maryland, after Proposition 13 passed

I AM NOT AN ECONOMIST.

But Milton Friedman, Arthur Laffer and Neil Jacoby are economists, and each one of them is widely renowned.

Milton Friedman, who taught for many years at the University of Chicago and is now a professor at Stanford University, won the Nobel Peace Prize for his work in economics. In a speech before the Americanism Education League in Pasadena on February 6, 1978, Friedman declared:

We are not going to get tax reform by a congressional committee in Washington or in the state house in this or other states voting lower taxes or voting an improved structure of taxes. That way is hopeless. It's a way we have been trying for years on end and it has gotten us nowhere.

The only effective tax reform is tax reduction.... The only feasible way of stopping tax increases is via constitutional limitation on government spending and government taxing.

In an interview with the Associated Press published in the *Los Angeles Herald Examiner* on March 31, 1978, Friedman stated that Proposition 13 is "the best chance we have to control government spending." He also said:

You know, we're all a bunch of suckers, unable to do anything about government overspending. It's in the self-interest of the people to have this pass.... Everyone knows that you simply do not get your money's worth for what you pay for government. If government has $7 billion less to spend, the public has $7 billion more to spend and will spend it more wisely....

Any business that comes out against Jarvis-Gann is absolutely insane. Business seems to have this inclination toward self-destruction.

Friedman also commented in an interview with Copley News Service, published in the *Fremont Argus* on April 18, 1978, that the most important feature of Proposition 13 might be the requirement of a two-thirds vote to increase taxes,because that would make it difficult for the legislature or local agencies to make up the tax revenues they would lose if 13 passed.

Having Friedman in our corner was a big plus. Even a small newspaper like the *Marysville Appeal Democrat* noted on April 29, 1978: "When an economist of Milton Friedman's status endorses the Jarvis-Gann property tax initiative, those who have scornfully dismissed the proposition as a screwball idea that would bankrupt California government are forced to give it more careful consideration."

That Copley wire story that quoted Friedman described him and Arthur Laffer as "California's two most prominent economists." Laffer is a young fellow—still under forty—who is a professor of business economics at USC. He told Copley: "Jarvis-Gann is excellent. There should be a limit on all taxes. This is a major first step."

Laffer made a study of Proposition 13 and concluded that it "would go a long way toward revitalizing California's economy." He also found that "with property taxes lower, businesses will expand their activities within the state. This expansion will create new jobs, more investment, and higher real wages. Sales, incomes and other forms of activity will expand. Sales taxes, income taxes, etc., all will rise. In addition, state outlays for social welfare will fall (unemployment compensation, rent subsidies, medical, etc.)."

I should point out that Laffer is the inventor of the Laffer Curve, an economic theory which says that if tax rates increase past the optimum level they actually result in decreased tax revenues for government, because prohibitively high taxes discourage consumer spending and business investment.

Both Friedman and Laffer also said that if Proposition 13 were to lose, it would be a signal to politicians in California and all over the rest of the country that they could raise taxes without fear of making the voters angry.

California's other leading economist, Neil Jacoby of UCLA,

INITIATIVE MEASURE TO BE SUBMITTED DIRECTLY TO THE ELECTORS

The Attorney General of California has prepared the following title and summary of the chief purpose and points of the proposed measure:

INITIATIVE CONSTITUTIONAL AMENDMENT--PROPERTY TAX LIMITATION
Limits ad valorem taxes on real property to 1 % of value except to pay indebtedness previously approved by voters. Limits annual increases in value. Establishes 1975-76 assessed valuation as base value of property for tax purposes. Requires 2/3 vote of Legislature to enact any change in state taxes designed to increase revenues. Prohibits imposition by state of new ad valorem, sales, or transaction taxes on real property. Authorizes specified local entities to impose special taxes except ad valorem, sales and transaction taxes on real property. Financial Impact: Would result in the loss of local property tax revenues of $7 billion to $8 billion annually and a reduction in state costs of about $700 million in 1978-79 and $300 million annually thereafter.

Ⓐ All signers of this petition must be registered in _____ County.

			For Official Use only
1	SIGN AS REGISTERED	PRINT NAME	
	REGISTERED ADDRESS	CITY ZIP	
2	SIGN AS REGISTERED	PRINT NAME	
	REGISTERED ADDRESS	CITY ZIP	
3	SIGN AS REGISTERED	PRINT NAME	
	REGISTERED ADDRESS	CITY ZIP	
4	SIGN AS REGISTERED	PRINT NAME	
	REGISTERED ADDRESS	CITY ZIP	

92

5	REGISTERED	CITY	ZIP
	ADDRESS		
6	SIGN AS REGISTERED	PRINT NAME	
	REGISTERED ADDRESS	CITY	ZIP
7	SIGN AS REGISTERED	PRINT NAME	
	REGISTERED ADDRESS	CITY	ZIP
8	SIGN AS REGISTERED	PRINT NAME	
	REGISTERED ADDRESS	CITY	ZIP
9	SIGN AS REGISTERED	PRINT NAME	
	REGISTERED ADDRESS	CITY	ZIP
10	SIGN AS REGISTERED	PRINT NAME	
	REGISTERED ADDRESS	CITY	ZIP

THIS PETITION IS INVALID UNLESS DECLARATION OF CIRCULATOR IS COMPLETED. Petition signers NEED NOT date their signatures. Circulators MUST.

DECLARATION OF CIRCULATOR (to be completed after above signatures have been obtained):

I am registered to vote in the County (or City and County) of _____ . I circulated this petition between the dates of _____ and _____ , inclusive. Each of the signatures to this petition was signed in my presence. Each signature of this petition is, to the best of my knowledge and belief, the genuine signature of the person whose name it purports to be. I circulated the petition in the above County (or City and County) and no other. I declare under penalty of perjury that the foregoing is true and correct.

SIGNATURE AS REGISTERED	DATE	PRINT YOUR NAME

ADDRESS AS REGISTERED	CITY	ZIP

Congress shall make no law . . . abridging the right of the people . . . to petition the government for a redress of grievances. Bill of Rights — First Amendment

STATEWIDE — PEOPLE'S PETITION TO CONTROL TAXATION

Sponsored By: PEOPLE'S ADVOCATE, P.O. Box 6113, Van Nuys, CA 91408, (213) 988-9737, P.O. Box 681, Carmichael, CA 95608, [916] 487-6114, PAUL GANN-Chairman, ORRIN STRATTON—No. California Chairman   UNITED ORGANIZATION OF TAXPAYERS, 6451 W. 5th Street, Los Angeles, CA 90048, (213) 938-4982, (213) 938-3316, HOWARD JARVIS-State Chairman, J. EARLE CHRISTO-State Vice Chairman

AREA TELEPHONE NUMBERS: LOS ANGELES COUNTY 988-4982 / 934-3316 / SO. BAY 320-1080 / 325-2769 / B.F. VALLEY 988-1080 / 841-2514 / 785-7912 / 988-4737 / 764-2500 / ALHAMBRA 284-5848 / COVINA 842-2239 / LANCASTER 942-0244 R. HEIGHTS 965-3005 / WESTCHESTER 776-3970 / 670-7150 / VENTURA COUNTY 647-3100 / SAN BERNARDINO COUNTY 912-4499 / SAN DIEGO COUNTY 440/027 / 852-3224 / VISTA 726-7409 / ORANGE COUNTY 542-7853 / 776-9053 / SACRAMENTO COUNTY 487-6114 / BUTTE COUNTY 342-0028 / STANISLAUS COUNTY 523-3051.

Co-Sponsored by

Return completed petitions to local sponsors or to addresses listed above.

DEADLINE: This petition must be in the offices of one of the sponsoring agencies no later than November 25, 1977.

INITIATIVE MEASURE TO BE SUBMITTED DIRECTLY TO THE ELECTORS

The Attorney General of California has prepared the following title and summary of the chief purpose and points of the proposed measure:

INITIATIVE CONSTITUTIONAL AMENDMENT—PROPERTY TAX LIMITATION

Limits ad valorem taxes on real property to 1 % of value except to pay indebtedness previously approved by voters. Establishes 1975-76 assessed valuation as base value of property for tax purposes. Limits annual increases in value. Provides for reassessment after sale, transfer, or construction. Requires 2/3 vote of Legislature to enact any change in state taxes designed to increase revenues. Prohibits imposition by state of new ad valorem, sales, or transaction taxes on real property. Authorizes specified local entities to impose special taxes except ad valorem, sales and transaction

$8 billion annually and a reduction in state costs of about $700 million in 1978-79 and $800 million annually thereafter.

To The Honorable Secretary of State of California

We, the undersigned, registered, qualified electors of the State of California, residents of _____ (B) _____ County (or City and County) present to the Secretary of State this petition proposing to add Article XIIIA to the Constitution, and petition that the same be submitted to the electors of the State of California for the adoption or rejection at the next succeeding general election, or at any special statewide election held prior to that general election, or as otherwise provided by law. The following is a full and correct copy of the title and text of the proposed measure.

THE AMENDMENT.

That Article XIII A is added to the Constitution to read:

Section 1.

(a) The maximum amount of any ad valorem tax on real property shall not exceed One percent (1%) of the full cash value of such property. The one percent (1%) tax to be collected by the counties and apportioned according to law to the districts within the counties.

(b) The limitation provided for in subdivision (a) shall not apply to ad valorem taxes or special assessments to pay the interest and redemption charges on any indebtedness approved by the voters prior to the time this section becomes effective.

Section 2.

(a) The full cash value means the County Assessors valuation of real property as shown on the 1975-76 tax bill under "full cash value", or thereafter, the appraised value of real property when purchased, newly constructed, or a change in ownership has occurred after the 1975 assessment. All real property not already assessed up to the 1975-76 tax levels may be reassessed to reflect that valuation.

(b) The Fair market value base may reflect from year to year the inflationary rate not to exceed two percent (2%) for any given year or reduction as shown in the consumer price index or comparable data for the area under taxing jurisdiction.

Section 3.

From and after the effective date of this article, any changes in State taxes enacted for the purpose of increasing revenues collected pursuant thereto whether by increased rates or changes in methods of computation must be imposed by an Act passed by not less than two-thirds of all members elected to each of the two houses of the Legislature, except that no new ad valorem taxes on real property, or sales or transaction taxes on the sales of real property may be imposed.

Section 4.

Cities, Counties and special districts, by a two-thirds vote of the qualified electors of such district, may impose special taxes on such district, except ad valorem taxes on real property or a transaction tax or sales tax on the sale of real property within such City, County or special district.

Section 5.

This article shall take effect for the tax year beginning on July 1 following the passage of this Amendment, except Section 3 which shall become effective upon the passage of this article.

Section 6.

If any section, part, clause, or phrase hereof is for any reason held to be invalid or unconstitutional, the remaining sections shall not be affected but will remain in full force and effect.

IMPORTANT — PLEASE READ

1. Any registered voter may circulate this petition.

2. Fill in the name of the county **IN WHICH YOU ARE CIRCU-LATING THE PETITION** in section (A) on the back of this petition and section (B) above then proceed to obtain signatures. Signers MUST sign as they are registered. USE PEN.

3. After all signatures have been obtained complete the Declaration of Circulator. If you circulate more than one petition make certain you complete the Declaration of Circulator on each completed petition.

4. Processing of petitions takes time. Please return petitions to any of the sponsoring groups **AS SOON AS THEY ARE COM-PLETED. THIS IS IMPORTANT!**

DO NOT XEROX (PHOTOCOPY) THIS PETITION.
(FRONT)

who once served as adviser to Presidents Truman and Eisenhower, was also solidly on our side. He gave a speech over in the San Fernando Valley on October 15, 1977, and urged everyone to sign our petitions. He also said:

> Property tax bills are rising much faster than family incomes. . . . They threaten to erode away that foundation of American society: the family-owned home. . . .
>
> We must deliver an unmistakable message to our elected representatives that no longer will we permit misuse of the property tax to finance welfare, health, educational and other governmental services that serve all of the people in our state. Such government spending programs should be paid for by revenues collected from all the people. . . .
>
> By curbing the widening flow of government revenue, it would compel our public officials to cut wasteful spending and stop giving outsized annual increases in the pay and benefits of public employees. . . .
>
> A 1% limit would still leave property tax revenues far above the level required to pay for property-related governmental services. . . .
>
> Politicians tend to spend all the revenue coming into the public treasury. Hence, the only effective way to curb government spending is to turn down the revenue spigot. Inflation has pumped up government revenue, and public officials have voted themselves higher salaries, put more jobholders on public payrolls, and fattened the compensation packages of government workers. This easy process of spending more and more must end.

Jacoby also pointed out that according to surveys made by the Economy and Efficiency Commission of Los Angeles County, property taxes yielded $9.4 billion in California during the fiscal year that ended June 30, 1977, but $5.5 billion of that—or about 60%—was spent on education and social services that benefited everyone, while $3.9 billion, or 40%, was used for property-related services.

As Jacoby said, "The property tax bill of the average California homeowner would be less than half its present amount if property taxes paid only for property-related services. This fundamental inequity in California taxation should be removed!"

In another speech at the UCLA Business Forecast Conference on March 16, 1978, Dr. Jacoby said that Proposition 13 is "the only hope we have for bringing economy, efficiency and justice to California's government. The time has come when heroic surgery is needed to excise the cancerous growth of property taxation."

He said in that same speech that Proposition 13

> would precipitate a revolutionary reform—one long overdue—in California state and local finance....
>
> People's incomes are not closely related to their ownership or use of housing. Hence, the present tax system unjustly burdens the young family with large housing needs and the older couple who want to live in their family home on their retirement pensions. Stability of home or apartment occupancy is an important social goal. The present tax system weakens our society by threatening to force people out of their homes.

I think I know as much about taxes as anyone. But the fact remains that I am still just a layman. But the words I have quoted here come from the experts. In addition to the clout they carried, I was flattered and proud to have the support of leading economists like Milton Friedman, Neil Jacoby and Arthur Laffer. In my judgment, their support proved that we were correct.

THE NUMBERS SHOW
WHY TAX RELIEF WAS NEEDED

Most people don't like statistics. Nevertheless, it takes figures to show why Proposition 13 was necessary, and what applies to California applies to most other states and the federal government. I'm going to list some important statistics in this section, so anyone who doesn't like to be bothered with numbers should skip it.

Here are some of the reasons why we needed tax relief:

—In 1950 there were 343,000 state and local government employees in California, and the population of the state was 10.5 million, or 1 employee for every 30 residents. In 1960 there were 620,000 government employees and the population was 15.5 million; 1 government employee for every 25 residents. In 1978 there were almost 1.5 million government employees, and the state population was 22 million. The ratio was 1 government worker for every 15 residents. (These figures are from the State Employment Development Department.)

—In the 1967–68 fiscal year the state budget was $5 billion. By 1977–78, 11 years later, it had tripled, to $15 billion. During that same period, the consumer price index in Los Angeles rose only 64%, or one-third as much as the state budget. In only three of those years was the increase in the state budget less than the increase in the consumer price index. (Figures provided by U.S. Bureau of Labor Statistics and the State Department of Finance.)

—Between 1957 and 1977, total state tax collections increased by 874%, while the gross personal income of California residents increased by 334%, according to the Republican State Central Committee.

—From 1968 to 1977, the cost of city government in the state rose 163%, but the population rose only 14.5%. During this same period, the city of Los Angeles had a 2% drop in population and a 159% increase in spending, according to the California Chamber of Commerce.

—During the 1977–78 fiscal year, which ended less than a month after Proposition 13 passed, local governments collected $10.3 billion in property taxes, an increase of 10% over the previous year, and the assessed value of taxable real and personal property in the state was $96.3 billion, or 15% higher than the year before, according to the State Board of Equalization. In that same year, the consumer price index rose only 5.8%.

—In 1968 the average property tax on a single-family home was $362. In 1978 the average tax was $811, according to the Board of Equalization.

—According to Neil Jacoby, as of March 1978:

> Government employees in California have a total compensation package—including paid holidays and vacation, pensions and job security—that is 25% higher than that of workers in comparable jobs in private industry. The average annual income of the California government employee today is substantially higher than the average income of the taxpayer—a case of the poorer supporting the richer.

—During the eight years before Proposition 13 passed, the cost of food stamps in California went up from $248 million to $5.5 billion, the cost of unemployment insurance increased from $2.5 billion to $14 billion, Medicare costs rose from $6.1 billion to $21 billion, and Social Security costs increased from $26.7 billion to $82.4 billion.

—The average person in the United States works 2 hours and 52 minutes out of every 8-hour day to pay taxes, according to the U.S. Chamber of Commerce. To put it another way: the average employee gives every dollar he earns from January 1 to May 11 to federal, state, or local government.

—As of 1975, 81 million people in the United States were supported by taxes, while only 72 million were supported by jobs in the private sector, according to a study by the Ford Motor Co.

Those were some of the conditions that created a need for Proposition 13. Again, while the details differ, in general, most of the other states and the federal government suffer from the same conditions, to a greater or lesser degree.

OUT ON THE HUSTINGS

It took a lot of years to get ready for this thing to happen. When it finally jelled, I was ready for it. I was keyed up for it. I knew we were going to make it this time. I felt the time was ripe. I knew as much about taxes and about California as anyone else. I felt it was my job to defend the gates at any cost.

I was ready to carry on the campaign—by myself, if necessary—in the last six months. I was on the road constantly. I even spoke two or three times on Election Day. On a typical day during the campaign, I would do a couple of interviews with the press, give a speech at lunch, cut a radio or TV spot, have dinner with the local tax leaders in whatever area I was in, and appear at an evening rally. And these appearances would be in two or three or four different cities and towns around the state. I also had to make sure the pro-13 campaign, the United Organizations of Taxpayers and the Apartment Association were all being run properly.

At times I felt like a lone eagle on this. I was the political strategist, the media man, the copywriter and the janitor. I was the driver of the tractor. Bill Butcher, a partner in Butcher and

Forde, the political consulting firm in Newport Beach that was guiding the campaign, said that the focus was on me, not on the campaign. And one of the leaders of the "no on 13" campaign said they could overcome everything except my personality.

Early in the campaign, people used to get up in the audiences and say they had heard I was a kook or a nut. I would say, "Well, you know, there was a fellow named Thomas Alva Edison who ran around telling people he could take a bottle and some silk string and make a light out of it that they could read by. Everybody said this guy was nuts. And one day the people who had said Edison was nuts could sit in their chair and turn on a light and it turned out that they were the nuts, not Edison."

I also used to tell 'em, "If I'm a nut, I'm in pretty good company, because a million and a half Californians, including Ronald Reagan, signed our petitions; Milton Friedman, Neil Jacoby and Arthur Laffer are supporting 13; and Friedman even taped some TV commercials for us at no charge." Before long, people stopped referring to me as a nut.

I was hitting a responsive chord in places like Orange County, where property market values had gone up an average of 20% in 1976–77, compared with the 2% a year limit that was in Proposition 13. And up in Santa Cruz, where they had about 1,800 surfers from all over the country, aged 16 to 34. They didn't do anything but surf and draw welfare and food stamps. The guy who owned a home got hit with a huge tax increase in order to support these surfers in the style to which they had chosen to become accustomed. Why should a guy who has to support a family also have to support these bums who surf eighteen hours a day, thirty-seven days a month? I told them that after 13 passed, the sun was going to come up the next day and all the surfers were going to evaporate. We found out there was one water district in the state that had not provided any water for years, but still collected taxes, and that one school district had enough money to pay for six electric typewriters, so they bought them—even though they only had one typist. But they had to spend the money so they could justify asking for a bigger budget the next year. Proposition 13 went over real well in those places and a lot of others that had similar situations.

I told the people that up until now we had given government an unlimited budget and they had still exceeded it. I told them that we didn't need to send our money to Sacramento to have it laundered and sent back to us—what was left of it, that is. And I pointed out that the state Revenue and Taxation Code is now about 1,500 pages long, and every one of those pages is filled with different schemes for taking our money from us.

I reminded them how when Abraham Lincoln was on his way to Washington to take office in 1861, he made a speech in Indianapolis and he said, "It's your business, not mine," in reference to government. This has been a creed with me since I read it about fifty years ago. I also told my audiences about something a very great man in this country had said back in the 1920s. His name was Al Smith, he was governor of New York and when I say he was a great man, I'm well aware that he was a Democrat. Al Smith said, "When I have a problem as a politician, when there's something I don't understand, I always give it back to the people. They have more brains than I do. Their collective judgment is better than the collective judgment of the legislature or the governor." I wouldn't let them forget that this was their one chance to take things back in their own hands.

Proposition 13 was needed mostly because property taxes are the only form of taxes that have no relation to the ability of someone to pay them. The three main forms of taxation are property taxes, income taxes, and sales taxes. Income taxes have a direct relation to the ability of the taxpayer to pay them. You don't pay sales taxes unless you decide voluntarily to buy something; if you can't afford the sales tax, you don't buy the item. But property taxes could amount to thousands of dollars on a house—even if the owner had little or no income: Some people would say that if the taxes on a house were that high, it meant the house was worth a hell of a lot of money and the owner ought to be able to pay the taxes. That's only half true. The house might be worth a lot of money on paper, but the guy who owned it might have been living there for forty years and might be trying to get by on Social Security. Just because his house is worth a lot of money is no reason to kick him out of his home. But that's what was happening.

Assemblyman Henry Mello—who is a Democrat—said many older people were going hungry in order to save enough money to pay their property taxes. Mello is the number-two ranking guy on the Assembly Revenue and Taxation Committee—the one Willie Brown is head of—and we tended to believe him when he made a statement like that that didn't really serve his own interest. Besides, we knew on our own about folks passing up meals so they could pay their property taxes. We also knew about some senior citizens who were eating dog and cat food to save enough money so they could pay their taxes. That's just plain criminal.

Hell, Jerry Brown himself went on KNBC-TV in Los Angeles on January 15, 1978, and admitted: "Where I've gone to meetings, people say, 'Why don't you tax me based on how much I make, not just take it from my house, which doesn't have any relationship to how much income I have every month?'" That's exactly the point I was trying to get across: not that incomes should be raised, but that all taxes—especially property taxes—should be reduced.

One of the things I said as I campaigned around the state was that passage of Proposition 13 would result in a two-thirds reduction in the tax impounds that banks and mortgage companies collect in advance from their mortgage payers to make sure the property taxes get paid when they're due twice a year. I also said that if 13 won, there would be significant reductions in utility bills all over the state. The opposition tried to argue that I was wrong, but they never stood a chance. On the utility bills, for instance, we had letters from officials of companies like Southern California Edison, Southern California Water, and San Diego Gas and Electric saying that if 13 passed and their property taxes went down, they would lower their rates for service. And just in case any utility companies didn't lower rates voluntarily, we also had a letter from Robert Batinovich, president of the state Public Utilities Commission—which is responsible for setting utility rates—which said:

"To the extent that passage of Jarvis-Gann would reduce a utility's property tax liability, that would result in a corresponding reduced need for revenues. If a study of this effect showed that a reduction in rates would be appropriate, we would not only permit such a reduction, we would require it."

Letters like those were pretty persuasive to the voters.

We also had a report from the H. C. Wainwright Company a Boston firm that was established in 1868, stating that if 13 passed and property taxes were reduced, it "would lead to an estimated $75 billion increase in California personal income" during the next four years.

The Wainwright report, which was dated June 1, 1978, also said the huge increase in personal income

> could result in more, not less, total tax revenues for state and local governments. Combined with the directly implied decrease in unemployment and social welfare spending, California's budget surplus would go up, not down. . . . Total tax revenues most likely would rise because the increase in general economic activity in California would produce significantly higher income, sales and other tax revenues.

According to the Wainwright report, the decrease in cost of owning property if 13 won would result in more construction of homes, apartments, and commercial and industrial buildings. The net result would be "a building boom" in California.

And in an updated report three weeks after 13 passed, the Wainwright people projected that personal income in the state would increase by an estimated $110 billion during the next ten years. These reports gave proof that we were going to be successful in one of the major goals we set out to accomplish: taking the money away from the politicians and putting it back in the hands of the people.

THE POLITICIANS' LAST GASP

Almost from the moment we began circulating the 13 petitions back in the summer of 1977, the politicians and bureaucrats started looking for ways to circumvent us if we won. Under their theory of taxation, a reduction in one form of taxes, such as property taxes, simply meant that they would have to find a way to raise other taxes to make up the money. They didn't understand that our goal was to cut taxes—not shift tax collections from property taxes to some other form. As early as September 26, 1977, a report prepared for Willie Brown's Assembly Revenue and Taxation Committee said:

> There is no indication as to how this measure [Proposition 13] will be funded. Is the intent to "cut" local government services by $7–8 billion? If so, what services will be eliminated? Police and fire protection? Parks and recreation?
>
> If the intent [is] to have the state raise state taxes by $7–8 billion, what state taxes would be increased to pay for these local services?

They were already assuming that we wouldn't mind their raising other taxes, just as long as property taxes were cut by the same amount. I suppose that's the kind of "reasoning" you'd expect from staff people who were hired by Willie Brown.

However, both Ronald Reagan and Senator S. I. Hayakawa understood what we were driving at. Reagan wrote in his syndicated column in March: "In Washington [and many state capitals] when the words are stripped away, 'tax reform' usually boils down to a little cut here, a little added tax there. The underlying assumption is that the cost of government can never go down, only up." And Hayakawa declared: "Government does not know how to cut. All Congress knows is how to add. The art of subtraction seems to be beyond its intellectual capacities. And the same applies, as we all know from experience, to state and local governments."

In plain English, what we were trying to accomplish was to put a fence between the hogs and the swill bucket. Virtually all of the howlers against Proposition 13 had their noses buried deeply in the public trough. They were on a gravy train provided by the taxpayers, and they wanted to ride that train at the taxpayers' expense until they reached the promised land of exorbitant pensions for the rest of their lives. They were trying to use the taxpayers' money to bankrupt the taxpayers at whose trough they were gorging themselves. Proposition 13 was intended to forge a chain around the necks of all elected officials and their coteries of bureaucrats so that they could be dragged away from the feedbag. We wanted to put the politicians and their comrades in the bureaucracy on a permanent diet that did not include large portions of the taxpayers' money.

Many years ago, Calvin Coolidge said, "Collecting more taxes than is absolutely necessary is legalized robbery." And highway robbery is what the political establishment had been getting away with for many years before Proposition 13 passed. The state had taken more money from the taxpayers than we needed to operate the government. That money belonged to the taxpayers, but when they politely asked Sacramento to return their money to them, the word came down from on high that the politicians would condescend to "give" a little over a billion dollars back to its rightful owners.

Of course, the party line from Sacramento was that the state surplus was "only" a billion dollars or two. But we knew better. We knew it was more like $6 or $7 billion. One politician who did tell the truth was Jesse Unruh, a Democrat who used to be the Speaker of the Assembly and is now the state treasurer. He said about six months before the election that the state surplus was $6 billion, and he was correct. That didn't surprise me a bit. During my many years in politics I had discovered that Jesse Unruh was one of the few politicians whose word was good. I should add that Unruh did not give his estimate of what the state surplus was in order to help us; he was opposed to 13.

There was also a question as to how much of a tax revenue loss Proposition 13 would cause. I said it was $5 billion. Roy Bell, Jerry Brown's finance director, said it was $7 billion. Let's use Bell's figure. That sounds like a hell of a lot to take away from government—except that they were collecting $40 billion a year, which amounted to $1,800 for every man, woman, and child in the state of California. All 22 million of them. Even if they lost $7 billion, they would still have $1,500 to spend on every resident of the state. That's enough to float this state in hundred-dollar bills. When we were able to get that point across—that 13 would still allow state and local governments to collect $1,500 a year from every person in California—we assured ourselves of a landslide victory.

We had given the politicians and bureaucrats an unlimited budget, and they had exceeded it. Now we wanted them to decide

how to save money—not look for new sources of revenue. Instead
of spending public funds in ways that were designed to assure
their own reelection, we wanted the legislators to spend the money
in ways that would best help the people. I have felt all along that
even after Proposition 13, the state would have plenty of money
to pay for all the necessary programs. School districts receive 47%
of their revenues from property taxes. Cutting property taxes by
57% means the schools will lose 27% of their money. Similarly,
counties get 40% of their money from property taxes and will lose
23% of their total revenues as a result of Proposition 13. Cities
get 27% of their money from property taxes, so they will lose
15%. Altogether, California state schools will have 73% as much
money as they did before 13, counties will have 77% as much,
and cities will have 85% as much. All of them should be able to
survive and provide all adequate services if they establish their
priorities properly. But they're going to have to take a careful
look at their budgets and say, "We can't afford to do these twenty-
nine things. We have to decide which seventeen of them we want
to cut."

Maybe government shouldn't be doing everything it has been
trying to do. Everybody agrees that one of the essential services
government provides is fire protection. But during the campaign
I frequently pointed out that Scottsdale, Arizona has no fire department. Instead, they contract with a private firm for fire protection. And the fire company has made many innovations in
fighting fires and has received national recognition because they
can put out more fires in less time and at lower cost than publicly
funded fire departments can.

During the campaign, I also told my audiences about the example that was set by Puerto Rico, where they reduced personal
and corporate tax rates by 5%. In one year the government went
from a deficit to a balanced budget, and with more efficient government they were able to reduce the interest rates they pay on
their bonds from 12% to 8%.

As I said over and over during the campaign, every appropriation bill should be put to the bottom-line test: who will benefit
from this spending? If the ultimate beneficiary is the people and
it involves a program they need and want, fine: the appropriation
should be approved. But if the beneficiary is a narrow special-

interest group or the bureaucracy itself, the spending should be eliminated.

In any event, we made it possible in 13 for government officials to raise taxes—but only if they could get a two-thirds majority in favor of higher taxes. We felt that was a positive limit. Before 13 it seemed like it was a lot easier to raise taxes than it was to reduce them. Every year the legislature introduced about 5,000 bills and passed about 1,500 and the governor signed 1,300 or 1,400 of those, but not a single one of those laws gave tax relief. Proposition 13 didn't close the door all the way on new taxes. But 13 did shut the door most of the way without making it impossible to raise taxes when necessary.

THE PUBLIC OPINION POLLS
MISREAD THE PUBLIC OPINION

Most of the politicians and the press were wrong about 13, so it's no surprise that most of the pollsters were, too. The first time a California poll was conducted on 13 by the "impartial," "scientific" Field organization in February 1978, the result was 20% in favor of 13 and 10% opposed. The opposition had no trouble rationalizing that poll by pointing out that 70% of the voters were undecided, and that it was only natural for the people who had signed the petitions to be strongly in favor of 13, which they said distorted the poll.

In mid-March the *Los Angeles Times* polled 1,348 Californians of voting age and found that 35% were in favor of 13, 27% were against it, and 38% had not made up their minds. Another Field poll conducted in late March and early April was probably the most incorrect of all. According to that survey, 27% were for 13, 25% were against it, and 48% either were undecided or said they were not aware of 13. Ridiculous! In the end, the California poll finally began to register accurate results. The last poll, taken a week before the election, gave 13 a lead of 57 to 34, which wasn't too far off.

The trouble with those polls is that the companies that take them, the newspapers that print them, and the politicians who believe them don't understand what the people are really thinking. They take consumer surveys in their offices that don't have any connection at all with what the general public is thinking. Either that, or else they deliberately concocted lies to influence the election. I would prefer to think that they are stupid about what the people are thinking—but I do think a lot of polls are fixed. There's a great question whether they should be allowed to be printed before elections because a lot of ignorant people who don't know anything about the issues or the candidates may—I don't say they will—but they may follow a phony poll.

And I was very concerned that the people not be misled by inaccurate polls. If newspaper reporters and other writers were fooled, that was okay. But not if the people were confused. I didn't mind a bit when a mouthpiece from the left like Richard Reeves reported in the May 23, 1978, issue of *Esquire*, just two weeks before the election, that "most knowledgeable Californians are predicting that the amendment will be defeated." Now Richard Reeves is based on the East Coast, and he has a certain following on the Georgetown cocktail circuit and the Upper East Side. But those "knowledgeable Californians" he mentioned were politicians who didn't want to believe what was happening. Reeves and writers like him don't know a damned thing about California, so they have to rely on politicians and other uninformed people.

Speaking of Reeves, I recently skimmed over another one of his ideas of what makes a story. He quoted Ted Kennedy as being shocked over the affluence in places like Newport Beach, while people in New England are cold and hungry. Here's Ted Kennedy, who wasn't born with a silver spoon in his mouth, he was born with a platinum spoon in his mouth—and he never earned a dollar in his life that didn't come to him because he was Joe Kennedy's son and Jack Kennedy's brother, here he is bitching about people who live well and own yachts because they worked their tails off. But guys like Kennedy say things like that, and guys like Reeves print them. Not even the California poll was as far off as Reeves was. And by the time his story appeared, practically every "knowledgeable Californian" knew that 13 was going to win big. By then even Jerry Brown had backed off and declined to campaign against 13 because he knew what was going to happen.

When those polls were indicating that the race was close, like that one that had us ahead by only 27 to 25, I just laughed. I said these guys have got to be nuts. *I* knew about the people. I was out there, you see. On March 15, the day after my arrest in Ventura, I went to Oceanside, and there was something like 2,700 people there. Jerry Brown went there about the same time to campaign against 13, and he had about 200. And almost everybody who was there supported 13, after listening to me. Oceanside was a damn good cross-section: poor people, some wealthy, some military. And when I spoke, there were twice as many people there as were included in those phony polls. Hell, the *Torrance Daily Breeze* published a long interview with me on May 7, 1978, and I predicted in there that 13 would pass by a mile. When they asked me if I had a poll to support that, I answered, "There's no poll except mine. Everywhere I go, people overwhelmingly support Proposition 13."

I was out there and I knew how the people felt. During the campaign, I debated a school superintendent in Southern California. He said, "Why, if you pass 13, we'll have to shut the schools down." And everybody stood up and clapped. They wanted the damn schools shut down. Even Richard Reeves wrote in that *Esquire* article of his that Paul Priolo, the Republican leader in the Assembly, said, "Whenever I tell an audience that Jarvis will bring local government to a halt, all I see is smiling faces."

Along the same lines, a May 26, 1978 editorial in the *Anaheim Bulletin* said that "One fed-up-to-here character in response to the threat to close down the schools, commented: 'Why wait till June 6? Why not now?'" And columnist Wayne Lee wrote in the *Simi Valley Enterprise Sun and News* on February 1, 1978:

> We relish the Jarvis initiative. We know that what Jarvis has done is nasty, morbid, dirty, a kick below the belt, dangerous, insidious and irresponsible. And yet we can't help but salute him. He has made everyone realize that the well is running dry. He is a drought.
>
> And we love the thought of it just to make other hemming and hawing politicians think.

And we had letters, like one from Dorothy Dallas of West-

chester (California), who wrote the *Santa Monica Evening Outlook*
on February 8, 1978:

> I am one of the 1.2 million voters who worked to qualify
> the Gann-Jarvis Initiative. The reason I worked is to save
> my home, not to "save money" as some of our opponents
> suggest.
>
> Saving money will be our next objective—if we succeed
> in saving our homes. . . .
>
> The bottom line is government is too expensive, and
> budgets have to be cut—drastically. Taxpayers are fed up
> with having their own living standards lowered by infla-
> tionary taxes in order to maintain or escalate those of our
> employees.

And from Norman I. Arnold, whose letter to the *San Francisco
Chronicle* was also quoted by Milton Friedman in his column in
Newsweek on April 10, 1978:

> We are saying that we know it [Proposition 13] will severely
> disrupt state and city governments. We are also saying that
> we want it to severely disrupt state and city governments.
> We are not anarchists, we are not radicals and we do not
> think we are irresponsible. We are simply full sick and tired
> of having our pockets picked at every level of govern-
> ment. . . .
>
> We want only the most necessary government "services."
> We want an end to the countless layers of useless bureau-
> cracies. We refuse to pay any longer for the parasites who
> are feathering their own nests directly out of our pockets.

And finally from Mr. and Mrs. A. G. Isgreen of Hermosa
Beach, who wrote the *Hermosa Beach Easy Reader* on May 25,
1978 that on May, 17, 1978, they picked up their assessment
notice and learned that the market value for tax purposes on their
house and two small rental homes had skyrocketed from $100,900
the previous year to $239,000; an increase of 140% in one year!
The Isgreens also said: "We have lived here for thirty-six years
and just retired. Proposition 13 must be passed or we will be wiped
out. *It's no joke!*" (italics theirs)

People like Wayne Lee, Dorothy Dallas, Norman Arnold, and the Isgreens spoke much more eloquently about why 13 was needed and why it passed than all the politicians, all the rest of the press, and all the pollsters put together.

All over California—and, for that matter, all over the United States—people universally want taxes and services cut because government is providing them with services they don't want. In terms of property-related services like police, fire, streets, and sewers, there's no more service to my house today than there was when I bought it in 1941. But the taxes have gone from $200 then to $1,800 before 13 passed.

The problem is that property taxes have been used to pay for the special interests that grew up within the government, such as social workers, food-stamp recipients, aid to dependent children programs—all of these people have lobbies of their own. *They* are the ones who want more services—not the people who pay the bills. The taxpayers have services coming out of their ears already. They don't use all these exotic services.

If twenty-nine social workers get out there and jump up and down, that's a big headline everywhere. So the press encourages it. But if twenty-nine homeowners demonstrate to complain about paying $3,000 in taxes and getting $300 in services so they're out 2,700 bucks, they don't get a line.

DOWN THE HOME STRETCH

During the last week of the campaign when I knew we were in by about 2-to-1, I insisted on spending $180,000 for television instead of the $90,000 which we had scheduled for that final seven days. We had the money—and I thought spending it was a damn cheap gamble. I have never forgotten what happened to Tom Dewey in 1948, and I've never let up an inch in any campaign until all the ballots were in. Suppose I had decided not to spend the extra $90,000 and we had lost by 500 votes! People sent us the money to pass 13. We didn't have any right to use it any other way. Some of my advisers nearly had hemorrhages when I told them I wanted to spend the extra $90,000. But I said, "I don't give a damn, I've been in this for fifteen years. People put in this money and, by God, if we let the election go by and we lose and we've still got this money, we're in trouble with those people. If we don't spend it for 13, we're in trouble even if we do win. We wouldn't be doing what we said we'd do. So I'd rather throw the $90,000 in the TV pot than put our whole operation in the delicate position of being open to accusations."

HOW SWEET IT IS!

The Proposition 13 election was on June 6, 1978. D-Day, the sixth of June. That was a significant date in 1944, and it was again in 1978. I campaigned right up until the polls closed at 8:00 that night and then went to our victory party to await the results. How sweet they were! We got 4,280,689 yes votes, or 64.8%, and 2,326,167 no votes, or 35.2%. We swept every county in the state, except for San Francisco—which was to be expected; Kern, which we lost by 650 votes out of 92,000 cast, and Yolo, which is just outside Sacramento. Many bureaucrats live there.

The passage of Proposition 13 made competing Proposition 8 moot; but just for the record, Proposition 8 lost anyway. The figures on 8 were: 2,972,424 yes votes, or 47%, and 3,345,622 no votes, or 53%.

The victory of Proposition 13 and the defeat of Proposition 8 were not the only notable events of the day. My friend Jimmy Ware upset Dixon Arnett in the Republican primary for state controller. The result was Ware: 1,039,435, or 52.9%; Arnett: 924,695, or 47.1%. Arnett was a very well known guy who had represented the Redwood City area in the Assembly for eight years and was Republican whip in the Assembly. In the words of the August 5, 1978 *San Francisco Chronicle*, Ware's "only claim to pre-primary fame was that he was closely associated with tax reformer Howard Jarvis." And that was true. Jimmy's entire campaign was based on his getting in newspaper pictures next to me as often as possible. Ware spent $3,050 on the campaign, while Arnett spent $236,000. In other words, Arnett, who was very well known, spent 77 times as much money as Ware, who was practically an unknown! And Ware won—just because people knew he was a friend of mine. Jimmy lost to the incumbent, Ken Cory, in November, but Ware's beating Arnett had to be just about the upset of the ages.

It was also significant that the two Republican candidates for governor who had belatedly endorsed 13, Evelle Younger and Ed Davis, finished one-two in the primary that day, while Pete Wilson and Ken Maddy, who were opposed to 13, were way back. For that matter, 13 ran way ahead of the gubernatorial candidates. We had 4.3 million yes votes, compared to 3.3 million for all the Democratic candidates for governor and 2.5 million for all the Republican candidates.

There was one more figure that meant a lot to me. A total of 6.84 million voters went to the polls on June 6: one-half million more than the number who voted in the 1976 primary. On top of that, 1976 was a presidential election year, when voter turnout traditionally is higher than in off years; and in 1976 both Ronald Reagan and Jerry Brown were running for president, which increased the turnout even more than in other presidential primaries. Nevertheless, we got half a million more people to take the time and trouble to register their opinions. That was really gratifying to me. Whether they voted for 13 or not, at least 13 made them care enough to go to the polls. And two-thirds of them *did* vote for 13. They showed the politicians that they cared enough to vote, and the way they voted showed they wanted to take matters back into their own hands. That was the real triumph of 13.

After all, a government is supposed to be run by the people. We've developed in this country an apathetic philosophy that says: "I'm only one person. I can't do anything—why should I take my time?" The lack of interest means the people have lost faith in their elected officials. They have lost faith in their capacity to be part of government. They have lost sight of the fact that if this system continues as it has, it's going to change American citizens into subjects.

What it comes down to is this: is it better or is it worse to get wide participation in the political process?

On the same day that 13 passed, a young conservative named

Jeffrey Bell ousted Senator Clifford Case, who was relatively liberal, in the New Jersey Republican primary. Bell, who was once an aide to Reagan, said his victory was due to "the tidal wave of tax revolt." And in Ohio, 117 of 198 school finance measures were rejected by the voters. Proposition 13 fever was catching.

At our party on election night, the band played "The Impossible Dream." And that's what it was.

MY OWN ASSESSMENT OF 13:
AN ACROSS-THE-BOARD TAX REVOLT

Time said on June 19, 1978 that 13 was "a middle-class tax revolt." I don't think that's accurate at all. This was across the board. We got 40% of the minority and lower-income vote. We got about 60% of the vote of the middle class. We got practically all of the vote of the wealthy. When you roll up a 65% vote in a state the size of California, there's no way to say that this was an action of any particular class.

I think the wealthy, the middle class, and the poor voted for 13 because I think people from every class resented the fact that the government was stealing too much of their money. I think the general idea in California and all over the country, with rich and poor alike, is that the government is too invasive; it has too much control; it passes too many laws; it curbs too many freedoms.

I was glad that 13 had so much appeal to wealthy people. More often than not, the rich make more money because they're brighter—as far as I've observed. I believe in the capacity of the man who starts at the bottom and gets to be president of GM. He doesn't get up there because he's a dummy. I think it was Lincoln who said that you can't help the poor man by destroying the rich man. I think it's sort of a sad thing in the United States that we permit ourselves to think that the rich are enemies of the country. There are undoubtedly some rich operators who are unscrupulous, but there are many labor leaders who are unscrupulous. There are many labor union men who cheat their employers, and there are many clerks who shoplift from the stores where they work. On balance, the rich guy is at least as good as anyone else.

I can look at myself and say, if I were wealthy, would I have voted for 13? Yes. If I were a black in Compton trying to buy a house, would I have voted for 13? Yes. If I were a carpenter sitting on my butt because there wasn't enough construction to provide me with a job, would I have voted for 13? Yes, of course I would. And that's how they voted.

MY ROLE IN 13'S VICTORY

I guess nobody chose me to lead the parade. I guess I chose myself. If I hadn't done it, I don't think anybody else in California would have done it. Nobody. The proof of it is, no one else did it.

My taxes don't worry me. I'm worried about the guy who can't pay his taxes. That was one of the big advantages I had over anybody in politics: I had no axes to grind. I went up before an audience of 200 or 50 or 2,500 and I told 'em just what I felt. If they didn't like it, the hell with 'em. I wasn't running for a damn thing. Anybody out there that I talked to, there was nothing they could do for me. What all these people were doing—if they did what I asked them to—was helping themselves. Whatever they did, they didn't do for me, because I'm not going to get a penny out of it. All I was doing was showing them how to help themselves. But politicians are afraid to tell the truth, because they're afraid they'll lose votes. I don't care whether I lose 4 votes or 4 million. If the people were not smart enough to save their own necks after I told them how, what else could I do?

So I kept plugging away. Estelle and many of my friends wanted me to give up. I was working my tail off and spending my own money, and for most of that time all I had to show for it was a bad press. Their cartoons implied that I was a thief or a nut or a fool. And so did their stories. But I have a hell of a thick skin. If the stories that appeared about me had appeared about the average guy in the street, they would have bothered the hell out of him. But they didn't bother me that much. They bothered Estelle a lot more.

I thought we could win. And we proved we could. Yes, we did it.

CHAPTER FIVE

Eureka!
Everyone's a Winner

The politicians have heard that the people are fed up. The people's mandate has been registered.

> —James Davidson, Chairman, National
> Taxpayers Union, after Proposition 13
> passed

As co-author and chief spokesman for the Jarvis-Gann initiative, he helped engender one of the most dramatic tax reforms in California political history. The passage of Proposition 13 allowed many who were being driven out of their homes by spiraling property taxes to keep those residences. And it has become the watermark for tax reform nationwide. This victory, capping a decade of crusading for less government, is deserving of our highest tribute.

> —KNX (CBS) Radio, Los Angeles, January 10,
> 1979, in naming Howard Jarvis
> 1978 Man of the Year

IN THE OLD DAYS—that is, before 13—people in general either laughed at me and called me a nut or ignored me altogether. All of that changed, starting at 8:01 P.M. on Tuesday, June 6, 1978.

All at once I was the darling of the press and the politicians. I was swamped with hundreds and hundreds and hundreds of requests for interviews from the media and with calls from politicians not just in California, but all over the country, who wanted me to meet with them, make an appearance with them, have my picture taken with them.

After all the abuse I had taken from the press, it was nice to finally get a little praise from them. *Time* said I was "a national folk hero" and put me on the cover of its June 19, 1978 issue. That same week, *Newsweek* had the Proposition 13 victory as its cover story and said the tax revolt had become "the new gut issue in American politics," and that "the California tax revolt had raced the middle-class pulse of the country as feverishly as anything since the invention of the station wagon." On July 17, 1978, *Business Week* decided that California had "staged the most significant tax revolt of modern times."

A couple of impartial polls showed we had struck a responsive chord nationwide, as well as in California. According to a Gallup poll conducted for *Newsweek* and published in its June 19 edition, 57% of Americans wanted their property taxes reduced, 30% did not want their property taxes lowered, and 13% were undecided. A nationwide *New York Times*-CBS poll published on June 28 revealed that there was even greater support for Proposition 13 outside of California than there was in the state. According to that poll, 53% of California residents said they would vote for a Proposition 13-type measure, while 34% were against, but nationwide the figures were 51% for Proposition 13 and 24% against, or better than 2-to-1 in favor. Meanwhile, the *Los Angeles Times* poll showed that support for 13 continued to grow in California, from a 41 to 34 margin in April, to 52 to 35 in May, to 56 to 36 in June, to 65 to 30 in August.

A few days after the election, I received a letter that meant a lot to me. It was handwritten, dated June 8:

Dear Howard,
    In over 30 years of observing the political scene in Cal-

ifornia and the nation I have never witnessed a more brilliant campaign against great odds than yours in behalf of Proposition 13.

Let us hope that California's message will be heard loud and clear in Washington as well as in states, counties and cities across the nation. The issue is, as you well know, much bigger than property taxes. People everywhere want to reduce government spending, the burden of taxes, and the spiral of inflation which is the cruelest tax of all.

Again—congratulations and best wishes for the future.

The letter was signed "Dick Nixon." I never expected it. I hadn't been in touch with him since about 1972. I thought it was a kind thing of him to do, having all the experience that he has had in politics, and all of his ups and downs. Later Mr. Nixon sent me an autographed copy of his memoirs, and I called him. We had a long conversation, about forty-five minutes or so, recalling our times together in politics.

A week or so after the election, Senator Hayakawa invited me to come to Washington to meet with the Republican senators, and I went. We had a long session, where a dozen or so of them asked me all about taxation and tax relief, and I told them about 13 and what I thought it meant: that the average citizen wants some relief from the burden of taxes.

Alan Cranston, the other senator from California, wanted to introduce me to the Democratic leadership on Capitol Hill, and I agreed to talk to them, too. Russell Long from Louisiana, the chairman of the Senate Finance Committee, impressed the hell out of me. He was about the sharpest guy I met in Washington. I feel that as head of the Finance Committee, he has more power than anyone else in Washington—including the President. One thing Russell Long said that impressed me: "The federal government is totally out of control. We do not know what we are doing here. We don't have any idea how much we're spending, how much we're taking in, how many agencies we have, how many programs we have. None of us know." He said there's only one solution, and that's to write "sunset laws, so that there's a date for every federal program that says, 'Expire, expire, expire'"— unless Congress takes specific action to keep the program in business. I also thought Ed Muskie from Maine was a nice guy, and he said he thought we were on the right track with 13.

The Democratic leadership of the House of Representatives had no one who impressed me nearly as much as Russell Long did. As far as I'm concerned, Tip O'Neill, the speaker of the House, is a run-of-the-mill political hack who has few scruples and not much of anything else to qualify him to hold power. He's a typical ward-heeler politician, a real wheeler-dealer. I don't think he was too anxious to meet me, but he didn't want to be in the position of letting it be known that some other Democrats wanted him to meet me and he refused. I do think he was pretty happy when I left—not only to see me go, but because he had learned a hell of a lot about taxes. He said, "Do you know how much you have shaken this Congress up?"

I said, "I hope so. You've gotten the first temblor, and you're going to get the real shock wave pretty soon."

Jim Wright from Texas the Majority Leader of the House, and a guy named John Brademas from Indiana, the Majority Whip—and a guy who is absolutely convinced that the Kentucky Derby is a hat—were there, and so was the rest of the House leadership. I think they understood when I got finished talking to them that this was dead serious, and they were just not going to be able to brush it off.

Evidently, Cranston or someone tried to make an appointment for me to see President Carter. I never said anything to anybody about my meeting the President. I never mentioned it, and I never intended to mention it. I thought it would have been presumptuous of me to ask to see the President.

I understand that the decision whether or not to see me presented a dilemma for the President. It shouldn't have. I think it's up to the President of the United States to do his job as he sees fit, and not the way that other people want him to. He decided not to see me, and that was fine with me. However, I would not have met with his staff unless he was there, too. The same was true of members of the Senate and the House: It was okay with me if they had people from their staffs there when I talked to them, but I wasn't going to meet with staff members alone. I had only so many days in Washington, and I wasn't there to hold remedial classes on taxation for politicians' aides. I was there to meet elected officials. Period. Elected officials are the only ones who could implement 13.

As I said, I felt President Carter should decide who he wants to meet, and I respect his decision not to meet me. If I had met him, I probably would have said, "Hello, Mr. President, I'm delighted to meet you," and I would have shut up. If he had asked me some questions, I would have answered them. But it wasn't my place to go in there and offer my opinion without having him solicit it, or to tell him what I had done or how smart I was. I wouldn't do that to the President of the United States, whether I liked him or not.

I agreed to let Senator Cranston introduce me to leading Democrats in Washington because it was to my advantage to meet as many officeholders as I could, regardless of party, and because I have known Cranston for many years. He and I are longtime political acquaintances, we've debated each other all over the state during the last fifteen or twenty years, and, unlike some other politicians, Alan Cranston never treated me like I was a kook. He's a decent man. That doesn't mean I agree with him; politically, on most things I don't. And I think he showed a lack of guts by campaigning all out against 13 and then turning around as soon as he saw the votes come in and start saying nice things about it. I think Alan Cranston always has been a big spender and always will be a big spender. I hope someone who is more fiscally conservative knocks him off in 1980 when his term expires. If I had been in his position, I would have stuck to my guns after 13 passed, continued saying how terrible it was, and taken my chances. I guess that's why I'm not in politics.

While I was in Washington, I appeared on NBC's "Meet the Press" on June 18. Imagine, Howard Jarvis from Magna, Utah, being interviewed on "Meet the Press" by Bill Monroe of NBC News; Jack Nelson, the Washington bureau chief of the *Los Angeles Times;* Neal Peirce of the *National Journal*, and Martha Angle of Newspaper Enterprise Association.

One night during my visit to Washington, I went to the Lincoln Memorial. I can't describe the sense of awe I felt, looking at Abraham Lincoln lit up there in the night. I knew that in my own small way I had accomplished something important, and now here I was, in the monument to one of the greatest Americans.

It was also while I was in Washington that a little old gal from California came up to me, put her arms around me, and said, "I just want to tell you you saved me $70 a month on my property tax, and with that $70 a month I can afford to put my son through college." I don't think very many people would know how to handle having people say things like that to them. I had never met that lady before, and I'm sure I'll never see her again, but what she said made the tears come to my eyes. I had a hard time answering her. The press and the rest of the people who don't know me like to describe me as a tough guy; a "crusty curmudgeon," as *Time* called me on June 19, 1978. How little they know.

As a result of Proposition 13, I met more great people—more honest-to-goodness fine people who love the country and want to help it. People who want to pay an honest amount of tax, but no more. They're not chiselers; they're not out to cheat anybody. It has been one of the inspirations of my life, and it helped make all the work, all the money and all the ridicule over the years worthwhile: there's a class of people in this country who are still honest-to-God 100% thoroughbred Americans, who don't lie to anybody, don't have any axes to grind, they don't ask anybody for anything, and they'll help you all they can if they believe in you and what you're doing.

I had some experiences after 13 passed that very few people are privileged to have. A few weeks after the election, I was in Chicago making the rounds of the talk shows. I had been on the go all day and half the night. I was tired. My voice was beginning to give out. Finally I said to the guy who was driving me around, "I've got to have a drink." It was late at night, dark and gloomy, and we weren't in a very good section of town.

My driver stopped in front of a little neighborhood bar called Claus's Bar. We walked in. There were four or five guys in there, none of them in suits or anything. There was a little guy behind the counter. I ordered a vodka and he gave it to me. He wasn't paying much attention to us. Then—all of a sudden—he looked up at me and he said, "It can't be. There's no way it can be."

I said, "What are you talking about?"

He said, "You look just like a guy named Howard Jarvis, but I know he wouldn't be here."

So I said, "Well, I'll tell you, it is."

I thought this guy was going to jump over the bar. He immediately got every customer in the bar to come over and shake hands with me. He went upstairs and got his wife and two kids to come down and meet me. He told me all about himself—he was born in Germany and was forced to serve in the German Army during World War II. He got captured and spent time in a prison camp. As soon as the war was over, he left for the United States, where he had heard there was freedom. He found freedom here, and he was as patriotic about this country as anyone I've ever met.

After a while, I laid down a $10 bill to pay for the drinks. Claus looked at me and said, "What am I going to do with that?"

I said, "What do you mean, what are you going to do with it? It's money. It's to pay for the drinks."

He said, "I can't take that money."

I said, "Why not?"

Claus said, "Well, because then I'll have to pay tax on it. I've never fudged a nickel on my income tax. I can't take your money because then I'd have to pay taxes on it, and I'm not going to use your money to pay taxes."

The topper was that later that night I told the story on a radio show in Chicago. I talked to Claus a couple of days later, and he said he had people lined up waiting to have a drink in his bar because I had been there.

I also received some official recognition that meant a lot to me. I won the Daniel Webster Award from the International Platform Association in Washington, D.C. It was given to me "for the most influential words spoken concerning our nation's most important problem: taxes and government spending."

The California State Senate Rules Committee, consisting of twelve members—both Republicans and Democrats—passed a resolution honoring Paul Gann and me for our "determination and commitment" to "the needs of California citizens. The people of this state have been heard, and through their perseverance, these needs will continue to be met in the future."

One of the most exciting things that happened to me after 13 passed was when I went to Owensboro, Kentucky, on June 24, 1978, to receive the Golden Plate award from the American Academy of Achievement. Several of these awards are given each year to "America's captains of achievement" who are "dedicated to the inspiration of youth, to raise their sights high, to excel in their endeavors."

That award put me in fast company. The other recipients for 1978 included Colonel Ulrich Wegener, who led the German military effort that resulted in the rescue of eighty-six hostages from a Lufthansa jet in Somalia; William H. Webster, the new head of the FBI; Stansfield Turner, the head of the CIA; Arthur M. Schlesinger Jr.; Tom Landry of the Dallas Cowboys; Judge Frank M. Johnson, who was nominated to be head of the FBI, but had to turn it down for health reasons; the Reverend Jesse Jackson; Gordie Howe, the hockey star; Armand Hammer of Occidental Petroleum; Clark Clifford; Steve Cauthen, the jockey; General Omar Bradley, and Attorney General Griffin Bell.

I never had such a thrilling time in my life. The banquet was beautiful. The guests were beautiful. Ed Asner was the emcee. It was a marvelous thing to have Edward Teller come up to me and put his arms around me and say, "Howard, you're the greatest man in the country." All in all it was just a fantastic trip, one of the highlights of my life.

Later, on January 1, 1979, *Time* named me one of four runners-up for the Man of the Year award. Me, along with President Carter, the new Pope, and—oh, yes, the Reverend Jim Jones. Here's how *Time* described what I had accomplished:

> In 1978, after 16 years of trying, he caught the crest of a national wave of discontent and succeeded spectacularly in selling his tax-slashing ideas. . . . On Election Day, voters by 2 to 1 approved Proposition 13, making it one of the most important political and sociological events of the year, and transforming Jarvis into a national symbol of middle-class Americans' mounting anger with expensive government programs that yield too few benefits, big budget deficits and intrusive government regulations.

And KNX Radio, the CBS station in Los Angeles, named me their 1978 Man of the Year because I

> helped engender one of the most dramatic tax reforms in California political history. The passage of Proposition 13

allowed many who were being driven out of their homes by spiraling property taxes to keep those residences. And it has become the watermark for tax reform nationwide. This victory, capping a decade of crusading for less government, is deserving of our highest tribute.

Since 13 passed, I have crisscrossed the country again and again to lead the continuing fight for tax reduction and to talk about what we had accomplished in California and are now beginning to accomplish nationally. Just to give you an idea, here's my schedule for a few days:

August 17: I flew from Los Angeles to Fort Worth. That night I addressed a rally sponsored by the Taxpayers Association of Fort Worth. Then I flew on to New York.

August 18: I held a news conference on the steps of City Hall. In the afternoon I taped interviews for radio station WOR and WABC-TV. Then I flew to Boston, and that night I appeared live on a radio show there.

August 19: I gave a newspaper interview, held a news conference at historic Faneuil Hall, and met with some people from the Boston area who are working to reduce taxes.

August 20: Traveled to Washington.

August 21: First thing in the morning, I appeared live on the Today Show on NBC-TV from Washington. Then I was the speaker at a Newsmakers' Breakfast at the National Press Club. After that I held a news conference on the steps of the Internal Revenue Service headquarters. At lunchtime I appeared live on a local television show. Later that day, I traveled to Philadelphia.

August 22: I started the day with a live appearance on a local television show in Philadelphia. Then I held a news conference outside Independence Hall. At noon I appeared live on another television show. From there I went to the airport and flew to Pittsburgh, where I held a news conference, taped a television interview, and then that night went on a radio program.

August 23: I appeared live on a television show called "Good Morning, Pittsburgh." Then I flew to Chicago. At midday I taped a television interview and held a news conference. In the afternoon I went live on one radio show, and that night I went on another radio talk show.

August 24: That morning I made live appearances on two Chicago television stations. Then I flew to Detroit. That afternoon I had a press conference in Detroit. In the evening I addressed the Michigan Tax Assessors Conference in Cadillac, outside of Detroit.

August 25: I flew from Detroit to Seattle, held a news conference in Seattle, and finally arrived back in Los Angeles that night.

I thrive on this kind of schedule, because fighting for a cause I truly care about keeps me fired up. I love it. When I stop giving speeches and holding press conferences and going on radio and television shows I'll be dead. Until then I'm going to keep at it.

THE END OF MY PARTNERSHIP WITH PAUL GANN

The end of the campaign also brought about the end of my relationship with Paul Gann. It was a relationship that was formed back in the summer of 1977 and had a goal from the very start: qualifying a property-tax initiative for the ballot and getting it approved. We did what we set out to do, but out partnership was to end on June 6, 1978; win, lose, or draw.

I wish that's all I had to say about the end of our partnership, but—unfortunately—it's not. Since then Gann has been quoted as saying I'm "irrational"; that I have "diarrhea of the mouth"; that I have "a very difficult problem with the English language. It's hard for him [me] to get above a two-letter word. He says 'I' and 'me' very well," and things like that. Gann also said, "Howard tried to climb the tree all his life and never succeeded. He was an utter failure until Proposition 13."

To set the record straight, let me start with Gann's last comment: that I was an "utter failure" before Proposition 13. Unlike Gann, I was a successful businessman, and I didn't go into tax reform in a desperate attempt to find a way to earn a living. I could have bought and sold Paul Gann any day in the last half century. I spent sixteen years of my life fighting for tax reduction, long before Gann knew what that meant. He was a Johnny-come-lately who arrived on the scene after I and the other members of the United Organizations of Taxpayers had done all the heavy work. We would have won with or without Paul Gann. But because I invited him to join us, he was able to share in the limelight. If I had not extended that invitation to him, nobody would have ever heard of Paul Gann. If we hadn't bankrolled him and carried him during the signature campaign, few would have ever heard of him.

Paul attacks me out of jealousy. Jealousy is a very sad disease. I'm sorry to say he suffers from it. I understand why he resented me all during the 13 campaign and why he does to this day, and I sympathize with him. Both of our names were on the amendment because we signed it together, although Phil Watson and I wrote it years before Paul Gann came along. I tried my best to see that Gann got his share of the publicity. Three times a week during the campaign, we put out press releases with both of our names on them. After all, it was the Jarvis-Gann amendment. But sometimes the press didn't mention his name. He was a little sensitive about that, which I understand.

There were two reasons why I got 90% of the publicity for 13. First, Paul was a newcomer. I had been in it for fifteen years and he was really in it for only one year. Secondly, I have a different kind of personality than he does. He's sort of a soft, farmer-type guy, which is fine. But I'm a different kind of personality. The press centered on me because I was more controversial and more outspoken and better copy and more show business and so forth than he was. Paul naturally felt that I was getting the lion's share of publicity. He didn't seem to understand—and I didn't care if he did nor not—that I had been getting this kind of publicity for many years.

During the campaign, Paul even went so far as to issue a press release saying I had hired the firm of Butcher and Forde to get me publicity because that's what I was after. I think Gann really thought that was the truth. But it wasn't that at all. I wanted Butcher and Forde in the 13 campaign because they could raise money and they produced the finest, most effective television commercials I've seen in my life. They hired top talent. It cost us about $25,000 to produce a thirty-second commercial for television. I thought that was a little high until I looked into it and

I saw what the opposition was doing for $10,000. Our commercials were effective for $25,000, and theirs were lousy for $10,000.

Gann also failed to understand that Butcher and Forde didn't charge us a nickel for their services—not a nickel. I met them through the campaign of State Senator John Briggs for Governor in late 1977. John Briggs was one of the first major candidates to endorse 13. Butcher and Forde thought they could piggyback John Briggs on the campaign for 13—or vice versa. They could send out mailers for both John Briggs and Proposition 13 at no extra cost—except the price of paper. They were just clever enough to see the possibility. So they came to me and put the idea to me. They were talking about 3 or 4 or 5 million mailers at virtually no cost to us. I'd have been a horse's butt to have turned them down. Once Briggs dropped out of the race early in 1978, Butcher and Forde spent full-time on 13. Just for the record, what they got out of the campaign was the commissions on the broadcast time and newspaper space they bought. They got a 15% commission on every ad they placed, which is standard in the advertising business. But if I, as a private individual, had handled the ads, I would have had to pay the extra 15% to the newspapers and the radio and television stations. That's the way it works. We couldn't have saved a nickel by handling our own advertising, unless we set up a phony advertising agency, which I refused to do. But Gann never was able to grasp the fact that Butcher and Forde gave us a great deal and we didn't have to pay them at all for what they did.

Still, I want to give credit where credit is due. Paul was a full partner on 13. He was out there collecting signatures and making speeches. Whether his speeches were good or bad, he was out there making them. But the fact remains that there has to be a leader. I was the guy that sparkplugged 13.

Gann had a little different objective in this than I did. He said to me many times that he wanted us to form a major national tax organization after the campaign for 13 was over. The way he had it planned, he and I would run this operation and become highly paid officials in the tax movement. I told him I couldn't do that. I told him I had established a long time ago that I was not going to be paid anything for my work on taxation, that nobody else in the United Organizations was going to be paid anything, and that this had to do with our credibility. If he wanted to put together an organization himself and have the members pay him, that was all right with me. He and I just had different viewpoints.

I'm a little skeptical about partnerships in so-called quasi-public affairs like tax reform, because then each partner is bound by what the other partner does. If you file a financial disclosure statement with a state or federal agency and your partner louses it up, you each get blamed for it. I know what the United Organizations does with our money. I know that when we make a report every dime is in there. There is no monkey business. There are no stamps taken out and no envelopes taken out. I *know* that.

Besides, after June 6, I decided to go big league and try this on a national scale, at the suggestion of Butcher and Forde. I didn't see any place for Paul Gann in something of this magnitude. We never had an argument or a bad word during the 13 campaign, but I became aware of his capacities. He thinks in terms of a few thousand dollars; we think in terms of millions. Some people think big and some people think small.

Paul has a right—just like I have a right—to do whatever he wants to do and to say whatever he wants to say. We are not together now; we have not been together since 13 won, and we are never going to be together again. Since 13 passed, I haven't been on a television show with Gann. I have had television stations invite me to be on with Gann, but I turned them down. I told them they could have Gann, *or* they could have me; but if they were going to have Gann, I didn't want to be on the show.

In November 1978, I heard that Gann had gone to the real estate people and convinced them to give him $50,000 or so to gather signatures for what he called a "Spirit of 13" initiative in California. The first part of that amendment provides that any increase in state and local government spending must be limited to the annual rise in the cost of living and the growth in state population. I can't support that because I think that having taxes and spending increase at the same rate as inflation is a big mistake. Government spending causes inflation. So if you allow spending to increase at the same rate as inflation, you're never going to curb inflation. It's like throwing gasoline on a fire.

Gann launched that petition drive with a lot of fanfare. He had hordes of realtors outside of the polling places on November 7, 1978, and he claimed they would collect enough signatures that day to qualify his initiative for the ballot. Then, after the election in November, you didn't hear anything about that for months. The reason was simple: they had a real hard time getting the signatures. Finally, on March 16, 1979—more than four months after Election Day—Gann announced that he had collected about 850,000 signatures. Later it was revealed that he and his group had spent $537,194 to get those signatures compared to about $28,500 it cost us to gather 1.5 million signatures for Proposition 13. His initiative will be on the ballot in November 1979. I don't expect to be involved with it.

THE CALIFORNIA SUPREME COURT UPHOLDS 13

On September 22, 1978, while I was observing my seventy-fifth birthday by speaking to a group of taxpayers in Cleveland, I received a delightful birthday present: the California Supreme Court ruled that Proposition 13 was legal. The only thing that marred their decision was a "concurring and dissenting opinion"— which is sort of like someone going into the polling booth and voting both yes and no on 13—by Chief Justice Rose Bird. Bird's dissent was based on her theory that the provision in 13 which allowed higher assessed valuations on property that changed hands after March 1975 "violates the equal protection clause of the Constitution by treating identical or similarly situated property taxpayers in an unfair and unequal way." That was the same old argument that had been used without success against us during the campaign. Whether Rose Bird and the other opponents of 13 want to admit it or not, there is nothing wrong with allowing a buyer to voluntarily determine his assessed valuation for tax purposes by deciding what price to pay for the house.

I expected the opposition to fight 13 in court after we won at the election, and they did. I expected the Supreme Court to rule in our favor, and they did. I wasn't even surprised that a leftist like Rose Bird—who was almost certainly Jerry Brown's worst appointment—would vote against us. But I had one hole card, just in case we had lost in court; I was going to call for a statewide revolt against paying property taxes if they had declared 13 illegal. If the court had ruled against 13, it would have been a political decision to thwart the will of the people. If the property owners had refused to pay their property taxes, the government couldn't have taken away their homes for five years. Long before then, the people who run state and local governments would have caved in if the people who voted for 13 refused to pay their property taxes.

PLAYING OFF JERRY BROWN AND EVELLE YOUNGER IN THE 1978 ELECTION

On November 7, 1978, Jerry Brown was elected to a second term as governor of California. Brown received 3.8 million votes to 2.5 million for Attorney General Evelle Younger, who was the Republican candidate for governor. Brown's total vote and his margin of victory were both state records. Even though I am a registered Republican and have considered myself a Republican all my life, I was one of the 3.8 million Californians who voted for Jerry Brown. It was a very difficult thing for me to do, but ultimately I felt that he would do a better job of implementing 13 than Younger would have.

I have known Jerry since he was on the Los Angeles Community College Board and was running for secretary of state back in 1970. I used to attend meetings of various boards and agencies, and that's how I met him. During that 1970 campaign, Jerry was walking from house to house, seeking votes, and he said that every other voter asked him about property taxes. One Sunday morning Estelle and I were home and Jerry called and said he wanted to talk to me about property taxes. He said, "I wonder if I could make an appointment with you to discuss them."

I said, "Sure. When did you have in mind?"

He said, "Well, you know how campaigns are—the sooner the

better. I'll take only an hour of your time." Of course I knew it would take a lot longer than that, but that's all he thought it would take. It was about nine o'clock in the morning, and I said, "How about this morning?" He said he would be right over.

Pretty soon Jerry arrived and I said to him, "Have you had breakfast?" He said he hadn't. So Estelle fixed him breakfast. Later on she fixed us lunch, and that night she fixed dinner for us. I spent all day telling Jerry everything I knew about taxes. I didn't care whether he was a Democrat, and Pat Brown's son. I would have spent that much time with anybody running for office on either ticket.

(Brown recalls: "I met Howard because he was around local politics. I went to see him that Sunday because I wanted to start an initiative to abolish property taxes for low- and moderate-income homeowners. Howard didn't like that because he wanted to give tax relief to all property owners, including business. I didn't think the state could afford that.")

Brown campaigned against 13 until the last few weeks before the election, when he saw it was going to pass. Meanwhile, Younger announced in late April, about six weeks before the election, that he was going to vote for 13 but he felt he couldn't campaign for it because it would be his job to defend it if it were challenged in court. Younger said, "My present intention is to vote for Proposition 13. However, I cannot take an advocate's role concerning Proposition 13 without diminishing the effectiveness of my efforts as the state's chief law officer. I can't be both a crusader and get my job done as attorney general." In my opinion, that was a lukewarm statement at best, and Younger was Caspar Milquetoast on 13.

The night 13 passed and Younger won the Republican nomination for governor, I stopped by his party at the Century Plaza. I said to Younger, "You had better get on 13, Evelle. I'll tell you what: I think you've got about an hour. If you don't come out right now, Brown's going to beat you to it." I also told Younger that night, "Inasmuch as Brown has campaigned against 13, the only chance you have in my opinion is to come out strong for 13, so you can make a campaign between yourself and Governor Brown on 13."

Younger said it sounded like a good idea, but he would have

to discuss it with his campaign committee. I knew right then he wasn't going to use 13 as his issue because his committee was like all Republican committees: if you take something up with a high-level Republican group, they'll be discussing it into the next century. All my life I have observed that the Republicans never knew when they had a good issue. They have rocks in their head. On many occasions when they had a good chance to knock off a Democrat for a change, the Republicans managed to be stupid enough to snatch defeat from the jaws of victory. Besides that, few Republican activists had much use for me, so I knew they wouldn't want to be in a position of having Younger's victory possibly be due to me and 13. I think a lot of them would rather have seen him lose—and they got their wish.

The night 13 won, Brown, who several months earlier had called it a "monster," said it presented a "great opportunity." He also said, "We have our marching orders from the people. This is the strongest expression of the democratic process in a decade. Things will never be the same."

I have always suspected that in the privacy of the voting booth, Younger voted against 13. I think he has been marinated so long in the political grease that he's against anything that cuts taxes. I think Brown probably voted against 13, too, but at least he didn't say he was for it. Besides that, I don't think Brown was all that unhappy when 13 won. After all, he came to office in 1975 talking about "an era of limits," and setting an example of frugality by driving a Plymouth instead of a limousine, refusing to live in the governor's mansion, and things like that.

Right after 13 won, *Newsweek* quoted one of Brown's unnamed critics as saying, "Within a month, you'll think it was Brown's proposition." Sure enough, a *Los Angeles Times* poll conducted three weeks after the election revealed that a majority of Californians believed Brown supported 13, and that more people thought Brown backed 13 than felt that Younger had been in favor of it. People started referring to Brown as "Jerry Jarvis," which, of course, amused me quite a bit.

While I was visiting Washington shortly after 13 passed, Senator Cranston called me and told me Brown wanted to talk to me. He gave me Brown's private number. I called him, and the first thing Brown said to me was, "Do you remember that Sunday when I came over to your house?"

I said, "I sure do, Jerry, I've thought about it many times."

"Well," he said, "I guess I missed the boat. I should have gotten on tax reduction then."

I said, "You're in a wonderful position to see to it that it's done now."

He said, "I'd like to have a couple of meetings with you at your convenience."

I said, "You're the governor—it's at your convenience." And later on we did meet a few times.

Then a little later, while I was in Chicago, Brown called me. "I just want to tell you employment in California has gone up 1½% since 13 passed, unemployment has gone down 1%, and inflation is going down in California, instead of up like it is in the rest of the country." Naturally, I was very pleased to hear that.

About six weeks before the gubernatorial election in November, I said publicly that Younger had defended 13 in court, that he had defended it successfully, and that he was entitled to credit for that. I also said in speeches around the state that Governor Brown had proposed a budget that showed a decrease for the first time in seventeen years, that he had put a cap on state employees' salaries, and that *he* was entitled to credit for what he had done.

On October 3 I went to lunch with Younger and some of his top aides. They asked me to tape a television commercial for him, and I did. I praised Younger for presenting "a brilliant legal brief" to the State Supreme Court, which helped persuade them to rule in favor of Proposition 13.

Meanwhile, Brown's people found out about the Younger commercial and they asked me to film one for Brown, too. And I did. In that one, I said, Brown "imposed a hiring freeze on state agencies. Then he did something really remarkable. He signed a budget which actually went down instead of up. Sure, I wrote Proposition 13, but it takes a dedicated governor to make it work." That was pretty much the script that Brown and his staff asked me to read.

When Younger and his group learned that I had made commercials for both candidates, they were furious. It created quite a little hassle, but I didn't pay much attention to it. All the Republicans started calling me and asking me why I had endorsed Brown, and Democrats were calling me and asking why I had endorsed Younger. I said to everyone who asked me about it, "You can't read, and you didn't listen to what I said. I didn't endorse either one. I never said at any time I was for either one. I never said at any time I was for either one of them. I said the public was entitled to know what each one of them had done with respect to 13, and I was just telling them what Brown had done and what Younger had done. After that it's up to the voters to make up their minds."

But, as usual, a lot of Republicans didn't understand what I was doing and didn't like what I was doing. Which was their tough luck. Just like when I did the commercial for Brown, a lot of Republicans had been incensed when I met with Cranston and some of the Democrats while I was in Washington right after the election. They would say, "We sure are disappointed with you. We hear you met with Cranston and talked to Jerry Brown on the phone. That's a fine thing for a man who has pretended to be a Republican all his life. You must be a fink. A faker. What right have you got to talk to Jerry Brown or Alan Cranston? What business have you got visiting the Democratic leadership in Congress?"

To people like that, I said "My object is to implement 13. And I have to implement it with the officers who are in power. It just so happens that Brown is the only governor we have. You may not know that, but he is. And Alan Cranston is the third most powerful man in the U.S. Senate. I don't agree with Alan Cranston's politics, and I never did. I'd like to see someone else in that seat. But as long as he's in it, I'm going to work with him if he will support tax reduction and work with me. I can't implement this thing with people who are not in office." But so many conservatives are so narrow-minded and dumb that they don't understand that. I'm not for Cranston any more than I ever was.

My job is to get support for tax reduction. I'm not part of any political party when it comes to tax relief. I've always been a Republican. I'm a Republican now, but the Republican party never did anything for me.

Neither the Republican nor the Democratic party ever turns down a vote. They don't say, "You can't vote for us because you're a gangster or a whore or a pimp or a garbageman or whatever." Everybody seeks votes wherever they can find them, and that's what we're doing. I am trying to get everyone I can, including and especially elected officials, no matter which party they belong to.

I made statements for several dozen candidates in the November elections. Some of them were Republicans, some were Democrats, some were from the smaller parties, and some were running against each other. But if they were for 13, I was for them. It comes back to the same point: only elected officials can implement 13, so I had to go with the ones who said they were for 13. Reporters and other uninformed people asked me how I could be for two candidates who were running against each other, and I replied, "How can I do it? Easily and in good conscience. Both of these candidates say they favor tax reduction, and that is my target."

I used the same basis for making endorsements all over the country: how the candidate stood on 13, not what party he belonged to. If candidates committed themselves to 13, I campaigned with them or sent out a letter asking people to vote for them, or sent them contributions. If they refused to commit to 13 or if they hemmed and hawed, I did what I could to defeat them.

One example of what I did during the campaign came while I was fishing in Wyoming in September. It was just before the primary there, and both candidates for the Republican nomination to the U.S. Senate came to visit me and seek my support within a few hours of each other. I made statements on behalf of each candidate. After Al Simpson won the primary, I reaffirmed my support for him. He won the Senate seat in November by a margin of 8-to-5 over the Democratic candidate, Raymond Whitaker.

In California in the November election, I campaigned for six candidates for Congress, four for seats in the State Senate, and ten candidates for the Assembly. As it happened, all twenty candidates were Republicans. I sent out letters telling the voters that these candidates had endorsed the idea of 13, and that their opponents were "a threat to our Proposition 13 victory." Fourteen of the twenty candidates I campaigned for in California won.

WHY I VOTED FOR JERRY BROWN
AGAINST A MEMBER OF MY OWN PARTY

A few days before the election in November I was home with the flu. There was a knock at the door. Estelle was out, I wasn't feeling well, and my first inclination was not to answer it. The knocking got persistent. Finally I opened the door, and it was Jerry. He had Gray Davis, his top aide, and another staff member with him. Jerry said to me, "I just thought I'd come by and have a chat with you."

I said, "Come on in." I had my pajamas on, and I put on a robe over them. I didn't have any shoes or socks on. So I was sitting there in my pajamas and my robe and my bare feet, talking to the governor. About an hour later, Estelle came home. She was awful mad at me because I hadn't gotten dressed.

Jerry and I proceeded to discuss every aspect of 13. I told him the only surplus being discussed was the state surplus, when as a matter of fact I had information that practically every city, county, and school district in the state had a surplus. There was something like 485 cities and 1,150 school districts in this state, in addition to the 58 counties, and if my information was correct, they were hiding another $2 billion in surpluses from the taxpayers. Brown said that sounded like something he should check into, and I think he did check and found out that most of what I said was true.

I pointed out to him that because most young people had not been able to afford to buy a home for fifteen years, the owners of residential property, not only in California, but around the country, are getting older and older and finding it more and more difficult to pay their property taxes, as their fixed incomes are eroded by inflation, on top of ever-steeper taxes. I said, "You've got to understand that from now on, the property tax will never be able to pay for more than the police and fire and the lights and streets and the sewage and garbage collection. Property tax revenues will *never* be able to pay for more than these basic property-related needs. So you must start looking for other ways of financing schools and welfare and all the rest." Jerry said that was the first time he had ever heard the people's dilemma expressed in those terms. He got the point, and that's why I like Jerry; he's fair and has an open mind.

We discussed the size of the state surplus, how much of it should be returned to the people; how to streamline government, and everything else under the sun. For several hours we sat there talking in my living room, me in my robe and pajamas, and Jerry in a sport shirt and jeans. Pretty soon it was about 4:30 in the afternoon, and a television show I had taped earlier was coming on. I said, "I want to watch this show I'm on, but you fellows don't have to stick around the see it if you don't want to."

Jerry said, "I want to see the show."

I had forgotten what I had said on the damn show when it was taped. So the show went along pretty good, but after a while, the reporter said to me, "What do you think of Jerry Brown?"

I said, "Well, I'll tell you: out here in Hollywood we used to have a horse called Hi-Ho Silver. And Hi-Ho Silver used to make circles faster than any animal that ever lived, but Governor Brown makes those circles even faster than Hi-Ho Silver did."

Jerry looked at me and he said, "Did you say that?"

I said, "I sure did."

He smiled at me and at Estelle, who was there, too, and he said, "Well, that's not too bad."

The last thing Jerry said to me that day before he left was, "Now, I don't want you to worry about me implementing 13. I'm going to tell you, I'm going to implement 13, both in the spirit and the letter of the law. I want you to know that. I give you my word." And, by God, I think he has been doing a good job of making 13 work. I think that everything he told me that day was the truth.

So I voted for Brown, even though as a lifelong Republican my feelings were toward the Republican candidate on everything except 13. The only trouble was, 13 was everything, as far as I was concerned. It was my litmus test: who was for 13 and who wasn't.

I just couldn't walk around Brown. In the final analysis, after he promised me he would do everything he could to make 13 work, which is what he had been doing for the five months since 13 passed, and when I knew Younger did not have a commitment to 13, I had to vote for Brown. The most important guy when it comes to implementing 13 is the one who holds the office of Governor of California. If Younger had won without committing himself to 13, he wouldn't have listened to me after the election. But Brown came over for 13, so I feel I'll get more out of Brown than I would have gotten out of Younger. I still think that if Younger gets elected, I don't get nearly as far with him as I do with Jerry. I think Younger's failure to get behind 13 cost him any chance he might have had to win the election. The thing that proves my point is that Mike Curb, who was absolutely new in politics, had no political background at all and was very young besides, Curb endorsed 13 and he beat Mervyn Dymally, the incumbent, by half a million votes. There were other factors in that race, but in my opinion, 13 was what won it for Curb. Younger blew it on 13. He was dead even with Brown in the polls in June; he let Brown have 13, and he lost big.

A few nights after the November election, I was out making a speech. About ten o'clock there was a knock on the door. Dolores, Estelle's sister who lives with us, was the only one home. She went to the door, and there's Jerry. She said I would be home about eleven and Jerry said, "Tell Howard I'll be over." But he didn't come over, so I went to bed.

A few weeks later, I made up my mind I was going to hold a press conference to call on Brown to return $2 billion of the state surplus to the taxpayers in 1979. But I felt I owed it to Jerry to call him before I had the press conference. So I did, and he said to me, "Howard, I'm a little worried about returning that much. I've got to have some flexibility in case the economy turns sour."

I said, "Okay, how about a billion and a half?"

He said, "I think maybe I can go for that."

I said, "Jerry, as strong as you've worked to implement 13 I'm not going to set your feet in cement or put you behind the eight-ball on this."

He said, "Would you please hold off your news conference until I make up my mind?"

I said, "Sure I will." He eventually wound up going for $1.2 billion. I think he's being too conservative on this, but I respect his judgment and his reasons. I also think that if the economy does as well as I think it's going to, I'll be able to talk him out of a little more of a reduction in taxes.

Jerry has certainly gotten onto lowering taxes and spending. I disagree with him on the balanced federal budget, as I'll explain later, but I think he's heading in the proper direction. It would really be interesting if he and Reagan are the nominees for president in 1980. I don't know what I'd do—I'd have a hard time opposing either of them. I think that if the Democrats don't renominate Carter, they're in a hell of a lot of trouble. When either party repudiates their president, they're going to have trouble getting the replacement elected. That's what happened with the Democrats in 1968. But if the Democrats do renominate Carter, they're in a lot of trouble. I don't know which way is more trouble. But you must remember one thing: every time the Democrats are certain to lose, the Republicans find a way to make 'em win. Every time.

CHAPTER SIX

What Really Has Happened
Since 13

[Proposition 13 is] the best chance we have to control government
spending.... If government has $7 billion less to spend, the public
has $7 billion more to spend, and will spend it more wisely.... It's
in the self-interest of the people to have this pass.... I strongly
support Jarvis-Gann. It does cut taxes. It does raise obstacles to
further increases in government spending. And it will not have the
dire consequences its opponents threaten.... If Jarvis-Gann is defeated, the legislature will be right back at its old stand.... Anything
which reduces the amount of money available for government to
spend is a good thing.

—Milton Friedman, Nobel Prize-winning economist
before Proposition 13 passed

The sweeping victory of Proposition 13 will be heard throughout
the land. The "brewing" tax revolt is no longer brewing. It is boiling
over.... The public refused to be bamboozled this time, as they
had been so often before while watching taxes mount and govern-

mental services deteriorate.... The populace is coming to recognize that throwing government money at problems has a way of making them worse, not better.

—Milton Friedman, after Proposition 13 passed

SHORTLY AFTER 13 PASSED:
—The city of Long Beach raised landing fees at Long Beach Airport and increased green fees at the municipal golf course.
—The city of Sacramento also increased fees at its golf course, as well as charges for docking in its marina.
—At Newport Beach docking fees were also increased.
—The cost of dog licenses in Los Angeles was raised.
—The city of Santa Barbara hiked the admission charge at its public swimming pools.
—The city of Arcadia increased the admission tax at Santa Anita Racetrack.

All of those things were not in keeping with what we hoped to accomplish in 13. Why should the homeowners have to pay higher property taxes to help subsidize the owners of small planes, yachts, and dogs? There's an old saying that if you have to ask the price of a big-ticket item like a yacht, you can't afford it. And if you can't pay the full share of docking fees or landing fees, you can't afford the yacht or the airplane.

Some people may criticize me for citing the higher charges for people who use Santa Barbara's swimming pools. The bleeding hearts say that swimming pools paid for with tax dollars are necessary to keep poor kids amused in the summertime. My response to anyone who raises that point is: Haven't you heard that Santa Barbara has miles and miles of beautiful public beaches? If the kids want to swim, they can go to the beach for free.

And as for golfers, I've been a golfer all my life. I've always paid my own way. And I expect all the rest of the golfers to pay their own way, too. Either that, or don't play. Why should property taxes be used to keep greens fees down. It's simple—they shouldn't.

Proposition 13 was intended to cut the fat and the frills out of government. That's why I was delighted when I read in *Time* on June 19, 1978, right after 13 passed, that in Monrovia, over in the San Gabriel Valley, fees were being increased for classes in things like yoga, jewelry making, and "Dancercise," to the point that "the users will pay the freight." That's exactly as it should be. Anybody who wants to take classes in yoga or jewelry making is welcome to. But don't expect the homeowner to pay for it.

The more time went by, the more proof there was that Proposition 13 was working. On June 14, 1978, Governor Brown announced that he was cutting $570 million from the state budget, including half a million dollars from the $3.4 miilion annual budget of the California Arts Council. I can't think of a better way to save $500,000. State Senator Bob Wilson from San Diego has been trying to abolish the use of tax funds for the support of the Arts Council, and in a letter to the *Los Angeles Times* on September 22, 1978, he gave some examples of tax moneys that were being wasted by the Arts Council. Wilson pointed out that the Arts Council used public funds to publish the following poem, called "The Three Stooges at a Hollywood Party." The poem, which Senator Wilson quoted in its entirety in his letter to *The Times*, is short, and I'd like to read the whole thing to you:

> the three stooges get an
> invitation to a big party at
> john wayne's house
> but besides the stooges
> the only people who show up are
> randolph scott
> glen campbell and
> stuart whitman who all drop acid and
> beat the shit out of
> john wayne just for the
> hell of it
> john wayne looks to the stooges for help
> but
> they're too busy
> melting down his oscar

I repeat: tax dollars were spent to publish that poem, the creation of one Paul Fericano. I even prefer the Beatles to that. According to Bob Wilson, the Arts Council also gave $5,000 to a filmmaker to produce a film about the Royal *Chicano* Air Force; $700 to produce art performances in laundromats; $1,200 to hold an art show that consisted of submerging 77 works of art in a river, and $1,000 so that some jerk could buy himself a wet suit, a typewriter, and some wood so that he could play music to mammals under water. The Arts Council has always been one of Jerry Brown's pet projects; this is one project I do not admire him for.

But, as I said before, Brown did a lot of things to implement 13 that I did like. In August he signed into law a $1 billion cut in state taxes—the largest tax reduction in the history of the state. Most of the tax cut was in the form of lower state income taxes. Brown said the impetus for the tax cut came from 13.

Brown also had the good sense to appoint David Janssen as the state's general services director. In August Janssen asked all state employees to return pens, pencils, and other office supplies that they might have "inadvertently" taken home. He also ordered a freeze on the purchase of new cars and office furniture for the state. And when he found out that one state agency had ordered $40,000 worth of signs costing $132 apiece, he rescinded the order. Janssen declared that "Business as usual cannot continue," and estimated his rules would save the state $17 million a year. We should have more public servants like him.

Also in August, Robert Alioto (who is not related to former San Francisco Mayor Joseph Alioto), the superintendent of schools in San Francisco, of all places, said that Proposition 13 "had a positive effect on San Francisco" schools by forcing the annual budget to be reduced from $190 million before 13 passed to $169 million. Alioto said in a speech that Proposition 13 "forced us for the first time to really tighten up our operation and to reevaluate our priorities." He said he had spent a year before 13 passed trying to talk the school board into closing down twenty-two unneeded schools. "But with the advent of Proposition 13, the board moved quickly to close nine additional schools and eighteen children's centers." I think Alioto is one of the few enlightened school people I've ever heard of.

I hoped 13 would reduce utility bills by reducing the utility companies' property taxes. That worked, too. For example, in September, the California Water Service Company notified its customers that the state Public Utilities Commission had approved the company's request for a rate reduction. "All water bills . . . will pass through to customers the Company's property tax savings in your community," said the notice from the water company. "During the 1977–78 tax year California Water Service Company paid $3.6 million in property taxes statewide. Of this total, approximately $1.6 million is being applied to reducing Company water rates."

Contrary to what the opposition had predicted during the 13 campaign, the impact of 13 on government services was "generally minimal," according to State Finance Director Richard Silberman, one of Brown's closest aides. In February 1979—eight months after 13 went into effect—Silberman said that the state had not been hurt by 13. Furthermore, said Silberman, "I sense no mood for increased taxes at the state or local level. I don't think they are necessary; I don't think they are possible."

Other studies about the effects of 13 reached even more optimistic conclusions than Silberman's. The U.S. Department of Commerce reported that in the third quarter of 1978—covering July, August, and September, the first three months after 13 became law—California had the highest increase in personal income among all fifty states. California's increase was 5.25%, compared to an average of 3% for the entire nation. Kenneth P. Berkman, a Commerce Department economist, concluded that the huge rise in the personal income of Californians "mainly reflected the initial effects of Proposition 13. Excluding these effects, California's increase would have been 3.5%."

Furthermore, retail sales in California during the last quarter of 1978 were 13.6% higher than they were in the last three months of 1977, which economist Eric Thor, Jr. of the Bank of America attributed to "the positive aspect of Proposition 13."

A study released in May 1979 reported that 13 had had another beneficial effect by channeling needed tax dollars from high-income suburbs to the needier central cities. The author of the study, William H. Oakland, a professor of economics and public administration at Ohio State, said that 13 "should increase the equity of California taxes, among persons and political jurisdictions." Oakland, who spent five months at the Federal Reserve Bank in San Francisco investigating 13's effects, added: "Since cities and rural areas have a larger share of the statewide property-tax base, tax [burdens] consequently would be shifted toward the suburbs," as a result of 13. "Given the poor fiscal condition of many central cities, such a shift would provide welcome relief." So much for the campaign lie that 13 would hurt poor people.

Another report revealed that while the national economy might be headed toward a recession in late 1978 and early 1979, California's was booming because of 13.

Still, as might be expected, the editorial department at the *Los Angeles Times* found grounds to fault us. In an editorial on September 28, 1978, the *Times* pointed out that the eighty-one branch libraries in Los Angeles County would henceforth be closed on Mondays. That meant the branch libraries would be open only five days a week, although nine regional libraries would still be open six days a week. The *Times* decided it was "distressing" that most libraries would have to close an extra day each week and that fees were up and attendance was down at museums and public gardens in the county since 13 passed. The editorial concluded:

> We were told, of course, that Proposition 13 would eliminate only the wasteful frills in government, and that there would be no cuts in "essential public services." We agree that the police cars, the fire engines and the rubbish trucks [not to mention the Hillside Strangler task force] are still on the streets in adequate force.
>
> But we do not agree that access to libraries, museums and gardens is an extravagance that a responsible community should forgo without protest.

I happen to feel it is not a hardship to have libraries closed two out of every seven days; people still have plenty of opportunity to use them. And people who visit the museums and public gardens should pay a substantial portion of what it costs to operate them.

Some of the stories out of California about 13's effect were very misleading. In my travels around the country, I came across articles claiming that in California we had been forced to lay off half the police and firemen and that Proposition 13 was responsible for everything from the damage done by the fires at Malibu in the fall to the failure of the Dodgers and the Rams to win championships. I talked to the fire chief, and he admitted to me that if they had had 75,000 more men and twice as much equipment, they still wouldn't have been able to do anything about containing the Malibu fires. The problem was that the unpredictable Santa Ana winds changed direction every five minutes. I told some newspaper people back East that the next thing you know, I'll be getting the blame for causing the Santa Ana winds. I said to them, "You ought to print that now, and you'll have yourself a scoop." They got a kick out of that, but I wasn't entirely joking.

There was one development after 13 went into effect that I heartily approved of: the city administrations in Hillsborough and San Marino asked residents to voluntarily give the cities more money than they owed in taxes, and many residents in each town did donate extra money. That's basically what 13 was about: that people should pay as much to governments as they could or as they desired, but that they shouldn't be coerced into paying more than they could afford. I realize that both San Marino and Hillsborough are very wealthy communities, and most other cities and towns would not be able to get much of a voluntary contribution from their residents. But I think they established a good precedent in those two places. There's nobody—including me—who has a right to say that taxpayers shouldn't pay as much as they want to—just as long as they aren't forced to pay more than they can afford.

13'S EFFECT ON THE JOB MARKET:
VERY ROSY

One of the worst scare tactics used against us during the campaign was the dire prediction—based on the phony UCLA study that Governor Brown and other politicians cited—that hordes of public employees, perhaps as many as 451,000, would be laid off if 13 passed.

Well, 13 did pass. And what happened?

Tax Revolt Digest is published in Sacramento by *California Journal*, which is published by, for, and about the Sacramento establishment. If any publication was consistently opposed to 13, and understandably so, it was *California Journal*. So it was with surprise and great pleasure that I read in the first issue of *Tax Revolt Digest* in November 1978, a story under the headline: "Prop. 13 Casualty Reports Much Lighter Than Predicted." The story began: "Compared to the predictions, the Proposition 13 casualty reports are quite light. There have been no massive layoffs of public employees or drastic cutbacks in governmental services in California." *Tax Revolt Digest* noted that four months after 13 passed, only 19,000 employees of local governments and school districts had lost their jobs because of 13. That's less than 2% of the 1.1 million people who work for local governments and school districts in the state.

Two months later, in its January 1979 issue, *Tax Revolt Digest* reported that 26,412 public workers lost their jobs as a result of 13, but that 9,324 were later rehired, for a net job loss of 17,088. So even a publication that makes no bones about its unhappiness with 13 had to admit that the public employees were not hit too badly by 13.

In February 1979 Richard Silberman issued a report in which he said that 3,500 out of 300,000 state employees—or 1%—were fired because of 13, and that about 17,000 local government employees lost their jobs, another 2,000 took early retirement and 93,000 jobs were vacated through attrition and were not refilled.

All those figures reveal that before 13, state and local governments had a total work force of nearly 1.5 million. And about 20,000 of those 1.5 million employees were terminated because of 13. That amounts to 1.5%. Somehow that doesn't seem too catastrophic to me.

Anyway, what if several hundred thousand had lost their jobs because of 13? The public employees—as we hear every day—are the most highly educated, the most loyal, the most industrious, the most dependable, and the most productive workers in the United States. Private industry is crying for people like that, and they all ought to be able to find a new job in about twenty minutes.

Actually, there is nothing special about public employees in my book. I don't recognize any difference between someone who is laid off by private industry and someone who is laid off by government. I don't think one is a sacred cow and the other is a piece of junk. We had something like 65,000 people laid off in California when they canceled the aerospace program and something like 54,000 laid off when the B1 bomber was canceled. It's not at all uncommon for some private company to close down a plant in California and throw several thousand people out of work. But I've never seen one schoolteacher or one bureaucrat shedding any tears when a large number of employees in the private sector lose their jobs. My heart doesn't bleed any more for public workers who get fired than it does for employees of private business who lose their jobs; much less, in fact. I'm not saying all public workers are bad, but I think there are too many of them who never do anything. A lot of them are cynical and arrogant and give lousy service. They have no investment in their job, no responsibility, and for many of them their sole objective is to avoid doing anything until they become eligible for a pension.

And taking into account new jobs in the private sector, 13 was a real bonanza for California—again, just as I had expected. In January 1979 there were 91,000 new jobs created in the state, compared to 30,000 the previous January. Eric Thor, the Bank of America economist, listed the new jobs as another significant result of the passage of 13. By August 1, 1979, according to the U.S. Department of Commerce, private employment in California had increased by 360,000 new jobs.

PROPOSITION 13 CLEARS SOME BIG SPENDERS OUT OF THE U.S. SENATE

Big-spending politicians felt the effects of 13 for the remainder of 1978. In September, Edward J. King upset incumbent Michael Dukakis, in the Massachusetts Democratic primary for governor. Bob Short upset Congressman Donald Fraser in the Minnesota Democratic primary for the U.S. Senate. Both Dukakis and Fraser were identified as big spenders, and their defeats were widely attributed to Proposition 13 fever. In Oklahoma, Governor David

Boren, who endorsed the Kemp-Roth tax reduction plan, won big over Ed Edmondson in the Democratic primary for U.S. Senate. Even in Democratic primaries, 13 was proving decisive.

In November 1978 the taxpayers' revolt took its toll on five fairly liberal Democratic members of the Senate: Wendell Anderson of Minnesota; Dick Clark of Iowa; Floyd Haskell of Colorado; William Hathaway of Maine, and Thomas McIntyre of New Hampshire, all of whom were ousted from their Senate seats. Edward Brooke, a liberal Republican from Massachusetts, also lost, but that was no doubt due more to reports about his personal finances and his divorce suit than it was to 13.

CHAPTER SEVEN

We'll Cut $100 Billion
in Government Spending,
Cut $50 Billion in Taxes

There is a revolt, and it is long overdue. . . . I think it will be an issue that Republicans certainly are going to run on.

—Bill Brock, Chairman of the Republican National Committee, on ABC's *Issues and Answers*, June 11, 1978

Those middle-income folks at $10,000 to $30,000 are on the verge of revolt. They want tax relief—and they want it now.

—Jim Jones, Congressman, D-Oklahoma, after Proposition 13 passed

Proposition 13 is one of the healthiest things that's happened in a long time. I thought California was the most overbloated state

government I'd ever seen, and the federal government is overstuffed
and can stand a lot of trimming down, too.

> —Sam Gibbons, Congressman, D-Florida, after
> Proposition 13 passed

WHEN PROPOSITION 13 PASSED, we did not win the war on taxes.
With Proposition 13 we won the first major battle in the war. The
war itself is continuing on three important national fronts:

First, immediately after 13 was approved, I launched the
American Tax Reduction Movement, of which I am chairman.
Our aim in this movement is to reduce federal taxes by $50 billion
over a four-year period and to cut federal spending by $100 billion
during the same period.

Second, I am trying to help angry taxpayers all over the country
gain approval of tax reduction measures, either through the ballot
process or by act of the state legislature, in their own states, just
as we were able to do in California with Proposition 13.

Third, I am working to secure the right of initiative to amend
the federal Constitution and the constitutions of the individual
states that do not now permit this procedure.

TARGET: A SIGNIFICANT CUT
IN FEDERAL TAXES AND SPENDING

The most important weapon in the war on taxes is the American
Tax Reduction Movement. With offices in Los Angeles and Washington, this organization is in a position to be the focal point for
all attacks on taxes.

By cutting federal taxes $50 billion over a four-year period,
or $12.5 billion a year, a large amount of money will go where
it should: back into the hands of the people. The major element
in this reduction is an across-the-board federal-income-tax reduction of 25%. Based on average figures for a family of four that
uses the standard deduction on their income tax form, a worker

who earns $15,000 a year will save $356 a year and $14,240 during his working lifetime under this plan; a worker with an annual income of $30,000 will save $1,352 a year and $54,080 in his lifetime, and someone who earns $50,000 a year will save $3,448 a year and $137,920 during the rest of his career. So this isn't chicken feed we're talking about; we think it will have a very meaningful effect.

In addition, income-tax brackets would be indexed to inflation, so that a raise in salary does not automatically result in a drastic increase in income taxes. As inflation rises, thereby diminishing the growth in purchasing power that a pay raise should mean, income tax brackets will reflect the changing economic conditions. The net effect will be that the taxpayer will owe less income tax than he would without tax bracketing.

These changes are very important. In 1972 the average taxpayer with a family of four had an after-tax income of $11,152. By 1977, after taking inflation into account, that same family's income had shrunk to $10,817. At a time when our nation was producing more goods and services than any nation since the dawn of time, the real income of the average American was actually declining!

Also, I want to reduce the capital gains tax from its current level of up to 40% to a flat 15%. This would free investment capital and result in increased productivity and a decline in unemployment.

Actually, if I had my way, I would eliminate the capital gains tax, instead of just cutting it to 15%. But you could never get that passed. All the liberals would yell and say, "This is a deal for the rich," which isn't true at all.

Japan and Germany, for example, have virtually no capital gains tax at all, and they have two of the strongest economies in the Western world. We don't need a capital gains tax here. We've gotten into a situation where people are so afraid of capital gains taxes that they're taking money that should go into the productive capacity of the country and putting it into tax shelters instead. Tax shelters are a coffin for money. If we can do something to make the capital gains tax more sensible, we'll get that money to go into the productive enterprise of this country. Economic experts inform me that substantially reducing the capital gains tax will create 3 to 5 million new jobs in this country. That way, our kids will have a job once they get out of school.

We've created a condition in this country where once people have made some money they're afraid to invest it in the stock market or anyplace else where it would be productive. The big thing they have gotten to because of our prohibitive tax rates is this: "We want to be damn sure we don't lose what we've got. We're not at all interested in making any more money if we can just keep what we've got." But if the capital gains tax is cut, there will be a little more spirit to gamble in order to make a profit. You can't have a capitalist economy without capital. Risk capital creates jobs. That's the name of the game.

Furthermore, reducing the capital gains tax should strengthen the U.S. dollar in the international monetary market. Don't forget: the Japanese yen and the German deutsche mark are among the strongest currencies in the world.

Speaking of Japan and Germany, a lot of people attribute our economic problems and the weakness of the dollar abroad to our dependence on foreign oil, which is becoming so expensive. There's no question that the price of the oil we have to import hurts. But Japan has to import almost all of the oil it consumes, and yet its economy and currency are in great shape. They have a huge surplus in their balance of trade.

So oil imports are not the real cause of our problems. The true cause is that the American economy has been crippled by a government that taxes too much, spends too much, and regulates too much. Since we reached our peak of individual prosperity in 1972, the average American's income, in inflated dollars, has grown 46%. And government spending has increased 77%!

The other major part of the American Tax Reduction Movement program is a $100 billion annual cut in federal spending, which will also be phased in over a four-year period. By cutting spending more than we cut federal taxes, we will end deficit spending—and, in fact, have enough of a surplus each year to reduce the national debt by 2%. As of 1977, the national debt had risen to $716 billion. Interest payments alone cost U.S. taxpayers $42 billion a year. That's a hell of a burden.

And deficit spending is the single most important cause of inflation, according to Milton Friedman, Neil Jacoby, Arthur Laffer, and other leading economists. If we can stop deficit spending, we can end the devastating spiral of inflation.

On September 26, 1978, the American Tax Reform Movement purchased a half hour of television time on about 120 stations that reached practically every large and medium-sized city in the nation. During that half hour, I unveiled our program to the country. Robert Reed, the television star, was host of the show, and Neil Jacoby, former U.S. Secretary of the Treasury William Simon, and several typical taxpayers appeared on it with me. I think that what Simon had to say was very important:

> The real issue here in America is whether or not the American people are going to be the ones that make the decision as to how they should spend their hard-earned money, or whether the bureaucrats in Washington should make the decisions for us. All these apologists for big spending who shriek, "This will bankrupt the country," don't want anything but more pervasive control over our lives and our livelihoods than they have already.

It cost us about $700,000 to produce that show and buy the time all around the country. We took in about $1.5 million as a result of our solicitation on the show, which enabled us to give money to candidates in the November elections who supported our program, to lobby for tax reduction in Congress, and to solicit more money by mail in order to keep our program going.

We spent several thousand dollars we had received from that show to take out a full-page ad in the *Washington Post*. The ad appeared in the paper on October 5, 1978, the morning of the day the House of Representatives was voting whether to override a veto by President Carter of a $10.2 billion federal public-works bill. We favored Carter's veto of the bill, which was nothing more than pork-barrel legislation so that members of Congress could provide unneeded dams and other federal projects back in their districts in order to grease their own reelection. We found out that most of the water from one of the projects the bill would have financed would have gone to a single catfish farm. In another case, a project would have given benefits to only sixty-nine families, at a cost of about $1 million per family in dollars taken from the taxpayers. As we warned at the end of our ad, "If the politicians don't change, we'll change the politicians," by voting them out of office four weeks later. I'm proud to say that the attempt to override Carter's veto fell more than 50 votes short of the two-thirds majority that was needed, so we helped save taxpayers all over the country more than $10 billion. That's exactly what we're trying to accomplish in the American Tax Reduction Movement.

In addition to campaigning for specific tax cutting legislation, the American Tax Reduction Movement has two other basic components:

—A research foundation to provide information to taxpayers everywhere who want to do something about reducing their taxes.

—A political action committee that gives money to candidates who are for the same goals as we are. I don't say there won't be candidates who will stand up and swear they're for our program, then, after they get elected, vote against it. But that's the chance we have to take. The only alternative is to leave things the way they are now, and we sure can't do that.

I do think that after what we accomplished in 13 and since, tax reduction is going to influence every election in the next few years, from president in 1980 down to elections for governor, congressional races, legislative elections, and local elections, all over the United States.

Within a few weeks after our television special in 1978, about 150 members of Congress and the Senate said they supported our program. In January 1979 the program proposed by the American Tax Reduction Movement was introduced into Congress by Robert Dornan, a Republican from Santa Monica, and Tom Luken, a Democrat from Ohio. That legislation, known as the American Tax Reduction Act, is pending in Congress. The number of the bill is H.R. 1000.

Let me emphasize that I don't get a dime out of the money we collect in the Tax Reduction Movement, and neither does anyone else connected with it. In fact, a couple of guys who tried to spend some of the money we received on fancy office furniture and expensive meals are no longer part of our organization. I'm not going to misuse any of the contributions we receive, and I'm going to see to it that no one else misuses them either. It's the same as it was during all the years we tried to reduce property taxes in California: every dime we get is going to be spent to reduce taxes. Period.

TARGET: PROPOSITION 13-TYPE TAX REDUCTIONS IN THE OTHER FORTY-NINE STATES

For the tax revolt, Proposition 13 was the shot heard around the nation, and, to some extent, around the world. *Newsweek* reported that in Colorado "little progress" was being made toward collecting 64,000 signatures needed by July 1, 1978, to qualify a property-tax-limitation initiative for the ballot—until 13 won. According to *Newsweek* (June 19, 1978), "The day after the Jarvis-Gann results came in, 250 people called to volunteer their help." In West Virginia, the *Charleston Daily Mail* asked its readers, "Would you approve abolishing a large chunk of state taxes knowing that it would mean curtailment of many public services?" The response to that poll was 552 yes votes and 38 no votes, or 94% in favor. This vote was reported in *Time*, June 26, 1978.

The first major test of how strong Proposition 13 sentiment was in other states occurred five months after the Proposition 13 victory in California. Here is how efforts to curb taxation and spending fared around the country in November 1978:

VICTORIES:

Alabama: Voters approved a constitutional amendment placed on the ballot by the legislature which reduced assessment rates on commercial and residential property that the courts had ordered reappraised.

Arizona: Proposition 101, a constitutional amendment placed on the ballot by the legislature to limit state spending to 7% of total personal income in the state, won.

Hawaii: Voters passed a constitutional amendment placed on the ballot by the legislature which limited state spending increases to the growth rate of the state economy and required a tax refund whenever the state has a surplus of 5% or more for two years in a row, in order to prevent the buildup of a huge state surplus like California's.

Idaho: An initiative virtually identical to 13—it limited property taxes to 1% of market value and restricted annual increases to 2%—was approved.

Illinois: An advisory referendum which was proposed by Governor James Thompson saw voters favor by a margin of more than 4-to-1 the placing of a mandatory limit on state and local taxes and spending in the state constitution.

Massachusetts: Voters authorized the legislature to establish different assessment rates for various categories of property, which overturned a court ruling that prohibited assessment of business and commercial property at a higher rate than residential. Residents unfondly refer to their stake as "Taxachusetts" because the state has one of the highest combined tax rates (property, income, sales, etc.) in the nation. Although I dislike the "split-roll" method of assessment, it's better than no tax reduction at all.

Missouri: A proposal placed on the ballot by the legislature which allowed the legislature to lower property tax rates if there is a statewide reassessment of property values and to reassess property without raising taxes won 2-to-1.

Nevada: Proposition 13's clone, Question 6, was approved by a margin of 3-to-1. However, it must win again in 1980 before it can go into effect.

North Dakota: Residents voted 2-to-1 to hand themselves some income-tax relief via an initiative that cut income taxes by an average of 37%.

South Dakota: Voters added to the state constitution an amendment that requires a public referendum or a two-thirds vote of the legislature before taxes can be increased.

Texas: Voters approved a "Tax Relief Amendment" to the state constitution that was placed on the ballot by the legislature. The amendment tied any increases in state spending to growth in the state's economy and required public hearings on tax increases of more than 3%. The margin in favor of the amendment was more than 5-to-1.

DEFEATS:

Arkansas: An initiative that exempted food and drugs from the state's 3% sales tax was rejected.

Colorado: Proposition 2, which would have limited increases in state and local spending to the rate of growth of the population and the Consumer Price Index, lost. However, a ceiling of 7% on growth of state expenditures that was adopted by the legislature in July 1977 remains in effect.

Michigan: The Tisch amendment, which was similar to 13 in cutting property taxes by 50% and limiting income taxes, was defeated. A proposal to prohibit the use of property tax revenues for financing public schools and replace the present system with a voucher system was also defeated. However, another initiative amendment that limited the growth of state and local spending was approved.

Nebraska: An initiative that would have limited local governments to a 5% increase in spending each year, unless the legislature approved exceptions by a four-fifths vote, lost.

Oregon: Voters rejected Measure 6, a Proposition 13-style initiative that would have limited property taxes to 1.5% of market value and reduced property taxes by an estimated 40%. Also defeated was Measure 11, which the legislature placed on the ballot and which would have granted tax cuts to homeowners and renters only and would have limited spending by state and local governments.

I campaigned from coast to coast for these measures in the fall of 1978, from Oregon to Massachusetts and from Michigan to Arizona. Our record was pretty good: eleven wins, four losses, and a split decision in Michigan. Of the amendments that were nearly identical to 13, two won (Idaho and Nevada) and two lost (Michigan and Oregon).

The election results in November 1978 showed what a tremendous impact 13 had made. Newspapers from California to

Europe were duly impressed. On November 9 the *San Francisco Chronicle* editorialized:

> The tax-cut message of Proposition 13, considered only six months ago to be a peculiarly California phenomenon, has struck a responsive chord across this country. Jarvis-like measures were submitted in 16 states, and...they...met with notable success....
>
> Proposition 13 may yet have a way to go before it becomes the political equivalent of motherhood. But it contains a telling ingredient for victory at the polls. That will hardly be ignored by politicians in the future.

Anthony Lewis, a columnist for *The New York Times,* wrote:

> This past election showed that people are fed up with government and its excesses in spending, bureaucratic confusion and rudeness. Indeed, a slick candidate who could come off as an "aginner" without being obnoxious had a good chance of ousting an incumbent.
>
> The citizenry thumbed its nose at government because of burdensome taxes, and Howard Jarvis and his Proposition 13 epistle were prophetic. As it turned out voters in 16 states approved 80 percent of the referendums calling for tax cuts and other handcuff devices for government.

His comments were reprinted in the *San Francisco Chronicle,* November 24, 1978.

During 1978 Norman Macrae, deputy editor of *The Economist* of London, toured the United States and recorded his observations. According to Macrae whose comments were reported in the *San Francisco Chronicle,* January 13, 1979:

> Anybody who has in the U.S. on the day when California passed Proposition 13 last June and at the time of the November elections had to notice a new spirit in the excited air.... This looks like a real turn of the tide against public-sector imperialism.

As of November 1978, great progress had been made in the eleven states where triumphs against taxation and spending had just been registered; in California, of course, and in Tennessee, where on March 7, 1978, almost 65% of the voters cast their votes in favor of a constitutional amendment that prohibited state spending to increase more rapidly than the rate of growth of the state economy and required the state to have a balanced budget. Between 1970 and March 1978, Alaska, Colorado, Kansas, Michigan, Indiana, New Jersey, Washington and Wisconsin adopted limits on taxes or spending, but some of those states are still taxing excessively. Two states where residents received tax breaks in 1979 as a result of the momentum generated by Proposition 13 were Wisconsin and Minnesota. Wisconsin taxpayers received a refund of almost $1 billion from a huge state surplus. In addition, the legislature and the governor agreed to declare a two-month moratorium on the payment of income taxes and to lower income-tax brackets. In Minnesota, state taxes were reduced by almost three-quarters of a million dollars a year. Minnesota, as well as Iowa, has taken action to prevent inflation from pushing state income taxpayers into higher tax brackets. Income taxes have also been reduced in Arkansas, Indiana, Kansas, Maryland, Mississippi, and Vermont. And Kentucky, New Mexico, and Virginia have limited the amount of tax revenues that can be obtained from property taxes.

The conditions are still fertile for tax revolt in many states such as Florida, Indiana, New Jersey, North Carolina, and Washington, each of which, it is estimated, will have a budget surplus of $100 million or more during 1979.

In terms of property taxes alone, the amount of tax grew at startling rates between 1966 and 1976 in Alaska (1,419%), Georgia (187%), New Jersey (140%), New York (147%), North Carolina (141%), South Carolina (190%), and Vermont (166%), according to the U.S. Department of Commerce. We hope to bring Proposition 13 example to all of those states.

New attacks on state spending and taxation have already been launched in many states, among them Florida, Georgia, Kentucky, Maine, Maryland, Minnesota, Montana, New York, Ohio, Oklahoma, and Utah. I'll be doing my best to spearhead efforts in each of those states, along with the states where we suffered defeats in November 1978.

One of our more recent victories occurred on May 8, 1979,

when Governor Edward J. King of Massachusetts signed into law a bill that provided for a 4% a year ceiling on local property tax increases in that state—the first such limit in Massachusetts history. Because of King's commitment to tax reduction, I had campaigned for him in 1978 and helped him unseat the liberal incumbent, Michael Dukakis.

The tax revolt has even caught on overseas. Most of the nations in Europe lack the mechanism we have in this country to amend their constitutions. As a result, many taxpayers have taken to transacting their business in cash so that they won't have to report their true incomes. Government officials are looking for ways to reduce taxes to a level that will be acceptable to the people they govern. In December 1978 I traveled to England and France to speak and advise on tax reduction.

I had an experience right after 13 passed that made me want to do anything I could to help the English. A chap from the BBC interviewed me, and after we had talked for a while he said to me, "If I could talk to the American people tonight, I would say, 'For God's sake, turn it around. You are following step by step every disaster that has befallen my country. England is down the drain, and England will never come back. But you in the United States have the resources, the power, you have everything except the one essential: you don't seem to have the will—the will to turn your country around.'"

I think what he said is absolutely true. I hope that the victory of 13 will give people in this country the will to turn things around, and I hope our example will give hope to people in Britain and other foreign countries. Actually, many foreign nations have much higher burdens that we do in the United States. The Organization for Economic Cooperation and Development, which is based in Paris, found that in 1976 in Sweden and Luxembourg total tax revenues amounted to more than half of the Gross National Product, while Norway, Holland, Denmark, Finland, and Belgium pay over 40% of the GNP in taxes. The OECD study covered twenty-one nations, all of which were in Europe, except for the United States, Canada, Australia, and New Zealand. The United States had the fourth-lowest tax burden among the twenty-one countries surveyed, with 29.3% of our GNP amounting to taxes. But that still isn't much consolation to taxpayers all over this country who feel—justifiably—that they are paying too much taxes.

TARGET: EXPANDING
THE RIGHT OF INITIATIVE TO
THE ENTIRE COUNTRY

Under the theory of representative government, candidates for public office state their views on important subjects. Then the voters choose which candidate they want to represent them. Once the candidate gets in office, however, he is under no obligation to vote as he promised during the campaign. And, of course, some major issues arise after the campaign and neither candidate has a chance to express himself on those issues before the election.

Elected officials have a responsibility to represent their constituents to the best of their ability. But there is hardly a better example of a conflict of interest than the difference between the best interest of the politician and the best interest of the people he has the duty to represent. The more taxes, the more money government has to spend, the more public employees the politician can put on the public payroll, the more power the politician has. And the lower the taxes, the less money government has to spend, the fewer the number of public employees and the less power the politicians have, the better off the people are.

The only solution is the right of initiative. I consider the right to change federal and local constitutions and enact law through the initiative process a more important right than the right to vote. At present about half the states permit some form of initiative. Most of the states where the initiative is allowed are in the West, where citizens of every state except Texas, New Mexico, Hawaii, and Kansas have that right. Among the Eastern states where the initiative is part of the political process are Michigan, Ohio, Maine, Massachusetts, and the District of Columbia.

The idea of direct citizen participation in deciding issues goes back to ancient Rome. One more recent example was the New England town meeting. I believe that every state and the federal government should permit that initiative.

Right now, campaigns are under way to win the right of initiative in many states. Among them are Connecticut, Georgia, New Jersey, Rhode Island, Texas, and Virginia. The best way to convince the state legislature to give people the legal right to petition to change the law is by circulating petitions and collecting the names of as many voters as possible. That's what keeps the politicians honest, or at least more honest than they would otherwise be: the knowledge that the people are interested in their government and that if they don't do the job, the people will reclaim their rights. That's why the initiative and referendum are important. I am working in every state where they need me to help them win these rights. In one state, Texas, they have been able to collect several hundred thousand signatures calling on the legislature to grant the citizens the right of initiative.

There is also a move afoot to win the same right in federal elections. In 1977 Senators Jim Abourzek, a Democrat from South Dakota, and Mark Hatfield, a Republican from Oregon, introduced a proposed constitutional amendment which would allow a proposed law to be submitted to the voters if 3% of the number of registered voters in the last presidential election signed petitions. The public would be able to enact almost any type of law—except for a declaration of war.

The requirement that the signatures of a number equal to 3% of the total ballots cast in the last presidential election be obtained would mean—if it were in effect now—that 2.5 million signatures would have to be collected nationwide. That sounds like a lot, but it's only twice as many as we got in California alone for 13. Gathering 2.5 million signatures from people all over the country should not be too difficult a task.

There seems to be strong public sentiment for permitting an initiative process in federal elections. In May 1978, right before Proposition 13, a Gallup poll showed that Americans favored by a majority of 57-to-21 the right of the public to propose and vote on laws. On the same day that Proposition 13 passed, voters in Los Angeles County approved by 2-to-1 Measure B, an advisory measure in favor of allowing a federal initiative. The percentages on Measure B were almost identical to the vote on Proposition 13 in the county, although half a million more people voted on 13 in Los Angeles County than the number who voted on Measure B.

WHY THE AMERICAN TAX REDUCTION
MOVEMENT'S PLAN IS THE BEST

There are several efforts under way to reduce taxation or spending by the federal government, but I think the plan we proposed in the American Tax Reduction Movement is the best one because it is the only one that deals with both taxes and spending. The other major plans under consideration are:

Kemp-Roth: Named after its sponsors, Congressman Jack Kemp, a Republican from New York, and Senator William Roth, also a Republican from Delaware, it would lower personal and corporate income taxes.

The Friedman Amendment: Advocated by Milton Friedman and the National Tax Limitation Committee, this proposed constitutional amendment would limit expenditures by the federal government.

A Balanced Budget: This is the plan that has received the most attention since Jerry Brown got behind it in January 1979, as one means of boosting his own presidential stock. The National Taxpayers Union has proposed that the Constitution be amended to require the federal budget to be balanced each year.

In theory I could support any of those programs—to reduce federal income taxes, limit federal government spending, or require a balanced budget—but only as a last resort, only if we can't win approval for our plan that requires reductions in both taxation and spending.

The competing plan that disturbs me the most is the balanced-budget amendment. Although we are required to have a balanced state budget in California, that didn't stop huge increases in both taxes and spending before 13 passed. If the government were required to have a balanced budget, all the people in Washington would have to do when they wanted to increase spending would be to increase taxes. It's that simple.

Second, the balanced budget concept does not speak directly to the real problem: cutting inflation. The only program that can have any meaningful effect is one that will require government spending to increase at a rate *less than* the rate of inflation. Otherwise, you're just adding fuel to the fire of inflation. If you enable taxes and spending to go up at the same rate as inflation or at a higher rate, it's just like carrying wood to a fire and saying, "I'm against the fire, but I'm going to keep putting wood on it anyway." I think that's irrational. One of the things that I think we have to do is to make certain that the cost of taxation does *not* keep up with inflation. That's the only way to break inflation. Inflation is the result of government extravagance and overspending, which causes them to print more money, which causes the devaluation of the dollar. And that's inflation!

A third objection I have to the balanced budget is that the requirement that the budget be balanced could be suspended whenever Congress decided there is a national emergency. There's nothing that would keep us from being in a permanent state of emergency.

Then there's the opposite problem: the government has to have some leeway, it has to have room to operate when there is an actual emergency such as war or recession. I've never been able to bring myself to support a hard-and-fast limitation on government spending. I don't think it can be done. I don't think anybody can write enough law to cover all emergencies, unless you put in so many loopholes that the law becomes meaningless.

I don't think the government should be shut down completely without access to more money when it really does need it. I never wanted to shut off the government absolutely. I consider taxes the number-one evil in the United States. But I think we also have to understand that we need a government. Government must be limited, but "limited" means to me that the government has to be allowed to operate in some areas, with reasonable limits.

I just don't think you can put absolute limits on government. Of course, when I say that, all the right-wingers get angry at me. But that's why we built some flexibility into 13. If someone can sell the need for higher taxes to two-thirds of the legislature or two-thirds of the voters, they can get it approved.

There's flexibility built into our American Tax Reduction Program. It goes into effect over four years, and there's no requirement that a certain amount be cut in any one year. And after four years, if necessary, we can try something else—I don't know what. But the first thing is to get the helicopter off the pad.

My biggest objection to both the balanced budget idea and the Friedman Amendment is that the way they're set up, if Congress refused to enact the amendment, a constitutional convention would be called. I'm very fearful of a constitutional convention. We could get a bunch of crazies in there and we might wind up with a constitution that's not nearly as good as the one we have now. I think the Constitution we have is marvelous. There is a real question as to whether a constitutional convention would have to stick to a balanced budget or whatever it was called into being to work on, or whether the delegates could start tinkering with any part of the Constitution that struck their fancy. There's a good chance that question would not be resolved until after the convention met, and that's too big a risk to take. But don't forget that the first constitutional convention was assembled in 1787 to amend the Articles of Confederation, and those delegates wound up drafting an entire new constitution. I urge all those who share my fears about the risks of a new convention tampering with our Constitution to write letters, speak out, and raise hell against this wrongheaded idea.

Also, I don't think the people who want to call a constitutional convention understand the political realities. Before you can hold the convention, you have to have two-thirds of the states in favor of it, and then three-quarters of the states have to approve any amendments that come out of the convention, according to Article V of the Constitution.

I think that's futile. Even if they could do it, it might take ten years, and we need tax relief now—not ten or fifteen or twenty-five years from now. But the thing is, I doubt if they could do it, within ten years or ever. See, if anybody could have done it, the ERA people could have done it, with all their clout. The women are the most powerful political force in this country, and they couldn't put over the Equal Rights Amendment, even without the need for a convention. If the women couldn't do it, how the hell is a bunch of taxpayers going to get it done?

Proposition 13's victory was elusive enough. It took us sixteen years. I don't want to chase any more butterflies like that. And besides, I don't have enough time left. I'm seventy-six, and I want to go with something we can accomplish fairly soon, like get a law through the House and the Senate to reduce taxes and spending.

Just to show how much I dislike the risk of a constitutional convention, I went to Sacramento in February 1979 to testify against Brown's proposal for a constitutional amendment to balance the budget. I went because I was invited to testify before the Assembly Ways and Means Committee. And who invited me? Leo McCarthy, of all people.

KEEPING THE HOME FIRES BURNING

Meanwhile, back in California, I'm fighting for my new initiative that would cut state income taxes in half. The maximum state income-tax bracket is now 11% for people who earn $32,620 a year or more; it would be cut to 5.5%.

As of 1979, the state personal income tax produces $4.8 billion in tax revenues. But the state income tax has been growing in recent years at double the rate property taxes were increasing before Proposition 13. In 1982–1983, if we continue on this same spiral, the state income-tax burden will be over $9 billion a year. Between 1974 and 1978, personal income in the state increased by 54%, but tax collections on personal income increased by 89%.

The other aspects of this initiative include:

—State income taxes would be indexed to inflation, so that cost-of-living salary raises don't force taxpayers into higher income-tax brackets.

—The state's business inventory tax would be eliminated to encourage businesses to move into California, which will further boost the state's economy and improve the job picture.

—Again, the idea is to reduce taxes—period—not to shift tax burdens from one form of taxation to another.

Before the end of 1979 I hope to gather the more than half a million signatures needed to qualify the income-tax initiative for the ballot in June 1980.

WE HAVE JUST BEGUN TO FIGHT

We have to keep working in order to keep government from being the only growth industry in this country. We have to keep working to make sure that government has what it *needs* to spend—not what it *wants* to spend.

I don't think the public interest in tax relief is going to diminish. And the public interest is very high. An Associated Press–NBC poll in December 1978 showed that all across this country 63% of the people wanted federal spending cut, while only 27% didn't want a cut; and the public favors cuts in federal taxes by a margin of 57-to-31.

Just in case the people do get complacent, there will always be greedy politicians to keep the fires of tax revolt going. A good case in point is Illinois. In November 1978, 82% of the voters said they wanted a ceiling placed on government spending. Right after that, members of the legislature raised their own pay 40%, to $28,000 a year; members of the Cook County Board of Commissioners—who work part-time—raised their pay 30%, to $32,500 a year; and members of the Chicago City Council voted to raise their own pay from $17,500 a year to $28,000 a year—a 60% increase—and then, after the public complained, the council members cut their salary back to $22,000—which was only 25% more than what they had been making.

As long as I'm around, I'm going to do my best to keep the ball rolling. I think there is always a danger that, having achieved a great victory like we did on 13, some people will say, "I've done it all—I don't have to work anymore." I think there will be a tendency toward a letdown in the wake of our victories in 1978; some apathy is only natural. But it's my job to overcome that, and that's exactly what I intend to do. A willingness to keep plugging away and working hard, no matter what, was something I learned many years ago, when I was growing up in Utah.

CHAPTER EIGHT

Shaped by the West— And How I Grew Up to Be Mad as Hell

If government doesn't cut rates, people have to do it. . . . By reducing business costs, Proposition 13 ought to spur business expansion and employment.

—Murray L. Weidenbaum, economist, University of Washington, after Proposition 13 passed

Jarvis-Gann is excellent. There should be a limit on all taxes. This is a major first step. . . . The rest of the nation will be watching. . . . Jarvis-Gann sends a message all around the country.

—Arthur Laffer, economist, University of Southern California, before Proposition 13 passed

My best guess is that the expansion of business activity caused by
the reduction in property taxes will yield an additional $3 billion
in revenue to the state in the first year.

—Arthur Laffer, after Proposition 13 passed

MERCUR, UTAH, WHERE I was raised, was a little mining town way
up in the hills about 50 miles west of Salt Lake City. The whole
town consisted of maybe 100 houses and 400 people. I was born
there and named Howard Arnold Jarvis on September 22, 1903,
and a week or so later the entire town burned down—every building. Nobody ever found out what caused the fire. In later years
all the survivors used to go out there and hold an annual picnic.
It was called Mercur Day, and it was a big, big event for us.

After the fire, my father and mother and I moved to Magna,
another small town of about 250 people located 18 miles west of
Salt Lake City. We rented a house for a year or so while my
father, who was a carpenter, built a house for us.

My father, J. R. (James Ransom) Jarvis, was born in 1879 in
Wilkesboro, which is in northwestern North Carolina. The Jarvises
settled in Jamestown in the early seventeenth century, and toward
the end of the century some of my ancestors moved to Albemarle
(which became North Carolina around 1700) and bought land from
the Indians. One of my forefathers, Thomas Jarvis, was Deputy
Governor of Albemarle from 1691 to 1694, and a relative of mine,
Thomas L. Jarvis, was Governor of North Carolina from 1879 to
1885.

My dad left North Carolina about the turn of the century, when
he was twenty or twenty-one. He had a large number of brothers
and sisters, but he and one of his brothers were the only ones who
ever left. I think my father left there and moved to Utah because
he came to the conclusion that there weren't many opportunities
back there. Life was very slow in North Carolina, and he was
always kind of a goer.

When I was six or seven my parents took me and my sister,
who was about four—my three younger brothers hadn't been born

yet—and we went on the train back to North Carolina to visit my father's family. We got a surrey with a fringe on top and a horse, and it took us six weeks to go through those hills and visit all his brothers and sisters. I'll never forget—we had chicken every night for dinner, no matter where we were.

Everyone in my father's family owned farms. Some of them had tobacco plantations—not big ones. They all chewed tobacco, even the women. I remember my grandfather had a thick beard all the way down to his waist, and he had a yellow streak right down the middle of it from the tobacco. He owned a farm, but he was also a Baptist minister. Of course that was the Bible Belt. And my grandfather fought for the South in the Civil War, but some of the family on my mother's side fought for the North.

My Southern grandmother was a typical old-fashioned farm woman, dressed in a long dress and a bonnet. I'm sure she never went to a beauty parlor or used lipstick or powder in her whole life. She chewed tobacco, too.

That was the only time I saw my grandparents or most of the rest of my father's family, although one of his brothers later moved to California, and I saw him occasionally out here. Compared to North Carolina, Utah was sort of bleak. It wasn't built up, and there's a hell of a lot of desert in Utah. But North Carolina was all green. It was just lush, and they had grapes back there like you wouldn't believe.

My mother was a lot like my father's mother. She was a farm woman, too, and I doubt if she ever had a manicure in her life. Her name was Margaret McKellar. Her parents moved from Glasgow, Scotland, to Illinois, and then to Eureka, Utah, where my father met her. Eureka was 30 or 40 miles from Mercur. The McKellars came to Utah because of the Mormon church. They were sold on Mormonism. My grandmother was very devout. My mother smoked cigarettes, which was very bad for her as a Mormon. My mother and my sister, who was always very religious, went to church every Sunday, but I didn't. The last ten years of her life, my mother worked as a volunteer in the Latter Day Saints Hospital in Salt Lake City, making bandages. She got on the streetcar and went to the hospital and made bandages all day long, six days a week.

My mother was always saying she would spank us tomorrow, but tomorrow never came. My father was the disciplinarian in the family. When one of us stepped out of line, he would tell you to go out and cut yourself a switch off a tree in the back yard. That taught you how to make decisions. A big one hurt more; but you knew if you got one that was too little, he'd send you back for a larger one and hit you a little harder.

The four of us boys got quite a few switches across the backside. There was Hugh, who was in the Air Corps in World War II and was killed in a plane crash near Washington or someplace. Keith was also in the Air Corps. He got a lung problem at Anzio and it finally killed him. Robert, who was an officer in the Navy, lives in the San Fernando Valley now, and is in real estate.

When I was about twelve, we got a small farm, just large enough to grow stuff to feed our family. I would get up at five in the morning and milk the cow, shovel manure, whatever else needed to be done in the garden or on the farm. Work was the name of the game. The cows had to be milked every day—Saturdays, Sundays, holidays, good weather and bad. We also raised some hogs and chickens, and I had to kill them. I was the guy who had to shoot the hogs between the eyes with a .22 and cut off the chicken's head with an ax. I was the oldest, and my father was kind of skittish about killing them. I was a little skittish, too, but I didn't have any choice.

That's the way you grew up in those days. Your father would say: "Here are the chores I want you to do," and that was one conversation that lasted five years. We did what we were told to do. We didn't consider it a drudge. As a matter of fact, we loved hard work. We loved to go out there and dig up the ground. And if we had a horse to plow, we thought that was a big thing. When the corn would come up, that was a great day.

The kids in our family hardly ever got into trouble—except for me. I used to get in fights at school. My father would go down to the school and get hold of the principal, whose name was Gardner. He'd sit me down and say, "Now, you tell your story," and then he'd say to the principal. "Now, what's the other side of this?" If my father was convinced I was wrong, he would wham it to me, but if he thought I was right, there was no way that he would back off.

There's no question about it: My father was the most important influence on my life. He was a very stern, righteous, but fair guy who had a set of principles by which he lived. Those principles were: you never lied to anybody, you never took anybody's money unless you had earned it, and education is essential. He would tell us that education was just like the cans on the market shelf: all you have to do is go take it off. But if you don't take it off, you're not going to get it. Nobody's going to hand it to you.

He expected everybody in the family to get straight A's. And if you didn't, he would say that you were wasting his time and his money. We had a library in the house. It was his private den, and you had to knock to get in there. If you didn't come home with an A, you were going to spend every night for the next two or three weeks in that library studying the subject with him. He would make you read it and ask you questions. Before you got through in there, you knew the answers.

He thought it was really inexcusable not to get straight A's because he said any dummy could do it. There was no excuse in my dad's book for doing the wrong thing. If you did something wrong, you had it coming. I'll never forget one thing he used to say: "In life, you know, it's easier to do things right than it is to do things wrong. You'll find out it takes just as much effort to do one thing as the other, so why do wrong?"

Nothing was more important to my father than us kids. But he was awfully busy, studying law at night and early in the morning, and working all day as a carpenter to support the family. If we wanted to see him about something, we would have to make an appointment—and you had better be on time, because he was always punctual.

When I was a boy, we had a Charter Oak range. I don't find many people these days who remember the Charter Oak range. It was a coal-and-wood stove—a big one—with chrome all over the front. We used mostly coal in Utah in those days. Once in a while we'd go up in the hills and cut a cord of wood and saw it up. There were no power saws in those days. It was not easy like it is today. That stove heated most of the house. Then we had a barrel-type fireplace in the living room. It got cold in that house at night. Back then we also had outdoor plumbing. In the winter we had to melt the ice and snow in a basin to get water, and we never thought anything of it because we didn't know any different. It was quite a while before we had running water inside the house. And we didn't have electricity until about the time I was in high school. Before that we used lanterns. The four of us boys handed clothes down from one to another. Of course, they were new when I got them, because I was the oldest. But we never considered ourselves poor. We always had everything we wanted.

The grade school was about a mile and a half or two miles from our house. In those days that was all farm country, and they had a typical red-brick schoolhouse with about four rooms. It was called the Hawthorne School. I used to walk down there to school; that was the only way to get there.

When I was in the sixth grade they built another school in Magna, only about three blocks from where I lived, and I went to the seventh, eighth and ninth grades there. Then, on the east side of town, they built the first high school in the Magna School District: Cyprus High School. Each year they added a grade. Four girls and I were in the first graduating class, so we were the first students in the tenth grade, then the first ones to take the eleventh grade, and so forth. It was a general run-of-the-mill small-town high school. They had none of these courses on sociology and all like they have in the schools today. They didn't believe in it, and I think they've been proven right.

When I was at the Hawthorne School, about the time I was in the fifth grade, my father got me a bicycle for Christmas. It was the first bike in town and that was the real jewel of Magna, to see me ride around on that bicycle. I was the cock of the walk. It was a black bike, and if I remember right, the price was $7.95. When I got up on Christmas morning, my father had assembled it, which wasn't all that easy, because he had never seen a bike before—except in pictures.

That bicycle got me in some trouble because all the farm kids used to come to school on their horses, and they were jealous of me and my bike. They beat me up pretty good, more than once. That got me started in the fighting business. There was another little kid whose father had a small furniture store, and he and I were about the same age. We got some boxing gloves and we used to box every evening. After a while we became pretty good, and one by one I licked all the kids who had beaten me up, those farmer kids, about eight or ten of them. They were about the same age as I was too, but they were bigger than me, maybe because they all worked on their family farms—we didn't have our farm at that time.

That was a great area for sports in those early days. In those towns that were generally mostly Mormon, sports was about the only thing there was to do for entertainment. Other than that all there was was a theater where they used to show a picture once a week. So we spent a lot of time in athletics. In high school we had a basketball team with only seven players on the squad because there weren't that many boys. We had a football team of sorts, but not much of one, and we had a scraggedly baseball team.

I never smoked a cigarette or had a drink or saw a pregnant girl either in grade school, or high school, or college. Never. When I was in high school, the coach would write on a piece of paper, "These are the rules," and hang it on the wall. And believe me, those were the rules. You had to go to bed at 9:00. You couldn't eat ice cream or pie. You had to report for practice at 3:35 every afternoon, for all sports. And of course we couldn't drink coffee or tea or Coca Cola or soda pop. It never occurred to us to disobey those rules.

We participated in sports outside of school, too. There was a canal from where the Utah Copper Company milled the ore up in the hills down through the town. It was a long, narrow canal, I imagine 15 feet wide and maybe 4 feet deep and maybe 2 miles long. It led down to what we called the tailings pond, where they would dump copper tailings (sand). Then they would pump the water out of the canal and flood the tailings pond to keep that fine dust from blowing over everything. We used to swim in the canal, and once in a while we would fish for carp in it. Then there was a lake out there. In the winter it would freeze up and we would skate on it, maybe three or four months out of the year.

I got my first job when I was twelve or thirteen, carrying buckets of water for the sidewalks that were being built in Magna. I worked a few hours a day, five days a week, and the contractor paid me fifty cents a day. I saved half of that and put it in the bank, a habit I learned from the Mormons and something I've tried to do all my life.

My father studied law by mail for several years and then became a lawyer. He had been town clerk back in Mercur, and later he was county treasurer and judge. I guess it's natural to idolize your father, and he was the most honest man I ever met. When he was county treasurer, if he had to make a personal phone call, he would leave his office and walk a couple of hundred feet down a long hall to use a pay phone. I'd say to him, "You take more time away from your desk than the nickel for the call is worth. Besides, who would know if you used the county telephone for a few of your own calls?" And he would say, "I would." And he kept on using the pay phone.

I remember when he first started filling out income-tax forms and I tried to get him to take deductions he was entitled to for this or that. He would say, "I won't do it. I don't need all the deductions." He thought the county needed the money. He was a very patriotic guy—a super guy on patriotism. Boy, I'll tell you, at our house on the Fourth of July that flag was out there.

While my father was a judge and I was studying law at the University of Utah, I would often go sit in his courtroom and follow some of the cases. I'll never forget one case. Around Salt Lake City there were a lot of mines, all through the mountains. On Saturday night a lot of gals used to go out to these mining camps and the guys would line up for the obvious reasons. There would be ten or twenty miners lined up in a row and they would pay maybe $2 apiece.

In order to make a good showing, the sheriff used to arrest a dozen or so of those girls out of about a hundred every week. They'd come into my old man's court, and he'd say, "What's your name?"

"Mary Smith."

"What do you do?"

"I'm a stenographer."

"What were you doing up at Gower Gulch?"

"Well, I was just visiting friends."

My father would give them a $3 fine or three days in jail. He knew what they were and he didn't believe their line. They didn't have any witnesses to testify for them, and it was up to him to say yes or no. They'd all pay the $3 and then go back about their work.

One Monday a little girl told my dad her name, and he said, "What is your occupation?"

"I'm a whore, your honor."

My old man was kind of a bluenose, and he said, "Do I understand that you're admitting to this court the practice of prostitution?"

She said, "I wasn't practicing, your honor. I'm a professional." That shocked the hell out of my old man. And he said, "Thirty dollars or thirty days."

When I got home that night I knocked on the library door and he told me to come in. He said, "Well, what can I do for you?"

I said, "I think you made a mistake today."

"What do you mean, I made a mistake?"

"Well," I said, "the only girl that told you the truth, you gave her the works. The rest of them you let off for three dollars or three days, but you gave her thirty dollars or thirty days, and I don't think that's fair."

He said, "I want to tell you something, son: you keep your nose out of my court business."

I said, "Yes, sir," and out I went. The next night he came home—in our house you didn't sit down to dinner until my dad sat down, and you didn't leave until he left—and after dinner he said, "I want to see you." I went into his library, and he said to me, "I just want to tell you I thought over what you said, and I reduced that girl's sentence to three dollars or three days." That's the kind of man he was.

My father always decided for the defendants unless the case against them was absolutely rockbound. If there was any hole in the state's case, he wouldn't convict them. And I never remember him being reversed. If he was, it's some cases I don't know about. I had the same damn philosophy as he. Later I was on the grand jury, and unless I was absolutely certain that the state could convict the defendant, I wouldn't vote for an indictment. I felt that the defendant should have the benefit of the doubt. If I thought that the defendant was guilty, but the state couldn't prove it, I wouldn't vote for an indictment. I know that a grand juror is supposed to vote to indict if he thinks there is probable cause a crime was committed by the defendant, but I didn't believe that was right.

Being indicted is a stigma that a person carries around for the rest
of his life, whether he's guilty or not. Besides, why should the
state waste money on a trial if they can't get a conviction?

My father was considered a successful man, although he never
made a great deal of money in his life. By the standards of the
area he was fairly prosperous, but he was never what you would
call wealthy. When I was young I think he made $376 a month,
and he had five kids. But he was looked up to and respected by
so many people that we felt the way he lived was the way to live.

I remember Dad and Mother's fiftieth wedding anniversary.
I went up there from California to Utah for it, back about 1950,
about five years before he died. They had one of the worst snow-
storms in Utah's history, but the ballroom of the hotel in Salt
Lake City couldn't hold all the people who came. How all of those
people got to the hotel in that weather, I will never know. I was
absolutely flabbergasted to think they would have so many people
in that kind of weather. That really opened my eyes to how far
the respect for my dad went in that state. That was some tribute.
I'll never forget it.

While I was in college I lived at home, rode the streetcar 18 miles
to the university in Salt Lake City and back each day, and then
seven nights a week I worked at the Magna Mill. At the mill they
ground up the ore and reduced it to copper and gold. The mine
from which they secured the ore was in a town called Bingham
Canyon, which was 20 miles uphill from Magna. They would load
the ore in railroad cars and send it down to the mill. It was one
of the largest mills in the world. They kept it open around the
clock and processed something like 350,000 tons a day.

I worked as a laborer in the tube-mill section, and earned $3.47
a day. The tube mill was one of the final stages. It consisted of
cylinders about 12 feet high and 30 feet long. By then the ore had
been reduced to pretty fine stuff, like sand. It would go in one
end of the tube where there was an acid mix and steel balls that
filled about half the tube. Then the mill would go around and the
ore would be ground finer and finer and finer until it could go out
over what were called flotation tables, which were made of long
corrugated iron sheets. The tables would shake, and gravity would

make the gold and copper go to the bottom. Then the metal would go over to the smelter. My job was to keep the tube mills running. It wasn't dangerous, but the grit got in your ears and eyes and nose and everywhere, which wasn't very pleasant.

One summer while I was in college, I decided to get a job in a silver mine near where my grandparents lived in Eureka, Utah. I was a mucker, which meant you got in the shaft and you went down a thousand feet or more to a stope, where we shoveled the ore into carts. That paid about a dollar a day more than my job at the mill had. It was hot as hell down in that mine. They had big pipes pumping air into the mine, but the air still wasn't very fresh.

One day there was a cave-in up above where I was working. Me and two other kids were locked in this stope, another tunnel off the main tunnel. We were in there for about two and a half days before we got rescued. We didn't have any food or water, but we didn't need any; we were too damned scared to eat, anyway. Even so, I don't think we had enough brains to know how much danger we were in. Later we found out that several of the miners had been killed. But none of the dead people were around us. As far as we knew, we were the only people left in the mine. We had caps with carbide lights, but we couldn't use the lamps because we were afraid we might cause a gas explosion. It was darker than hell down there. We sat in the dark for almost three days, without even knowing how much time had passed. We didn't dare move, so we just stayed where we were. When they finally got us out, it was about four o'clock in the afternoon and the light hurt our eyes, but just seeing the sunlight again was marvelous. My grandparents didn't even know about the cave-in until I told them; the news traveled slowly in those days.

I should have had sense enough to quit then, but I didn't. The mine was closed for about two weeks, but then it reopened and I went back to work. After another couple of weeks or so, the state made them shut it down for safety reasons.

The silver mine reopened about a year later, but I didn't go back there. The next summer I did something even more stupid. I went out to the coal mines, where I had heard they would hire you to shovel slack coal out of a railroad car. In those days they didn't sell the slack, they'd throw it out of the cars from a trestle over a canyon. You got 30 cents a ton to shovel it over the side, using a big scoop shovel. And there was 40 tons in a car. If you could shovel out a car in a day, you made $12. It was great pay. But it was a bitch to shovel 40 tons out of that car because every time you shoveled it out over the side of the car, the wind would blow half of it back in your face. And when you got down near the bottom of the car, you had to shovel the slack real high to get it over the top of the car. That job was a backbreaker.

There was a guy working in the office at the mine named Claude Stone. He had been one of my teachers in high school. I worked all summer there and I had my money, about $400, and I thought, "Rockefeller never had that much money." I took a freight train home because I didn't want to pay the train fare. I gave my money to Claude Stone to take home for me so I wouldn't have it on me while I was with all the hoboes who were in the freight cars. I never saw Stone again, so I had to go back to school broke. What a jackass I was. I thought, "I'm not taking any chances by giving my money to a schoolteacher."

What with going to college in the daytime and working in the Magna Mill at night, I didn't have much chance for social life during the five years I was at the University of Utah, going through college and getting my law degree. But I was active in sports there, too.

In football I played quarterback and started a few games. Four guys stood in a line side by side in the backfield. I didn't carry the ball much, and I didn't block at all, because I was too little. I passed some, but on many plays all I did was call the signals. I never made a touchdown, everybody else made touchdowns, but not me. I was in and out because I wasn't big enough. But I got a letter.

I taught boxing in college for three years. I was sparring every afternoon. I boxed with Jack Dempsey twice in exhibitions where he didn't try to hit me and I didn't hit him. We were just staging demonstrations in the boxing room of the gym at the university, trying to show the college kids how to box. I weighed 135 and he weighed 189. All he had to do was swing, and the air would have knocked me clear to Great Salt Lake. He just pushed me around a little. It was kind of an entertainment deal. And he was a nice guy. Later, on July 4, 1923, I went up to Shelby, Montana, for his fight with Tommy Gibbons. Dempsey won a fifteen-round decision. I was there at ringside. The people in Shelby thought they were going to make a lot of money, but that fight bankrupted the town. There was a lot of financial finagling going on there. Dempsey and his manager, Doc Kearns, left town within an hour after the fight. I ran into someone from Montana recently, and he said the town has never recovered. I'm afraid that's wat the 1984 Olympics might do to Los Angeles, in spite of all the guarantees by the politicians that the Olympics would not cost the taxpayers anything. Anytime politicians say something is going to be free, that's the time to start worrying.

Starting when I was eighteen in 1921, I had many amateur and professional fights. I only fought a few times as an amateur, but I had twenty-one fights as a pro, all over Utah. I fought Billy Wallace a twenty-round fight on the Fourth of July in the afternoon in Delta, Utah. We fought to a draw. I was in marvelous condition—absolutely perfect condition.

I never lost a fight, had a couple of draws. I retired undefeated. I decided when I got past 135 pounds I'd be a damn fool to fight. Actually, my dad decided. He said, "I don't want you to fight at all because you'll get your head beat in and you'll be a stumble-bum."

I got a big purse for that Delta fight: $600. But usually I would get $100 or $125. Tom Burke was my manager and trainer. He ran a pool hall in Magna—my father didn't appreciate that either. I trained out in the yard with a heavy bag and a speed bag hung from a tree. Mostly, I taught myself to box. There was a fighter named Kid Davis in Salt Lake City who knew a lot about the art of boxing. He said to me, "When you swing your right hand, don't swing it at your opponent's chin, swing it at his right shoulder. Because he'll duck—and that's where his chin will be." And I did that. I knocked out probably fifteen guys. I never fought less than six rounds, mostly ten, and a couple of fifteen's and a couple of twenty's. We wore four-ounce gloves.

I got hit hard only once. It was in a fight with a guy named Cat Grant. I weighed 135 and he was supposed to come in at not more than 145. He came in at 165. We weren't going to fight him, but there was a big crowd gathered. So I finally said to my manager, Tom Burke, "I'll tell you what, let's go downstairs so I can watch this guy shadowbox for a couple of minutes." Well, we went down, I saw him shadowbox, and I said, "I'll take him." During the fight Grant swung a punch way over the top—he was several inches taller than I was—and hit me on top of the head. It broke the tips of some of my teeth off. We didn't wear mouthpieces in those days. Breaking my teeth made me mad. Boy, was he big. And he was unorthodox—like a girl throwing a baseball.

He would come in like a bus and I would hit him with a left jab and then grab him. He was stronger than an ox. But I had these broken teeth in my mouth. And they hurt like hell, and I was mad. So I just kept jabbing him and grabbing him. And then one time he was coming in, and I faked the left jab and hit him with a right cross on the chin. Broke his damned jaw in two places. They had to take two of his teeth out and he had to drink his food through a straw. They wired his jaw shut. He was the nicest guy you ever saw, and it just crushed me to think I'd hurt this real nice farmer kid. That fight was held in a church gymnasium, of all places, in Hunter, Utah, where he lived. It was about five miles from Magna, just another little town. We had a terrific crowd, about 300. I got about $90 for that fight.

I never had a cut, never got knocked down or out. The problem with most boxers, and it's still true, is that they don't get in prime condition. All I had to do was to go out there and box four or five rounds and not get hurt, and the other guy was usually set up. There was nothing to it, because I was a hell of a puncher and I was very fast. I had a good left jab and I understood that the left jab is the most important thing in boxing. I never aspired to be a champion. My dad convinced me that fighters always wound up mentally mixed up, punch-drunk. He didn't want me to fight at all—under no circumstances. But I was kind of a strong-willed guy too. At that time I was eighteen, nineteen, twenty—I fought about once a month for two years—and I wanted the money. And I had found out how to get it. It didn't seem to me like there was even any risk. I never felt a punch except for that one in Hunter, Utah.

I always loved boxing, and about ten years later, while I was in the newspaper business in Magna, I was a manager for a while. I had a couple of boys. One was Maynard Neilsen, and the other was Frank Broadbent, who I nicknamed Jackie Ray. I didn't think the name "Frank Broadbent" was any good for the ring. And this boy had talent. He could have been a world's champion. He weighed about 135. He was a good-looking kid, seven or eight years younger than me. The other boy, Maynard Neilsen, was going with a girl in Magna by the name of Glenda Titcomb. They went into a hotel and for some reason or other he shot her and shot himself. Why they ever did it, I don't know.

Then I had only Jackie Ray left. He really had promise. Salt Lake City was a great fight town then. I got him through the preliminary stage and into fighting contenders. But he started running around with a lot of women, and he got set up. He didn't tell anybody, not even me. And the first thing you know, he was finished. I knew there was something the matter with him, but I didn't have any suspicion what it was. I cut down on his schedule, I thought maybe he was training too hard or something. Finally I found out what it was, but they didn't have an effective cure for it. He just went downhill, and I stopped booking fights for him.

I just managed those kids because they were small-town kids like me and they needed some help. I liked them and I loved boxing. I didn't take any of their money. Whatever they were paid to fight, that's what they got. In addition to being their manager, I was their trainer, and I sparred with them every day.

While I was in college I also played semipro baseball, in a very fast league called the Utah Copper League. We didn't get paid for playing ball, but they gave us a job at the copper mill. During baseball season we didn't have to do much work, but we still got our paycheck. The guys on the ball club, we'd check in at the mill in the morning, and then we'd just sit around all day until three o'clock, when we had practice. I still have an old newspaper clipping that says Jarvis was "a chunky right-hander with plenty of zip on his fast ball, a wicked break to his curve ball and a nice change of pace. He outsmarted many a Utah Copper League batsman."

One summer I pitched for the Salt Lake City Bees, who later

became the Hollywood Stars in the old Pacific Coast League. I played for them until my father found out what was going on and made me give it up. He went to Portland with me and discovered that all the ballplayers did (most of them were a few years older than me) was drink, gamble, and chase women. That ended my baseball career real quick. I was just a dumb green boob, a squirt.

We played in San Francisco, Oakland, Seattle and other cities. I was a relief pitcher and I had one experience that stands out in my mind. We were playing at Portland and we were ahead 5-to-0 in the bottom of the ninth. Portland made four runs and had the bases full. The manager, Duffy Lewis, took out our pitcher and put me in. The batter was a guy by the name of Whiffy Cox, who later became a big star in the majors. The first ball I threw he hit out of the ballpark. I can still see it going out. We had a pretty good team, though. The infield went up intact to the Chicago White Sox the next year. And Tony Lazzeri, who later was a star with the Yankees, played for us.

During those college years, I coached my old high school basketball team one season and also refereed high school basketball games for several seasons. I got paid for being a referee, but I didn't really do it for the money. I did it because I loved sports. Then, now, always.

BUSINESS AND POLITICS IN UTAH:
1925–1935

In 1925 I graduated from the University of Utah, where I was the first graduate of Cyprus High School to get a degree. My major was law, and the next year I got my law credentials. In those days they didn't have a separate law school; I just went on and took more law courses after I got my B.A.

I had been looking into the legal profession while I was in college, and I came to the conclusion that it wasn't for me. I could see myself in a little 8-by-10 office, sitting there for six months without a client. I thought, "The hell with that." There wasn't enough law business in Magna for there to be another lawyer. And the law business in Salt Lake City was all pretty well tied up. I was offered several jobs as a high school basketball coach, but I couldn't see that leading anywhere.

I had worked a little bit in high school and college writing stories for newspapers, just regular small-town stuff, nothing that ever amounted to anything. I liked it because it was exciting, and every day there was something new. So I thought, "Why the hell don't I go into the newspaper business?" I just didn't know what else to do.

I found out the man who owned the local weekly, the *Magna Times*, wanted to sell. His name was Clem Porter. He wanted to go to Washington and work for the Government Printing Office. He was asking $20,000 for the paper. I had hardly any money, but I finally got him to agree to a price of $15,000. Then all I had to do was get the $15,000.

I went over to the bank, where I had a savings account with $40 or something like that in it. The guy who ran the bank, Brigham Young Hardy, was a direct descendant of Brigham Young. I went in and told him, "I want to buy the newspaper." He asked me what I knew about the newspaper business and I told him the truth: "Nothing."

Originally I was to pay Porter $7,500 down and the other $7,500 in monthly payments, so I asked Hardy for the $7,500 I needed for a down payment. Hardy looked at me and said, "You're going to have to make two payments every month, us and him. How are you going to make the two payments?" I told him I didn't know. He said, "I tell you what: if I decide I want to loan you the money, I think I'd better loan you the whole $15,000 so you only have to make payments to one place."

He said, "Will your father sign the note for you?" I told him I didn't think so, but I would ask him. So they made out the note and I took it to my dad and asked him if he would sign it. He said, "No. You're over twenty-one, and I've got four other kids to raise. You're on your own, kid." I thought that was very cruel. But it wasn't cruel at all. It was the best thing that ever happened to me. Only I didn't have brains enough to know it then.

I went back to the bank and told them my father wouldn't sign the note. Hardy said, "I didn't think he would either. Do you think you can make a go of it?"

I said, "Sure, I think I can make it go."

He said, "I'll give you the note for $15,000." I signed the note—I think the payments were about $75 a month—and I went and took over the paper.

I had just gotten married. There was an apartment behind the newspaper office, and my wife and I moved into it. When I left home, my father gave me some advice: "One: you'll never go broke taking a profit. Two: never kick a jackass—you'll only break your foot."

My wife's name was Corinne Fickes. She worked in a drugstore. We'd been going together for about a year before we got married. Going together—what the hell, in those days if you saw a girl one day a week, that was going together. You took walks around the town, and if you were lucky, you went to a picture show once in a while. Her parents were from Ohio. Her father worked for the copper company. The copper mine was a few miles up in the hills and they'd bring down a trainload of eighty cars of ore. Mr. Fickes would be in the weigh station and he would check the number of the car to the pounds of ore. He could remember ten years later the exact number of pounds in each car.

Corinne and I moved into the apartment behind the newspaper office. It was downtown, which was just a wide place in the road. (In 1935, when I left Magna, the population had grown to about 4,000.) It wasn't much of a deal. Our newspaper office was also in the same building as the movie theater, the Gem. When there wasn't enough power, either we'd have to shut off the presses, or they'd have to shut down the projector. Fortunately, there wasn't much conflict because they showed most of their movies at night and we did most of our printing in the daytime. Before I left Utah for California, Corinne and I split up. We were just two young kids who didn't know any better. That's the way life goes. You get some kicks in the rear.

When I first bought the paper, I had an old fellow named Gus Bushman who ran the linotype and the press. I was the writer, and I sold advertising and made out the bills and did everything else. One day Gus said to me, "I don't think you know how to run this paper, so I guess I'll have to leave you." He stayed for two weeks more and taught me how to run the linotype and the press, a big flatbed. Then he left. He was absolutely right—I didn't know how to run a newspaper.

So there I was. With a wife and a newspaper, and I had to do it all myself. Sink or swim. At night I operated the linotype machine and put the newspaper together in steel chases. I wrote ads for everybody that didn't know how to write their own ads. And made out the bills. And collected the money. And wrote out the stories. And carried the trash. And swept the place out. For a while I didn't have anybody else—except my wife. She folded the papers, because we didn't have a machine to do the folding. Of course at that time we had only 900 circulation, and the paper ran six pages a week. Then I went to eight pages because I learned it was cheaper to print in four-page runs.

After two or three months, I hired another guy to run the press and then I bought a new Goss Comet rotary press. One day we couldn't get the press to start and I was underneath it. I had my assistant there and I said to him, "Now don't touch that damn switch until I tell you." While I was feeling around in one of the gears, he threw the switch by mistake and cut off most of my left index finger. I didn't know anything about the presses or anything else. So when the press stopped I tried to figure it out. I had my hand in the wrong place, and this dumb kid turned the motor on. "Cachook!" And I was minus a finger. I crawled out and put a towel around my hand. I knew the doctor was playing golf, so I drove out to the golf course, went out on the course and found him. We got in my car and drove back to his office, where he put me under an anesthetic, cut off the rest of my finger and sewed it back together. By then golf was my sport, and luckily, losing a finger didn't affect my game a bit.

Arthur Brisbane was then the leading newspaper columnist in the United States. He was carried in a daily paper in Salt Lake City, but not in any other papers in the area. I convinced them that a weekly paper out in a small town was no competition for a daily in a city like Salt Lake, and I was able to buy both the Brisbane column and Will Rogers' column, which I believe distinguished my paper from every other weekly in the country.

But pretty soon I found out there wasn't enough business in a town like Magna to support a paper and make it pay. That's why Clem Porter wanted to sell it. He thought he had a sucker, and he did.

Then I found out there was a thing called national advertising so I decided to go to New York to see if I could sell some.

I just barely had enough money for train fare to New York, and for a fleabag hotel and food. The day after I got there I walked into N. W. Ayer, one of the biggest advertising agencies, and I found out there was such a thing as a space buyer, which I hadn't known before. I got in to see the space buyer, and he told me they appropriated money every year for weekly newspapers; but they never placed any ads because they could never get back the bills or the tearsheets. He said he admired my drive for coming all the way from Magna to New York and he would like to do business with me, but he was sorry to say he couldn't. He said if anyone ever came up with a way to solve the problem, maybe they would change their minds.

I went back to my fleabag hotel and I thought about it all night. Finally I had an idea that I thought might work. The next morning I went down to Times Square to a tiny printing shop—it was just a hole in the wall. I asked the guy to print me up one envelope. He looked at me like I was nuts, but he said he could do it. I had him make up an envelope addressed to N. W. Ayer. On the outside of the envelope I put "From the Magna Times, Magna, Utah, Insertion order no. so and so, Tearsheet, Billing dept. so and so." It was a blue number-10 envelope.

I went back to the buyer at Ayer and I said, "I think I've got it solved. If you'll give me some space, you'll be the only one in the whole United States who will have a blue envelope like this. And here's what it will say on the outside. I'd like to make a deal with you: if you'll give me a schedule, the first time I miss one billing, you cancel me out."

He looked at me and said, "I would have bet $1,000 nobody could do this, but I think you've done it. Okay, I'll give you some space."

Then he said to me, "By the way, would you like these ads in mats or electrotypes?"

I said, "Well, if you were me, what would you have?" I didn't know the difference between mats and electrotypes, or even what electrotypes were.

He said, "You had better take electrotypes." I said, "Well, if you say so." I walked out of there not knowing what the hell size ads we were going to get or how much I was going to get paid. Our ad rate was 25 cents a column inch, but it turned out the national ad rate they paid me was 60 cents a column inch.

Then I had envelopes just like the first one made up, only in different colors. I went to all the other big advertising agencies, showed them what I had, told them N. W. Ayer had already signed up, and they all agreed to give me ad schedules.

While I was in New York, I was like Alice in Wonderland. I never dreamed there were buildings like that or offices like that. I went up to the Waldorf-Astoria for dinner—that's what everyone did when they got to New York. I ordered a baked potato, and it cost a dollar. I couldn't believe it. We sold potatoes like that at home for 50 cents a bushel. I'll never forget that—a dollar for a baked potato, and this was over fifty years ago. I thought it was absolutely outrageous. I thought even 25 cents for a potato was a lot of money because I had picked potatoes and topped beets, too. That's a job. Boy, I'll tell you, nobody has ever really worked unless they've thinned and topped sugar beets. I think thinning beets is harder than shoveling ore. I got $2 a day for thinning beets. After I passed the test and became a basketball referee in 1924, I used to officiate three or four games a week, get $5 for each, and I thought I was in clover. Even after I was making money in the newspaper business, I continued refereeing basketball. I loved it. And it was a change of pace from the business world.

Anyway, a dollar for a baked potato. New York was an expensive place, even back then. I was there for eight or nine days, and then I had to wire my father for $50 so I could pay the fare back home.

I got home and those national ads started rolling in. First thing you know, I had a big paper. I went to 16 pages, then 24, then 32, finally 44. Then I started a paper in Garfield. And then I bought the one in Bingham Canyon. Then as the years went by I started one in a town called Sugarhouse. Then I bought one in Helper, and another in Price. Within about five years I wound up with 11 papers with combined circulation of 30,000 and more national advertising than the Salt Lake City daily.

As soon as I acquired a new paper, I'd write advertising agencies in New York and ask them for an ad schedule, since it was a new paper in the chain. They didn't know the chain was made of celluloid. By golly, they all came through, with ads from R. J. Reynolds, Coca-Cola, Kellogg's, Ford, Chevrolet, J. C. Penney. And of course, when J. C. Penney came in, some of the other stores like Sears and Montgomery Ward had to come in, whether they liked it or not.

First think you know, I had a big office and I'm sitting there smoking cigars. And the money was coming in so fast I didn't know what to do with it. I was making $30,000 or $40,000 a year, which was a lot of money in those days. I didn't have any idea how much it was. I took the first money that came in and paid the bank on my note. If the payment was $50, I'd give them $100. That made my credit pretty good.

The printing was very simple. You just change the headline, change a couple of slugs, and there you go—you've got another paper. I loved crime stories. The beautiful thing about a good crime story was it could go in all the papers. All eleven papers were virtually identical, except they had different type for headlines and I would rearrange the stories. You see, I'd set all the stories the same length and just use them interchangeably. After all, these towns were all close together and all the people were interested in the same news.

There were two girls in the office, a linotype operator, a pressman, a general guy to set the hand type, a guy to cast the mats, a guy to clean the place up. Altogether, I had about ten people working for me. Then, in each town, I had a lady who would give me the local social news. All the papers were printed on that Goss Comet press I lost my finger in, but we had a little office in each town where we did commercial job printing, which was very lucrative. People who wouldn't have given us printing if we didn't have a newspaper gave it to us because we did have a paper. Without a newspaper, you're just another printer. But if you've got a newspaper, you're something special—you have a little muscle.

Pretty soon everything was running smoothly. My building was right next to the fifth hole of the golf course. I'd come in about seven o'clock in the morning and get everything lined up. Mail would come in about nine. I would read the mail and get the shop started. Then about ten I'd go down and hit a hundred golf balls. I'd come back to the office for a while and then go for lunch and have a sandwich and hit another fifty balls. Then I'd knock off from work about three thirty and play nine or eighteen holes. The papers were put to bed on Thursday, and on the weekends I would either go over to Jackson, Wyoming, and go fishing, or play golf—thirty-six holes. Saturday and thirty-six on Sunday. I had taken lessons from Bryon Nelson, who many people think was the greatest golfer of all time, and I got to be pretty good. I won some tournaments and some money betting on my golf game. In one tournament, the May leg directors' cup at the Utah Copper Golf Club, I beat a guy named Clarence Mitchell 6 and 5, and another guy named Jack Robbins 4 and 3. Both of them were "low-handicap players," according to the local newspaper story about the matches.

Fishing was another of my great loves. In 1929 I caught the largest fish taken in a stream in Utah, an 8¾ pound rainbow trout. I still go back to Wyoming and fish every fall. And during Labor Day weekend in 1978 I went fishing for marlin for the first time, off the coast of San Diego. My first time out, I caught a 160-pound marlin and got my picture in the San Diego paper. What a thrill catching that fish was! People tell me a lot of fishermen fish for marlin for years and spend thousands of dollars without catching one. I guess 1978 was just my year.

The first thing you know, I began to be elected to almost everything: Utah State Press Association; Chamber of Commerce—back before I knew what it was; International Order of Foresters; Lions Club, Young Republicans. And I became president of all of them. So I was off and running.

It all began with the Press Association. At the time of the 1927 meeting I was the youngest member of the association, and a story in the *Salt Lake City Tribune* described me as the "baby" of the association and as the editor of "three prosperous weekly papers"— the *Magna Times*, the *Garfield Leader* and the *Bingham Bulletin*. The *Tribune* asked me to put together a little story about small-town newspapers during that 1927 convention, which I did. Since

I first made my fortune, such as it was, on small-town papers, my feelings about them were very important to me:

> The field of the country newspaper and the country publishing business offers unlimited possibilities to any individual who is seeking a work that is eventful and full of interest.
>
> The country weekly can, and generally does, yield a tremendous influence for good in its particular locality. Almost invariably it is a staunch supporter of all constructive movements for betterment in its community and a medium upon which its readers may depend for information that is vital to them.
>
> Country newspapers have arrived at the point where they are reliable, energetic, hustling business institutions and the future of the country editor and his publication is of the most optimistic hue.

In 1931 I was elected vice-president of the Press Association. The next year they elected me president, succeeding Abe Gibson, an old friend of mine who was publisher of the *Nephi Times-News*. In September 1978, while I was on my way to Jackson to go fishing, I passed through Nephi, a little town of about 2,500 in central Utah, and I stopped by the newspaper office, which is right there on the main street. Abe has been dead for a while now, and his nephews run the paper. It's still just a little weekly, like it was back in my day. Right across from the high school, where I used to referee in basketball games. I really got a bang out of going into that little paper in Nephi and seeing them with a big $20,000 computerized VDT. During my newspaper days it was a big deal when I bought an $8,000 linotype machine. The truth is, I've never gotten the newspaper business out of my blood.

While I was in the newspaper business I made many speeches about publishing and visited about 300 papers in Utah and other western states. One time I was invited to speak at a meeting of the Idaho Editors' Association in Pocatello and I told them, "The ideal newspaper will be thoroughly independent, devoted to the protection and advancement of broad human interests, and fearless on all issues, with an optimistic, hopeful viewpoint."

I meant what I said about being fearless. I had that instinct of a newspaperman, and I loved to break a good story. In Bingham Canyon, where I had one of my papers, there was only one narrow street in the whole town, which is about 40 miles south of Magna and 50 miles from Salt Lake City. They had the largest copper mine in the world there, the Utah Copper Mine. This was during Prohibition, and some people had tipped me off that the sheriff's deputies were running liquor into Bingham Canyon from Wyoming.

My information was that they were going to bring the liquor in one day right after dawn. So just as it got light I climbed up on top of a building, which was about two stories. A skyscraper in Bingham. I had a $4 Brownie with me. I got a few pictures of sheriff's deputies riding herd on this truckload of whiskey—one on each side and one driving. The street ran uphill into the mountains, so they had to go slow and I had time to get some pretty good pictures. Not great ones, but they looked good enough on the front page of my papers. The *Desert News* in Salt Lake City picked it up, and you can imagine what a stink it caused. Whiskey. During Prohibition. Being smuggled by the sheriff's deputies. In that Mormon state. It caused a hell of a stink. The Governor raised hell, and they called for a grand jury investigation. A few deputies and some others wound up in jail.

Then one time I was getting license plates for my car and I noticed quite by accident that when the clerk issued truck licenses he didn't ring the money up. Instead, he put it in his own pocket. I dug into that and I found out that the clerks in the Secretary of State's office were stealing the truck license money. I broke the story and the Secretary of State and several of the clerks went to jail. The real clue was, in the State of Utah all the constitutional officers like the Secretary of State had to be bonded. The State Treasurer held the bonds. But the Secretary of State, who was head of the license department, never deposited his bond in the Treasurer's office. He never had a bond. When that came out, all hell broke loose.

I led a fight against a guy who wanted to be county assessor and serve in the state legislature, too. I crusaded against him in my newspapers, and I won that fight. I just thought that having someone drawing two public salaries at the same time was wrong. Also, I couldn't see how a guy could perform two jobs. I got the Press Association to pass a resolution that said: "In recent previous sessions of the legislature, numerous members of school boards, school officials and councilmen of cities and towns and others occupying positions of trust under the laws of the State of Utah were elected and served as members of the legislature, contrary to the state constitution." Therefore, the resolution said, the Press Association "will protest issuance of any certificate of election, the administering of the oaths of office or the seating of any legislator who is ineligible" under the constitution.

In 1933 I came across a rash of stock schemes and phony pyramid letters. They flourished to beat hell at the time. Some of the people who didn't know any better had been giving money to these high powered promoters. So I wrote in my papers:

> Why people continually fall for the "slicker" stock salesman is one of the unsolved mysteries of the universe. How some individuals who are apparently good thinkers in all other lines of endeavor succumb to the appearance of a gilt stock certificate is one of the unknown measurements. A number of Magna people have purchased stock in ventures which upon the slightest investigation they would have saved their money. . . . How foolish it is to take the word of a stock salesman, no matter what he may be selling. Don't be carried away with the enthusiasm of anything. Keep your money in your pocket until you find out what you are buying and what chances you have to make a profit on your investments.

Not long after I got into the newspaper business, I started running ads for Western Air Express, which was the forerunner of Western Airlines. They used to pay us in scrip instead of money, so I did a lot of flying in order to get something of value out of it. I was the second passenger they ever had. The first was a woman. I would fly all over the state to visit the different newspapers. They just had one passenger at a time. They flew deHavilland biplanes and other planes of that vintage. You would wear a fur coat—they didn't have heat in those days—and sit on a sack of mail. Sometimes when I knew the pilot we would fly over an island in the lake and shoot revolvers out of the open cockpit at timber wolves. Six months after Proposition 13 passed, I went to England and France to give some speeches, and I flew on the Concorde. What a difference from those old planes I used to fly on!

One time a few years later I was flying south from Salt Lake City on one of these early passenger planes during the winter and we hit a mountain near St. George, Utah. That was about 1927 or 1928. We had been in the air for about an hour and a half or so when the wings got all iced up and we couldn't make it over the mountain. We didn't have any idea that the plane was going to crash. There was no notice from the pilot. They didn't have loud speakers in the planes in those days, or seat belts. There were 18 of us on the flight, but we couldn't see anything outside, the snow was too heavy. The snow was in drifts about 40 feet deep, and the pilot just mushed into one. We were only going about 50 miles an hour when we landed. And the snow cushioned it. Nobody got hurt, except for one gal who broke her nose. All the rest of us got shook up, but not seriously. The plane wasn't even wrecked. We sure were lucky. If we had run into a tree we would have all been dead, but those drifts covered most of the trees. Not far away there was only two or three feet of snow, but the pilot put it down in just the right place.

We crashed about 4 o'clock in the afternoon. The pilot had sent out a distress call over his radio, but we had to stay up there on the plane all that night, all the next day, and all the next night. It was pretty cold. We stayed in the plane and there were enough blankets for everybody to have one. I was a hero because I had a quart of whiskey with me. A friend of mine and I used to go to Wyoming and buy 40 gallons of whiskey and bring it back to Salt Lake City. I had an apartment near the capitol that I used when I was there on business, and all the politicians used to come by and have a drink. At that time I didn't drink myself, I just had it for my friends. Anyway, I was carrying a bottle with me to give to the publishers I was going to visit. We measured it out among everyone on the plane during the night, when it was cold as hell. Everyone got a spoonful. They had a bunch of sandwiches on the

plane, but no coffee. After the plane crashed the radio wasn't
working, so we didn't know the rescuers were on their way with
dog sleds and mules. We sat there for almost 48 hours, just about
scared to death but not able to get ourselves out of there. Anybody
who left the plane would have gotten lost in those mountains, with
all the snow. Finally, about 2 o'clock in the afternoon on the
second day after we crashed, the rescuers reached us. They had
had a hell of a time. They put us on canvas sleighs and took us
down to a little town called Richfield, which was right at the base
of the mountain. It took about three hours and we got there about
nightfall.

MY INVOLVEMENT IN UTAH POLITICS

My father was a Democrat. He was originally from the South,
and he had been brought up as a Democrat, but he was fiscally
conservative, like a Republican. Most of the businessmen I associated with were Republicans, and in those days I always thought
Republicans had the best people. We had two Republican senators
from Utah that I thought a great deal of. One of them, Reed
Smoot, was one of the most eminent members of the Senate. So
I gravitated to the Republican side.

Although I was a Republican, I knew Utah's Governor, George
H. Dern—who was a Democrat—pretty well. At one time Dern
had been a mining engineer in Mercur, and he and my father were
good friends. In 1931 Dern named me as a member of an advisory
council of 100 citizens to make suggestions about how to deal
with unemployment in the state during the Depression.

In 1928 Dern appointed me a delegate to the Press Congress
of the World, which met in Havana. The featured speaker at the
congress was Franklin D. Roosevelt. That was the year he was
first elected Governor of New York, but he had been very prominent for years; he had served in the Wilson Administration, been
the Democratic nominee for vice-president in 1920, and nominated
Al Smith for president at the 1924 Democratic convention. Roosevelt made a speech in Havana in which he said he favored
virtually eliminating the tariff on sugar imported to the United

States. That was an important issue, especially in the West, where so many people made a living from the sugar-beet industry.

During the next four years I was very active in politics, and in 1932 I was elected president of the Young Men's Republican Club of Salt Lake City County and publicity director of the Republican State Central Committee. It looked like Roosevelt was going to be the Democratic nominee for president, so early in 1932 I wrote him and asked for a copy of the speech he had given in Havana in 1928. On February 26, 1932, he wrote me from the governor's office in Albany and sent me a copy of the speech. He expressed "cordial thanks" to me "for your expression of good will," that I had included in my letter to him. Little did he know why I really wanted the copy of that speech.

I also got hold of a copy of the *Havana Post* which quoted from Roosevelt's speech. Then I immediately got in touch with Stephen Walter, the Republican National Public Relations Chairman in Washington, and told him what I had. He asked me to send the speech itself and the newspaper clipping to him.

Using the information I had provided, the Republicans were able to have Congressman Gilbert N. Haugen, a leader of the House Agricultural Committee, put out a statement during the Roosevelt-Hoover campaign charging that

> Governor Roosevelt has already in advance of election day sold out the western beet sugar industry to the Cuban sugar interests, [which are] largely financed from New York City. The Democratic candidate had the effrontery to publicly sign his name to the bill of sale.
>
> On August 24, the *Havana Post*, an English language newspaper of which I have a photostatic copy, carried a story stating that officials of La Casa Grande, a large mercantile establishment interested in Cuban sugar, had written Governor Roosevelt congratulating him upon his nomination as Democratic candidate for the presidency and stating that they were glad to note his statement, in which he declared as confiscatory and dishonest the duty of two cents per pound on Cuban sugar and that in his opinion, this duty should be reduced to 20% ad valorem or less.
>
> The Cuban newspaper then quoted Governor Roosevelt's

reply as follows, "Thank you for your hearty congratulations. It gives me a great deal of pleasure to discover that my political ideals are understood and appreciated by my friends in neighboring countries."

It may give the governor "a great deal of pleasure to discover that his political ideals are appreciated in neighboring countries." In fact I am sure that if the Cubans could vote Roosevelt into the presidency of the United States, they would do so. Certainly the Mexicans, with their surplus of livestock, would be delighted to vote Roosevelt into the presidency of the United States. None of them, however, would be likely to vote him president of their own country.

Competitive tariffs are always welcomed by other countries. But they are poison to American producers. The political ideals most appreciated abroad are exactly the political ideals which would deprive the American producer on the farm and in the factory of his market.

I also received a letter from Henry J. Allen, director of publicity for the Republican National Committee, in which he wrote:

This is to congratulate you on digging up the Havana, Cuba, sugar story, from which we were able to put on Mr. Roosevelt a declaration in favor of a reduction of the sugar tariff to 20% ad valorem. Photostatic copies of the newspaper story in the *Havana Post* of August 24 have been widely circulated wherever sugar beets are grown, and will be helpful in swinging the election in many states. I want to express my appreciation of the initiative and cooperation expressed in this instance.

I had done my bit. Unfortunately, Mr. Allen's prediction that the sugar tariff story would prove "helpful in swinging the election in many states" from Roosevelt to Hoover turned out to be a little optimistic. I know; I was there.

While I was working on the story, the Republicans had invited me to come to Washington to talk to them. Hoover was going to campaign on this train from Des Moines, Iowa, to Elko, Nevada. I was a newspaper publisher. As a result of that sugar-beet story they asked me if I would be the press man on Hoover's train. Of course, I accepted. They didn't pay me anything, but I saw it as my duty. I slept in an upper berth in the next car down from Hoover's.

They told me what I had to do. It was very simple. When the train stopped, I had to go out and talk to the press; and when Hoover was ready to come out, I would say, "The President will be out in a minute."

I think they appointed me press man because nobody else would take it. It was a real bitch. There would be people out there waiting for Hoover, and they would throw rotten eggs and tomatoes.

I would have to stay out on the rear of the train and field the stuff the people in the crowd were hurling until I thought they didn't have any more. Then the President would come out on the rear platform of the train. We would keep the doors on the sides of platform shut so everyone would have to stand out in front where we could see them. I was up there with a pillow so I could knock down anything else they threw at him. I was an advance man in the true sense of the word. I'll bet I saved him from getting hit with 500 tomatoes. It stood me in good stead for Proposition 13.

I spent a week on that train, campaigning across the country with President Hoover and some of his aides. We would pick up a senator or a congressman a few miles before we got to a town, then they would ride in with us and get off. Hoover and I used to sit out on the observation deck and talk when we weren't going through towns. He talked to me like I was just a young, inexperienced fellow that wanted to listen to him. Which was true.

Hoover was a plain, simple genius. He was a very, very fine, bright, honest man. As a candidate, his only drawback was that he was not a politician. I don't think he considered the political situation at any time. He wouldn't make a statement that would result in political advantage for himself. I felt he knew the whole time he was going to lose, and that was not important to him. What he did care about was that he should not say anything that would hurt the next president or the country. Hoover wasn't much of a speaker. He didn't have a flair for dramatics like Roosevelt did. But in that campaign, that's all Roosevelt was—an actor, with a flair for dramatics, and, in my opinion, not much more. Hoover had a yellow pad and he would write out what he was going to say at the next stop and then go out and say it. It was as simple as that.

Hoover's main problem as president was that he had a Democratic congress to deal with and they wouldn't enact anything he proposed. As a matter of fact, he proposed the Reconstruction Finance Corporation, he proposed many of the things that the Democrats wouldn't put through then, because they simply wanted to win the election. All they wanted to do was take over the political power. The Democrats had no compunction about doing anything, they just wanted the Republicans out of the presidency.

During the campaign, Roosevelt said a lot of nasty things about Hoover's policies having caused the Depression. Hoover was hurt by what Roosevelt said, but I wouldn't say he was angry. I never saw any indication of anger or frustration or any of those things in Hoover. He was a very kind man; soft, compassionate, and a true patriot and gentleman. I have always thought Hoover was one of the most capable men to serve in the White House—at least during the sixty years or so I've been following politics.

I was with Hoover all the way until the eve of the election. I still have a badge he pinned on me while we were outside of Echo, Utah, a tiny town northeast of Salt Lake City, on November 7, 1932, the day before the election. We went on to Elko, Nevada, and that was it. From there I went back home and Hoover went on to his home in Palo Alto to vote. The night before the election we were talking about what was going to happen. We were talking about the states and Hoover would talk about each state and then say quietly, "I don't think this one is in our column." I think I was more sorry about it than he was, and he tried to cheer me up, seeing how young and downcast I was. On Election Day it was a rout. Hoover carried only six states: Pennsylvania, New Jersey, and four in New England. Roosevelt got all the others, including all the ones Hoover and I had been through.

In that same election I was on the ballot too, as a state representative for the Eighth District, where Magna was. And I lost— to my father, who was running for the same seat as a Democrat. Actually, I was my dad's campaign manager, and I was telling everyone to vote for him. While I was with Hoover, I wrote letters to my father about our campaign. And he would write me to towns where he knew I was going to be and I would go to general delivery to get them. We both ran because we wanted to make sure that one of us would be elected to represent our area. Each of us won his nominating convention. That was quite a thing: a father running against his own son.

Running against my father wasn't the only unusual thing that happened during that campaign. Before I started going around with Hoover, I was in Tennessee campaigning with Hoover's vice-president, Charles Curtis. He was from Oklahoma, and what an orator he was. Once Curtis and I were riding in a big, top-heavy sedan on a country road that had a crown in the middle so the water would run off. We were going about 25 miles an hour, and the guy driving this big sedan went too far over to the side of the road. The car rolled over, sort of in slow motion. I was riding in the back seat with Curtis and I wound up sitting on his head. We were both embarrassed. And here we were out in the middle of nowhere, with the car over on its side. Then a farmer came along with about six buddies, and between them and the three of us we got the car turned back upright.

On July 10 and 11, 1934, the Republican National Executive Committee had a meeting at the Palmer House in Chicago. I was still publicity director of the Utah Republican State Committee, as well as past president of the Young Men's Republican Club of Salt Lake County, and I was named as a delegate.

By that time I had made a few bucks in the newspaper business, so I took a suite with two bedrooms. Not long after I checked in, the manager called from downstairs. He said they were full, they had a delegate from California they'd like to take care of, I had the only extra room in the hotel, and would I mind letting this delegate use my second bedroom. I said, "Sure, if he's a delegate and he needs a room, send him up." Pretty soon there was a knock at the door and here was this tall, good-looking guy wearing a straw hat and an overcoat and carrying a straw suitcase. He said, "My name is Earl Warren."

I introduced myself and invited him in. He was very grateful to me for letting him use the room. He thought it was a big thing

I had done for him. I didn't think it was anything at all. We went to dinner and we went to the meetings together. We were there for a few days, and the whole time he talked about California. He said, "Someone like you could do fine in California. You could go into politics; you could do anything you want." I had been to California before, but I had never thought about moving there.

The more Warren talked about California, the better it sounded. At that time he was district attorney of Alameda County. When we were getting ready to leave, he said, "Instead of going back to Salt Lake City, why don't you come back with me and visit in Oakland for a while?" So I went with him and stayed for a few days in his house. It was at Vernon and California Street, as I recall. All the time we were riding across country on the train, and then while I was at his house, he kept on selling me about moving out there. Finally he suggested that if he were me, he'd go back to Utah, liquidate, and come to California. After I went back to Utah, the more I thought about it, the better I liked it. So I finally decided to do it. It was the best thing that ever happened to me.

I sold all the papers except the one in Bingham, and that one I gave to my father. I surprised him at a little family dinner the night he retired from politics. I told him, "I can't ever pay you what I owe you, but here's a down payment," and I gave him the deed to the paper. He got a lot of satisfaction out of running that paper. He owned it for about ten years until he sold the paper and moved into Salt Lake City, which was closer to where mother was working at the LDS Hospital.

THE LASTING IMPRESSION
MY YEARS IN UTAH HAD ON ME

So I left Utah. I haven't lived there since 1935—although I visit there every year—but I've never forgotten the way life was there. It was a very different atmosphere from what it's like on the West Coast and the East Coast. Back in Utah, nobody locked their car, nobody locked their house, nobody locked their office, never. We didn't even bill local people when they bought ads. They would always come around and pay us.

We had a little town where all the businessmen, whether they were competitors or not, were warm friends. We had a marvelous sense of fellowship and cooperation. And we had marvelous times. Taking our wives dancing, everybody wearing white tie and tails, in Salt Lake City, on Saturday nights. Playing golf and cards, fishing and hunting together.

Right before Thanksgiving, all the businessmen in Magna, about fifty of us, would go out with shotguns. We'd string out in a great big line and walk out to where the jackrabbits were. We'd kill maybe a thousand jackrabbits. Then we'd bring 'em into Garfield and Magna, and we'd pile them on the sidewalk. People would come and help themselves, and by God, within two hours there wasn't a single rabbit left. Rabbit made good eating if you killed them in a cold winter when they were fat and healthy. A dressed jack would weigh six or seven pounds. And then every year you'd put $50 in a hat and they'd draw a few names and the winners would get to go out to Antelope Island in Great Salt Lake and shoot a buffalo. I did it one year. It was like shooting a cow.

I do my best to be as open and honest as I can. That lesson from when I lived in Utah has stuck with me ever since. After Proposition 13 passed, I had lunch with Herb Caen of the *San Francisco Chronicle*. He had been zinging me in his column, which he had a right to do. But I knew he was pretty liberal and perhaps didn't like me—even though we had never met—and I was wary of meeting him, after what he had written about me. I found out that he's okay, and if you level with him, he levels with you. I felt that if he had any animosity toward me, he turned around; and I can tell you that if I had any animosity toward him, I turned around.

I grew up in one of the freest parts of this free country. We lived in Utah and Idaho and Colorado and Wyoming and Montana. We were Westerners, where a man's freedom and his privacy were considered number one. Where there wasn't a man or a woman for a hundred miles who wouldn't fight for this country at the drop of a hat. Where they taught patriotism in the schools, instead of tearing the country down. Where everybody had an opportunity to climb up the ladder, no matter who he was. Where they had fewer problems than the rest of the country did.

There's no question in my mind that the Mormon influence had a tremendous amount to do with all that. The Mormons are a very self-reliant people. I don't think anybody can honestly say that the Mormon church hasn't provided the best attitude, the best discipline, the moral leadership, the responsibility, the Americanism, probably more than any other institution in this country.

I think the Mormons established an attitude of conduct that makes a big difference. I think they understand the virtues of liberty and freedom. They understand the importance of education, and I think they have the best educational system in the country. All of this adds up to a great sense of citizenship. They have created an atmosphere in Utah that makes for honest progress, and I have always respected that. And the more I see of the rest of the world, the more I respect it. If the character of the people of the United States today was as strong as the character of the people of Utah, we wouldn't be in any trouble at all. Comparing Salt Lake City to Detroit or San Francisco, for instance, is like comparing a temple and a stable. The Mormon credo is like a tree that grows straight up. I go back there every year, and there's always the same atmosphere—clean, invigorating, industrious, ambitious, and yet not selfish. That's ingrained in those people. That's what enabled them to build a great state out of a wilderness.

There's an awful lot I don't know about the Mormon religion but there is one thing I do know: If you are a Mormon and if anything happens to you, the church would take care of you. After I had moved to California, my parents' house burned down. My father escaped with his false teeth and my mother with the bathrobe on her back. And that's all they had.

Of course, they could have called me in California and I would have gone right back there and taken care of them. But they didn't tell me what had happened. They didn't want to worry me. The Mormons built them a new house. I've seen so many instances of people who run into hard luck in Utah. If they're in the church, the church comes in and sees that they're fed and they have a place to live and clothes to wear. The church takes care of its people.

There are some things about the Mormons I don't comprehend. They probably don't even consider me a true Mormon. That's okay. I still believe in many of their ideals, such as their moral code, their fantastic educational system, their industriousness, their taking care of their own people, and the fact that they created a garden in Salt Lake City out of the desert. I still consider myself a Mormon, even though I never go to church.

I was friendly with many leaders of the Mormon church when I lived in Utah. I used to referee basketball games with Harold B. Lee, who later became president of the church. But I was never what you'd call an A-number-1 Mormon. I was always busy doing something else. I like to play golf on Sunday. I like to take a drink, although I never drank until I was about thirty-five. Besides, I thought those church benches were too hard.

Not being a devout Mormon wasn't much of a handicap to me when I was in the newspaper business in Utah. My family criticized it more than the people I did business with did. The fact is that financially I was doing good. And money talks.

Although I don't go to church myself, I do think we need religion to keep us adhering to some positive moral standards. I think moral standards are vital to the well-being of our country. I don't think we can have a strong country without strong moral standards.

During those years when I was in the newspaper business, I cut out a poem I saw in a magazine and pasted it into my scrapbook:

> Age is a quality of the mind.
> If you have left your dreams behind
>   And hope is cold;
> If you no longer look ahead
> And your ambitious fires are dead,
>   Then you are old.
> But if from life you seek the best,
> And if in life you keep the jest
>   And love you hold.
> No matter how the years go by,
> No matter how the birthdays fly,
>   You are not old.

Little did I know then how true that would be for me, that the highlight of my life wouldn't come until I was almost seventy-five. Everything that poem talked about came true for me. And I still believe every word in it.

At seventy-six I find all of the sugar is in the bottom of the cup. I wish the same for everybody.

CALIFORNIA, HERE I COME

On my way to California I stopped off in Las Vegas. I thought I would look at the newspaper in Las Vegas and see about buying it. I had sold my papers in Utah for a lot of money, and I had it with me in cashier's checks.

They were just finishing up Boulder Dam. There were a lot of cheap little gambling houses and a bunch of guys sitting around playing poker and shooting dice, but gambling had no appeal for me, even then. I thought to myself, "Hell, this is all the town will ever be: twenty guys running the dam and nothing else here." It wasn't much of a paper, and I thought, "I don't want to get stuck in a town like this." So I decided not to buy it. I could have had it for peanuts.

But I looked around a little more. I went in a couple of real estate offices to see what they had. A guy tried to sell me the block east of the railroad depot, which had a few buildings and a hotel called the Sal Sagev—that's Las Vegas spelled backwards. This guy said he could sell me the whole block for $50,000. I looked at it and I finally said to myself, "You've already made a decision to get the hell out of this town."

But he was a hotshot. After I said I didn't want to buy the block with the hotel on it, he said, "I can sell you a mile on The Strip for $5,000."

I went out and looked at that mile of land, and it looked like the Sahara Desert. I said, "What the hell am I going to do with all that sand?" So I didn't buy that either. I don't think there was anything out there except a road—the road to Los Angeles—just like there is today, only now it's a little wider.

So I kept on heading west, into California. Even though Earl Warren lived in Oakland, I had made up my mind to go to Los Angeles because I thought it had better weather and even then, more opportunity than the San Francisco–Oakland area. I had been to California many times in the past few years, usually to Los Angeles, and I had always liked Southern California.

One of my best friends in Utah was a lawyer named Ray Brady. He had been on the track team at Notre Dame. I had a lot of advertising scrip for hotels, and we used to go out to Los Angeles every other year for the Notre Dame–Southern Cal football game. Can you imagine two guys so nutty as to drive all the way from Salt Lake City to Los Angeles to see a football game, and then to turn around and drive right back? But that's what we did, and often we went out for the Rose Bowl, too.

One year we were going back after the Notre Dame–USC game and when we got up to El Cajon pass out of San Bernardino, it started to snow. The highway patrol was there and they required everyone to put chains on their tires before they would let them go over the pass. Having grown up as country boys, we had everything you can imagine in the trunk of our car: chains, picks, a shovel, you name it.

While we were putting our chains on, along came Will Rogers, riding in a red and cream Cadillac coupe with no top. Another cowboy was driving it. And they didn't have any chains or money with them.

I went up to Rogers, and I'll never forget: he was wearing Levis, a mackinaw, and an old gray hat that the sweat must have soaked through ten years before. At the time he was one of the most famous men in America—this was a couple of years before he and Wiley Post got killed in that plane crash. I said, "Mr. Rogers, my name is Howard Jarvis. I own some newspapers in Utah, and I run your column in them. I'm glad to say hello to you." He was eating raisins out of a big sack, and he said, "I'm glad to say hello to you, too. Have some raisins. You know, I haven't got any money on me, and they tell me I've got to have chains."

I went over to the guy at the gas station and asked him, "Hey, how much for a pair of chains?" It was a few dollars, and I said, "Listen, I want to pay. This man here is Will Rogers." When they found out who he was, they let him have the chains. They knew he would pay them back.

Rogers said to me, "You guys aren't going over that pass tonight, are you?" And I said, "We sure are. We're going all the way back to Utah before we stop." He said, "I'm on my way up here to see some cattle. But you guys must be pretty tough to be going on a trip like that on a night like this." Hell, it didn't mean anything to us—that was the way we lived.

Rogers and the fellow he was with left ahead of us and started up the hill. Ray and I had a sandwich and then we started. We got up near the top, and there was Rogers and his friend. They had slid off the road. It wasn't serious. But it was snowing, and their car didn't have enough traction to back up and get back onto the road. They were both standing there looking at each other. And here we come.

We had a Packard that looked like it was about fifty feet long, and the farther it went back, the higher it got. Damndest car you ever saw. It was a monster, but it wasn't much of a car. But at least this night it was doing okay. We got a big chain out of our trunk and hooked it onto the Cadillac. Then all we had to do was to back the Packard down the hill about ten feet and pull the Cadillac back onto the road and they were all set.

Ray had on this Notre Dame letter sweater with a big "ND" on it. By then Rogers knew who we were, and he said, "I'd like to take you guys to the football game two years from now." We said we would love to go. We had a nice little chitchat. Then we got in our car and they got in theirs, and off we went.

That's the last we thought about it until two years later, when we were back in Los Angeles for the Notre Dame–Southern Cal game. We were staying at the Alexandria Hotel, as we always did; I had so much of this advertising scrip that I usually stayed in the presidential suite there. Rogers had given us his private number at the ranch, and we had brought it with us. I wanted to call him, but Ray said, "Oh, nuts, he won't remember us. Let's not bother him. We've got tickets to the game anyway."

Finally, I decided to call him. When I got Rogers on the phone, he said, "I'm all set for you. You come out to my house at ten thirty on the morning of the game. We'll have some brunch, and then we'll go to the game." He had three seats: him in the middle and Ray and I on each side. Of course, he was a bigger attraction than the game. Afterwards we went back to the ranch and had a little snack, and then Ray and I went back to the Alexandria. That's the last time I saw Rogers. He was killed not too long after that, in a plane crash in 1935.

Another time Ray and I were out in San Francisco. The Union Pacific subpoenaed us in a railroad-rate case. One of my newspapers in Utah was a paper of legal record where the railroad had to publish its rates, and Ray had helped prepare the rate schedules as an attorney. They put us up at the Mark Hopkins and paid us $100 a day for expenses. That was a lot of money in those days. And they were paying for our meals. We would go to court every morning at 9:00, and the judge would excuse us for the day. So we would go out and play golf, come back and have a sauna, and then go out on the town every night. This went on for about six weeks, and finally I testified for an hour or so. My testimony was on the authenticity of the Union Pacific's notices; the question in the case was whether they had violated the ICC requirement of publishing their rates. After that we went back home. The railroad eventually won the case.

After I arrived in Los Angeles in 1935, I was trying to decide what to do. I heard the *Pasadena Star-News* was up for sale, and I went out and looked it over. I talked to the guy who owned it, and it looked like we were going to come to a deal. I had enough money to make a large down payment. But at the last minute he sold it to his son-in-law, Charles Paddock. Paddock had set a world's record in the 100-yard dash when he was at USC, and won a gold medal in the Olympics. He was the first guy who was known as the world's fastest human. He was killed in a plane crash during World War II.

I was living in an apartment at the Chalfonte, which was right behind the Ambassador Hotel. There was a golf-driving range alongside the hotel, and they had a lunchstand there. I would go over there and have my breakfast and read the paper and hit some golf balls. The owner was an old man from Scotland by the name of John Duncan Dunne. He and I took a liking to each other. His golf range took up a few acres, and one day he said to me, "How would you like to own this land?"

I said, "Well, I'd like to, but I don't know if I can afford it."

He said, "I tell you what I'll do. I'll sell you this land for $30,000. I don't want you to give me the money now. When I die, I want you to send it to my niece in Glasgow. From now until then, all you have to do is pay the taxes on it."

I was new in town, and much as I liked the sound of the deal, I wanted to check with my bank for some advice first. I went down to the bank, and they didn't like it. They didn't have any confidence in the town. The man at the bank—a very distinguished white-haired banker—looked me right in the eye and said, "You might as well understand something: this town is never going west of LaBrea." I'll never forget it as long as I live. That land is where the Tishman Buildings stand now. I think it sold several years ago for about $10 million.

But you see, I didn't know much. I had never had a lot of cash until then. And the bank said to me, "You must be absolutely certain not to lose your money." And they drilled that into me, and drilled it, and drilled it, and drilled it. So I was scared to do anything.

A little while later, after I had started to get a feel for California, I went out and looked at a piece of ground in Venice between Lincoln Boulevard and Redwood Avenue, not too far from the ocean. About 80,000 square feet was being offered. Part of it was swamp, and the price was 17 cents a square foot, or a little more than $13,000 for the whole thing. I was intrigued. I went back to my bank and they said, no, they didn't think it sounded like a good buy.

I went to buy some golf balls on Pico Boulevard, and I walked past a store where they had rolls of linoleum in the window. It was on sale for 19 cents a square foot. I thought to myself, "This linoleum isn't very thick, but it costs two cents a square foot more than that land in Venice. The land goes all the way through to China, and it's close to the beach. To hell with the bank."

I went to the bank and drew my money out. When I told them

what I was going to do with it, I thought they were going to have fits. They said, "We just can't understand this."

And I said, "Well, gentlemen, I'm sure you can't. And you can't understand a lot of things either, in my book." And I took my account out of that bank, the Farmers and Merchants—they were supposed to be the geniuses of the world—and moved my money to Security Bank. I held onto that land for a few years and more than doubled my money. Land in California was gold then, and it still is.

After a few months, I met Charles A. Dundas, who was a millionaire in this town. He had an apartment house on Seventh and Alvarado, across the street from what was then Westlake Park. At that time, Alvarado was probably the most important street in California because a lot of famous people in motion pictures lived there. Dundas had a company called the Glenwood Investment Company. He had a lot of property in Los Angeles and Riverside. He was getting on in years, and he asked me to be the treasurer of Glenwood Investment and to assist him in managing it. I was his right-hand guy. I took care of his properties, banked his money, spent a day a week in Riverside. I had a very pleasant association with Charlie Dundas for two or three years until he passed away.

After that I became general manager of the Servex Company, a place in Hollywood where they manufactured drugs and drug supplies. I ran the whole operation, even invented a plunger-operated syringe and got a patent on it. That was in 1937.

The Servex Company was located at the corner of Selma and Cahuenga. There was an underground garage next door where I parked my car, a new Packard 120. I didn't know it at the time, but Clark Gable and Gary Cooper parked their cars there, too. One day Gable backed his Duesenberg into my car and scratched mine a little. He asked somebody who owned the automobile he had hit, and he came into my office and said to me, "I scratched your car. I want to pay for it."

Of course I knew who he was. I said to him, "Let's go take a look." It was a little, fine scratch. I said, "I don't see a scratch there."

He said, "What's the matter? It's right in front of you."

I said, "I don't see any. And what's more, if I did see one,

I wouldn't let you pay for it. I can't see the scratch, and I can't ask anybody to pay for something I can't see."

Well, that turned into a big laugh. We got to be friends, and once every few weeks, Gable and Cooper would stick their noses in the door of my office and say, "Hey, let's go to lunch." There was a little Irish bar down the street with only about two tables in the joint. Most of the time we sat at the bar and ate our sandwiches and had a glass of Irish beer. Gable was a hell of a guy. And Coop was out of this world. I was under their spell. They were such fantastic characters.

Those were the great days in Hollywood, the heyday of the film industry. Working and living in Hollywood, as I did then, you'd run into all the big names in motion pictures all the time. They were famous, but they were also local business people, the same as anyone else. The big thing in those days was the Hollywood fights. They were held every Friday at the Hollywood Legion and I used to go every week. Claude Raines, Coop, William S. Hart, Roy Rogers, Buster Keaton, and all of them used to be there. I'd see them every week and I got to know 'em all.

I got to be starstruck, and I wanted to be a part of the film business myself. I put up some money for a film called *Ten Little Indians*. It was undoubtedly the worst picture in the history of the world. I don't think it ever got off the ground.

About the same time, I invested $100,000 to finance the major part of an oil well in Bakersfield. The well flowed at the rate of about 10,000 barrels a day for maybe three days. Then it all turned to salt water. I tried my best to find a market for that salt water, but nobody would buy it, and I lost my money.

After a few years, I got into an argument and left Servex. It was owned by several men, including Dr. John Vruink, who was then the top gynecologist in Hollywood. I wanted to expand the company. Vruink and the other stockholders weren't interested. They didn't particularly care about the money. They all had their own things and they didn't care that much about Servex. I wanted to add some new products, and I had worked out a deal with Hedy Lamarr to go into the cosmetic field under her name, but they wouldn't go for that either. I also wanted to go on a national advertising campaign. Finally they got themselves another boy.

While I was at Servex, I was involved in getting famous actresses to allow the use of their photos to be reproduced on 3-by-5-foot metal signs that were placed outside gas stations as a gimmick to lure customers. Through that I did some business with the Neuner Printing Company in downtown Los Angeles. They found out that J. Paul Getty was looking for someone to help him write the history of the Getty family and their involvement in the oil business. They appreciated the fact that I was a veteran newspaperman, introduced me to Getty, and I wound up writing some of the book.

Getty and I worked together on that book almost every day for nearly a year. We worked in the basement of his mansion at Wilshire Boulevard and Larchmont. It was damn cold down there because he didn't like to turn on the heat. I wore a sweater every day. The house was filled with all this white statuary Getty had imported from all over the world. He had so many statues that the floors were shored up with huge posts like telephone poles. It looked like a mine shaft. I guess I was one of the first outsiders to see most of those statues.

The room where we worked had stuff strewn all over the floor. It looked like a room in a college dormitory. Getty was a very strange guy, but I liked him. He never gave any indication that he was rich. He liked to eat at a little hamburger stand or some place like that. A lot of times he didn't have any money at all. I would pay for his lunch, and he would pay me back the next day. And if he picked up the tab, he would never forget to remind me the next day that it was my turn. Or if he gave you a cigarette or something he would let you know that you owed him one. And he had this ten-year-old red Ford convertible with no top. He drove it himself. He didn't have a chauffeur.

Getty's father's name was George F. Getty, and the name of the book, which was published in 1938 or 1939, was *The History of the Oil Business of George F. and J. Paul Getty*. The book was for him and his friends, and he had about 1,200 copies printed. He wanted the book to last a thousand years, so he had some of the copies printed on handmade parchment from the Vatican and bound in ramskin that came from there too. The paper and the ramskin cost a fabulous amount of money—about $50 for each book, which was a lot of money in those days.

We had big arguments over almost every word and comma in that book. He was a real stickler for certain kinds of detail. If he didn't like the way a sentence was written, he'd change it. And then, by the time I got the copy set in type, he would change his mind again. I thought most of the changes were unnecessary.

When I had time off from working on the Getty book, I would go over to the Biltmore and dance all afternoon. Then we would have dinner and then go out to a Latin spot and dance until two o'clock in the morning. I did that for years. A lot of people won't believe it, but most of the real dancers were not out for sex—either the men or the women. You didn't make a pitch at one of those girls if you had any brains. I danced with real sharp girls for years, and I never knew their last names, much less their phone numbers. The people who followed that route were all great dancers. If you weren't a topflight dancer you couldn't get a dance. That's what they were interested in. That crowd is all gone now. It has all disappeared from the face of the earth.

I was going to the Biltmore Hotel practically every day. There were a bunch of people who used to have a drink or a sandwich together. One day a fellow I had become friendly with there said he wanted to come up to my office, that he had a way of making money. He meant that literally. He said he had a machine, and if I would furnish a place so nobody would find out where we were, we could make a hell of a lot of counterfeit money and get rich.

I acted interested, and I invited him to come to my apartment on Whitley Avenue in Hollywood to give me a demonstration of how the process worked. Then I called the FBI and told them what was going on and when this guy was coming over. They said I should go through with the appointment, and they staked out my place and bugged it.

The guy showed up with some plates and some chemicals. As soon as he arrived, I said to him, "Now, I want you to explain to me in detail just exactly how you do this." He went all through this rigamarole of how he did it, and even showed me some $20 bills he made by what he called a "reverse transfer process," in which he used the chemicals to obtain impressions from genuine

$20 bills. His product looked like the real thing—I'll have to say that for him. After he finished telling his whole story the lawmen outside knocked at the door and said, "FBI." With that, my "friend" grabbed a metal bookend and made a lunge for me. I punched him in the stomach, but he hit me with the bookend and cracked some of my ribs. At that point, the FBI broke down the door to my apartment, and all at once about four of them burst in and grabbed the guy. They decided to break down the door because they were concerned about me, and I was too.

It turned out this man's name was Herslick Borensztajn, alias Harry Miller. The FBI and the Secret Service also arrested four of his accomplices; two in Beverly Hills, one in Compton and one in San Diego. I was credited with helping the government break up what they called a "highly successful" counterfeiting ring that had passed large amounts of phony money in Southern California. I believe that was the first time my name ever appeared in the *Los Angeles Times*, on February 20, 1937. I never saw the guy again. There never was a trial because he pleaded guilty and went off to the pokey. The doctor charged me about $35 to tape up my ribs, which hurt like hell, and the FBI reimbursed me.

At that time I was playing a lot of golf, and I had a two handicap. One time I played in a Pro-Am golf tournament at the Riviera Country Club in Los Angeles with Ben Hogan, Lloyd Mangrum, and Tommy Bolt. Hogan hit an incredible shot out of a sand trap while I was playing in his foursome. About three months after 13 passed, I was visiting some friends down in Fort Worth, Texas, and Hogan was there. I reminded him that we had met once before—it must have been forty years ago. I said to him, "Do you remember when you hit a ball out of a sand trap at the Riviera to about three feet from the cup with a three-iron?" He said, "Yeah, but it wasn't a three-iron, it was a four-iron." What a great guy. And he really made a lot of dough. I think he made his money manufacturing golf equipment. Someone down there told me he still plays great golf, although he never enters tournaments anymore.

Back when I was in the newspaper business, I had noticed how noisy all the machines were and how annoying it was. After I left Servex and finished up with Paul Getty I opened my own company, where I produced a padding material to muffle all that noise. My plant was located at Eighth and Santa Fe Streets near downtown Los Angeles. James A. McDonald, an engineer I had become acquainted with, was in it with me. We made pads to go under typewriters and other business equipment. We ran big rolls of felt through a conveyor belt. Then one spray gun would shoot granulated cork onto the felt, and another gun would shoot liquid latex for the cork to stick to. I traveled all over the United States, and in about six weeks I had national distribution.

That business lasted until World War II broke out. About three days after Pearl Harbor, somebody from the Government came into our plant and said they had to confiscate our latex for use by the Government. Latex was the heart of the rubber business, and the supply of latex to the United States was cut off because it came from Java, which the Japs had captured. Of course, nobody knew at the time that synthetic rubber was going to be invented. So we were out of the padding business.

The worst part of it was that the Government never used the latex they took from me. After the war somebody from the War Production Board gave me a tip that if I wanted to see my latex, he could tell me where it was. Just out of curiosity, I went. The latex was stored in a warehouse on Santa Fe Avenue near downtown Los Angeles. I knew it was mine because we were the only place in Los Angeles that used that much latex. Latex is a liquid. It came in barrels and looks like milk. But after sitting in that warehouse for a few years, my latex was just like a big ball of mush. All the water had evaporated out of it. And it took me about three or four years before the Government paid for it. It has always been a hell of a job to get money out of the Government, no matter what you do. They lose the forms. Or they forget. Or it just takes them a while to get around to paying.

My employees at the plant lost their jobs when the Government took my latex and closed me down, but they found new jobs right away. Hell, anybody who could stand up could get a job during the war. I was restless and I tried to get into the Marine Corps as a combat correspondent. They wouldn't take me: I was thirty-eight when the war broke out—just a little over age. I had a little pull. I knew some senators and some other politicians, and they tried to help me get in the service, but they couldn't.

I was out of action, and I sure as hell didn't want to be out of action during the war. So I got in my car and started driving around the state, looking for some way to help out in the war effort. Finally I got to Oakland and I found out that the Moore Drydock there was having an awful time installing degaussing systems on the ships. I didn't even know what degaussing meant. It turned out to be a process to demagnetize the hulls of ships so they wouldn't be so susceptible to the magnetic mines the Germans had planted in the water. The Germans had invented a magnetic mine and the gravity pull of the hulls of our ships would set off the mechanism in the mines, which would be propelled into the convoys. We were losing ships faster than we could build them. To make matters worse, during the long peacetime years in the Navy, every time the captain didn't have anything for the crew to do, he would tell them to paint the ship. Before long there was a heavy layer of highly flammable paint on the ship. And if you put those ships into combat and they got hit with just one mine, they would blow up like a bomb, because this paint they put on them was just like TNT.

One of the main problems they were having in building ships was degaussing them. The shipyards had contracts with the electrical unions under which no one but the members of the electrical union could install anything electric or touch a screwdriver. Nothing. These cables that were needed to degauss the ships were about 5 inches in diameter and they weighed 80 or 100 pounds to the foot. They had to go around each deck of the ship, and there were a lot of sharp curves and up and down and one thing and another. It was backbreaking work, and the union guys just refused to muckle those heavy cables around. So with that contract in effect, if the union guys wouldn't do it, the shipyard was in one hell of a mess. And they didn't know what to do about it.

The president of Moore Drydocks, Joe Moore, was in his eighties then. I had never met him, but I walked in off the street and asked for an appointment with him. I don't know why, but his secretary let me see him. When I got into his office I said, "I understand you're having trouble installing this degaussing."

He said, "That's right."

I said, "Well, I've never been in shipbuilding or anything like that, but I'd like to have a crack and see if I can solve the problem."

He said, "How the hell do you expect to solve the problem if you don't know anything about ships?"

I said, "Well, it's obvious that the people who know all about ships haven't been able to solve it."

Moore was desperate by then, of course. After a minute, he said, "What do you need?" I told him I needed a set of blueprints to look at. He said, "Come over tomorrow and I'll give you a set of prints." So I went over in my car, and the blueprints were enough to fill a truck. So I just left them in a pile there and went and rented a truck. Then I loaded all those blueprints in the truck by myself because I didn't have anybody to help me. And then I had to find a place to spread them out so I could look at them. I had some trouble, but then I remembered that many hotels had a few display rooms for salesmen. These rooms didn't have any beds in them—just space to set up displays. I went to the Leamington Hotel in Oakland and the guy at the desk said the only thing they had was a penthouse up on top of the hotel that hadn't been used for years. It was a good-sized room, but it was being used for storage, and the whole room was filled with boxes from floor to ceiling. The guy told me I could have the room for $50 a month if I cleared the boxes out. Today it would cost $1,000 a month. I hired some roustabouts and cleared out the room. Then I put in some drafting tables and lights. And I called Mac down in Los Angeles and told him to get up to Oakland as fast as he could.

I knew that if anybody in the world could figure out a way to solve the problem, it was Mac. I have hired many engineers in my life, and Mac had more brains in his little finger than all the rest of them put together. There wasn't a thing he couldn't solve. Sure enough, in about three weeks Mac figured out a way to take care of the problem with those cables they used for the degaussing.

It was so simple it was funny. The problem was when you had to make a sharp turn with this heavy cable by hand, it was almost impossible. Mac devised a cast-iron pulley big enough to handle the cable and he designed brackets for it. We went around the ship, and we welded brackets on wherever the cable had to make

SHAPED BY THE WEST

a turn. Then we strung half-inch stainless steel cable through all the brackets, attached the cable to a power winch and pulled four large cables through. The whole job required less than a day per cable, where up until then it had been taking weeks.

When I went in and showed what we had come up with to Mr. Moore I thought he would fall out of his chair. He said, "Okay, I'll give you three ships. And if you get these done on time I'll give you the other forty-nine I have." These were cargo ships weighing 20,000 tons or so. Mac and I went into business as the James A. McDonald Co., of which I owned 75%. We got people and we went to work. We worked like hell night and day and we did the three ships on time. And I wound up losing $350,000, which was all the money I had and all the money I could raise by mortgaging my house and everything else. It turned out I had seriously underestimated the cost of the project when I made my agreement with Mr. Moore. We had about 900 employees. It was Friday and my payroll was due and I didn't have the money to pay it. I had a loan from my bank, but that was the end of my credit.

I went to Mr. Moore and I told him what my predicament was. He asked me if I knew how to play pinochle, and I told him I did. So we played three or four games. The sweat was running down my back and I was scared to death. All of a sudden he pushed a button and said to one of his people, "Hey, give this guy a check for $350,000—no, make that $450,000." Then he asked me who my bank was and I told him the Union Bank at Eighth and Broadway. He called my bank in Los Angeles, and talked to a friend of mine named Herman Hahn, who was the manager, and asked him all about me. Moore finally said to Hahn, "I'd like you to set his line of credit at a million dollars and I'll guarantee it." Then Moore said to me, "You did these three ships, and I'll give you the other forty-nine. Now, how much?" I still didn't know. We finally settled at a price of $450,000 for each ship. Neither one of us knew how much it was going to cost.

Then he said to me, "You're not as damned smart as you think you are—do you know that?"

I said, "What do you mean, Mr. Moore? I don't think I'm so smart. I was flat broke just now until you gave me this money."

He said, "You had me right by the short hairs, and you didn't have enough sense to know it."

I said, "I don't understand that."

"Well," he said, "you've got all the fabricated steel for the other forty-nine ships over in that yard, haven't you? There isn't any more steel to be had. All you have to do is refuse to turn that steel over to me, and I'm out a million dollars a day."

I said, "You know, Mr. Moore, I've got two brothers in the service, out there fighting. If I had known I had all the fabricated steel in this area cornered I wouldn't have done anything. I'm not in this business to get rich. I'm in it to help us win the war." Well, from that the James A. McDonald Co. got something like 950 ships. We did them at every shipyard on the West Coast from Seattle to San Diego. Bremerton, Portland, San Pedro, all of them.

Most of the patriotic businessmen like me didn't charge nearly as much as we could have, and there was very little objection to the cost of the war, but still it would have cost a lot less, except for the arrangements between Franklin Roosevelt and labor. With Roosevelt's blessing, organized labor laid down the rules. They limited production. They mandated overtime, double-time, and triple-time. It was terribly wasteful. And make no mistake: it wasn't Roosevelt's policies that got us out of the Depression, it was the war. The Depression really lasted until the war got the economy going again.

During the war there came a time when the Navy decided they had to invade Leyte to start taking the Philippines back from the Japanese. I got a telegram from the Maritime Commission saying, "We have assigned you to wire ten cargo ships as A-1 priority. The price will be cost plus a dollar per ship. You can pick up the blue prints for these ships at the Naval Station in San Francisco. The ships will be towed to Moore Drydock and these ships must be completed by such and such a day."

Mac and I had never wired a ship before in our lives. But we had an order to do it, and we never had any doubt that we were going to do it. We couldn't get any electricians; all of them were already working. My superintendent said, "I'll get you some men." He went down to Mississippi and Arkansas and he hired 1,100 black men. We were delighted; we really needed manpower. We brought them all out to California and we gave each one of them $17 to go and join the union. They went and the union turned them down because they were black; they came back and gave us back the $17 and we hired them—because there was a labor-contract stipulation that if the union wouldn't take them we could hire them until the union could furnish the men, which they were never able to do.

Then we had to make electricians out of them. How do you make an electrician out of someone who has never had a wire cutter in his hand? Mac solved that problem, too. He had a foreman start on one end of the ship with a ball of red twine. He strung it all over the ship and put a mark everywhere a switch had to go. For a different type of switch, he used yellow twine, and so forth. We showed these men how to install the switches, and all they had to do was install a switch everywhere the twine was marked. That's how we got our ten Leyte ships wired.

We paid these men electricians' wages because they were doing electricians' work. The union was awful mad about that. I told the union to go to hell. Soon I got a notice to meet the union head in his office in Oakland. I waited a couple of hours, and finally he got around to seeing me. I said, "What do you want to see me for?"

He said, "We want you to get all those men out of your shipyard by nine o'clock tomorrow morning or we're going to strike the whole shipyard." I called him some names, some pretty strong ones, starting with traitor. And I told him that as far as I was concerned, all the union guys did was sit on their asses and cause trouble.

I went back to this little shack about eight feet square in the shipyard where I had my office and a cot. Aside from going across the road to the lavatory, I hardly left that shack for several weeks while we were working on those ships, not even to change my clothes or shave. They brought my food in. I looked like a bum.

After thinking over what this union boss had said to me, I decided I had better go over to San Francisco and talk to the admiral at the Naval Command. I went in and told the secretary I wanted to see the admiral. She said the admiral didn't see people unless they had an appointment. I said, "I've got a real problem.

I need to see him." I told her who I was and what the situation was. She said, "It does sound serious. I'll let you talk to the admiral's aide."

In a few minutes, the admiral's aide walked through the door. It was Carlos Badger, a guy I had gone to school with at the University of Utah. Here we were, old college buddies. I told him my problem, and he said, "I'll take you right in."

I sat down and told the admiral my story. He had two girls come in and take it down verbatim. When I got finished telling the story he said to me, "Is every word in this true?"

And I said, "Yes, sir, it is."

He said, "Well, if it isn't, I'm going to skin you alive."

He called the head of the union on the phone and he said to him, "I've got a man by the name of Jarvis here. I want to read something to you, and when I get through reading, I want you to tell me whether or not it's true." He read my statement word for word, and then he said, "Is it true or not?" Evidently, the union boss tried to avoid the answer, because the admiral said to him, "I just want you to tell me whether Mr. Jarvis' statement is true or not." Then the union boss finally admitted it was true. The admiral said to him, "I want to tell you something. You're not going to strike that shipyard tomorrow, because if you do, five minutes after you strike, the Navy will be the union, and you'll be in jail."

That ended the strike. After the war, believe it or not, the union tried to get the Government to disallow as legitimate expenses all the money we had paid to the blacks. They didn't win, but they sure tried. They brought an action before everybody they could, and I had to go to Washington to defend it. Ever since then, I haven't been what you might call the biggest booster of unions.

I had given Mac a share of our company; I put up all the money, but he provided the knowhow. But after the war he wanted his money, so I bought him out. About four years later, I got a call from the Internal Revenue Service saying that Mac hadn't paid his income taxes on his share during the years we were in partnership. They told me I owed the $40,000 Mac hadn't paid. Well, I had always paid my taxes, and I was damned if I was going to pay any more. So I flew to Philadelphia and got Judge Learned Hand, who was one of the best lawyers in the whole country, to take my case. Pretty soon after the IRS found out that I had hired Hand, they stopped trying to collect from me.

Another year went by. I hadn't seen or heard from Mac all this time, which wasn't really unusual. Mac was just like that. Then one day the IRS called me and said, "Mr. Jarvis, Mr. McDonald is going to be in our office tomorrow at ten o'clock to discuss his tax situation, and we thought you might want to be there." I hadn't seen Mac for a few years, so I decided to go.

At 10:00 we were all there, these Internal Revenue agents in the pinstripe suits, and me. And no Mac. A few minutes late, in breezes Mac, all 4′ 9″ of him. There were some preliminaries, and then one of the agents said, "Mr. McDonald, you owe $42,366.79, and we'd like to know what you intend to do about it."

Mac said, "I'm not going to do anything about it."

The agent said, "We don't understand that."

Mac said, "I'll make it clear for you. All you guys can go fly a kite, because I'm not going to do a damned thing about these taxes you say I owe. What do you think about that?"

And he got up and walked out.

That was the first time I saw a real tax revolt. I followed Mac out onto the street. We talked for a few minutes then we shook hands, and that was the last time I ever saw Mac. Several years later, I heard he was running a bar in Crestline, a little town up in the mountains. I heard he operated that bar for five years, never got a license, and never paid the state any money. I assume Mac is far away now; otherwise, I'm sure he would have gotten in touch with me after this tax thing got all the publicity. What a great engineer he was. His slogan was: "Find the simple way." I'll never forget him.

During the war I had been at a cocktail party in Washington, and the maid couldn't keep up with all the garbage the guests were producing. The hostess was helping her, and she asked me to take some of the stuff out. It was a very swanky place. We had to go out the door and put the garbage down a chute. There was a drunk leaning against the refrigerator, and he said, "There ought to be

something under the sink that would just eat up all that garbage."
I didn't think anything of it at the time. But about six months
later, when I was back in California, what that drunk said occurred
to me, and I thought to myself, "Why not?"

I called an engineer I knew—not Mac, who was gone by this
time—and told him I had to have a motor that stood on its end
and had a little plate with bumps on it, so that when you put the
garbage in it, the garbage would get ground up and go down the
drainpipe. I asked him if he could draw me up a set of plans and
how much it would cost, and he said he could do it for $500. So
I opened the Jarvis Manufacturing Co. at 757 Venice Boulevard
in Los Angeles and started making garbage disposals.

I carried on that business for quite a while and then sold it to
a group of people, which was a big mistake. They later sold it to
one of the big companies and made a good profit. I should have
held on to that garbage-disposal business, but I didn't realize how
big it was going to become.

The garbage-disposal thing wasn't original, so it wasn't a patentable idea. I knew that because I was in the process of learning
a great deal about patent law at the same time. Back in the 1940s
I had a friend in Los Angeles named LeRoy J. Leishman. He had
invented push-button tuning in radio and he needed some financing, so he came to me. And I invested in it. He had applied for
several patents, but they hadn't yet been issued.

After we got the models made satisfactorily and we had about
four patents pending, and two patents had been issued, Leishman
and I went to Cincinnati to show the tuners to Powell Crosley III,
who was the president of Crosley Radio. We showed him and his
people there this push-button device, and they absolutely went
wild over it. They loved it. They said they would pay us royalties
of a cent a button, which amounted to about $3 million. We went
on to Philadelphia and talked to the folks at Belmont, which was
the biggest manufacturer of radios, and they loved it too. We went
back to Los Angeles happier than hell, while Crosley and Belmont
were drawing up the contracts.

Neither one of them ever sent us a signed contract, and they
both applied for patents immediately on what we had. When there
are two patents applied for on the same thing, the man who applies

first can get what is called an interference hearing. Leishman had been the first to apply for the patents. We wound up in about ten interference hearings and won them all. In the meantime, we had applied for seven or eight more patents. And RCA and Crosley and Belmont and Majestic and all of them started equipping their sets with push-button tuners. So we filed suit for about $20 million, which is what a penny a button would have amounted to over a period of a few years.

A judge named Benjamin Harrison from San Bernardino who Roosevelt had appointed to the bench was assigned the case. He heard this case for about six weeks, and then he ruled that we didn't have a patentable item or invention, even though he told us he might be wrong, which I have felt to his day he was. So we went over to Oklahoma in another federal district court and we tried it before another federal judge there: same case, same plaintiffs, same defendants. On the morning of the third day the judge said, "I have decided this is a valid patent, it has been infringed, and I order an accounting and royalties to be paid to the plaintiffs"—me and LeRoy Leishman.

When you have two different decisions that conflict in two different federal courts, you can get a writ of certiorari to the U.S. Supreme Court, which is what we decided to do. I went to Philadelphia again to see Learned Hand to get him to take our case to the Supreme Court. We had good lawyers, but the other side had the best, and we wanted the best, too.

Learned Hand said to me, "You've got an absolute case. You've got a patent—there's no question about it. But Roosevelt has decided that there will be no patents held valid because most of them are developed by big corporation, and he doesn't want these big companies to have a monopoly on all the patents in the United States. If you go to the Supreme Court, you're going to lose the decision, and for that reason I won't take your case."

LeRoy Leishman and I went ahead anyway. It was about eighteen years from the time we started the case until we got the final decision, and we lost, just as Learned Hand had said we would. At one time or another during these court proceedings, we were involved in cases with Crosley, General Instrument Company, Radio Condenser Company, the Richards and Conover Company, and some other companies. In the end, all the courts decided that Crosley and the others had developed their push-button tuners "independently" and had not "borrowed" LeRoy Leishman's invention. The high point for us came on February 15, 1943, when we won a ruling in the Supreme Court, ordering a lower court which had refused to grant us an appeal to hear our case on the merits. The lower court, the U.S. Ninth Circuit Court of Appeals, heard our case again, but ruled on August 11, 1943, that our patents, "if valid, are not infringed." All the Roosevelt appointees voted against us. As far as I was concerned, Roosevelt was under the misapprehension that patents are developed by corporations, which they are not. The man who usually makes the invention is some little guy in a garage somewhere. Corporations hardly ever invent anything. I had 50% of the rights, and so did Leishman. We would have won fabulous amounts of money. As it was, I spent $100,000 or $150,000 on that case. The case dragged on until 1952, when we lost our final appeal to the Supreme Court. By the criteria they are supposed to apply in those cases, I believe we definitely had a patent, and the courts took it from us. It was strictly a political decision by the courts, which, at Roosevelt's direction, were trying to create a new social structure in the United States.

After the war, I was manufacturing an electric iron called the Erla. The Office of Price Administration was then functioning, and we were trying to make an iron that would sell for $5.95. It cost my company, the Erla Company, about $2.50 to make, and the OPA wouldn't let us sell it for more than $3.95. That made it impossible to produce the irons. I went to Washington to argue my case, and I got shunted from one agency to another. The longer I was there, the sillier it got. Finally somebody close to the Truman White House said if I'd give them $50,000, they'd get me the OPA price "tomorrow." I didn't like that one bit, and I told them to go fly a kite, but maybe not quite in those words.

So I got myself a market in Mexico and went ahead and produced the irons in spite of the OPA. And the American consumer wound up paying a lot more for the irons because the Government had to make it their business. After I made the irons in my plant in Los Angeles, I shipped them to a firm in Mexico. They immediately shipped them back into the United States through El Paso, Texas, and sold them for $14.95 apiece. It was a marvelous business for me because it was all cash in advance. I couldn't fill all the orders I had—there were checks and orders stacked up on my desk so high, I couldn't reach over them. My flatiron business was a gold mine until after a few years I heard the General Electric was tooling up to make electric irons out in Ontario. When I saw GE getting ready to enter the field, I got out. I knew I wasn't going to be able to touch them.

At the same time I was manufacturing irons, I was also making car coolers at my Erla Company for Firestone. That was the car cooler you put on the window of the car and filled it with water, so that when the wind blew through it there was a cool breeze in the car—which was really an illusion because all it was was wet air, not cold air. After a while, somebody developed the same kind of a car cooler you've got in cars today, and I decided to go out of that business.

In that same period I was also making gas heaters at the Jarvis Company on Venice Boulevard. They had a grid made out of Nichrome wire, which is a combination of nickel and chrome. These heaters were unique because they didn't leave an odor of gas in the room, the way most other gas heaters did in those days. We tooled up in 1948 to make the heaters and put them into production, and pretty soon I was manufacturing more than I could sell.

I went to Chicago to the home office of Sears Roebuck to try to sell these heaters to Sears. The buyer looked at me and he looked at my heater and he said, "That thing looks like a chicken coop to me. I don't see where Sears could do anything with it. I know you're in the business, but the desert is covered with the bones of people who tried to make gas heaters and failed."

I said, "You don't think it's any good? I'll tell you what I'd like to do: I'd like you to give me ten feet of counter space, and I don't care if you stick it in the worst corner in the store. I just want a board about chin high. We'll cover it and I'll bring in 250 heaters and sell them myself. Just give me a pipe that I can hook gas up to. Let me do it for a week, and we'll see how many I can sell."

He agreed. It was winter then in Chicago, and of course it was cold as hell. I stocked two gross of those heaters—288. The first day I sold nearly a hundred, and by Saturday night I had sold them all. I didn't really have to do much selling. When people saw how well they worked, they just carried them off.

I kept copies of the sales slips, and Monday morning I went in to the buyer and I said, "I sold 288 heaters and here are the receipts."

He couldn't believe it. Then he said, "Okay, I'll give you an order—ten stores, sixty heaters to a store."

I told him, "No way. I want an order for every store in the country, so I can ship truckloads at a time. You want this heater? I showed you what it would do and how it would sell. If you don't want it, okay, I'll go over to Montgomery Ward and sell it." The Sears buyer gave me the order I wanted. I shipped Sears a truckload of those heaters every week, and it was very successful. It was one of the few products that Sears sold under the brand name— the Jarvis gas heater—instead of under the Sears name. That went on for a long time until the Korean War came along. I couldn't get the Nichrome wire any longer, so I was out of the heater business.

Toward the end of World War II, I had started a firm called Femco, where we manufactured aircraft parts and subassemblies, such as wing assemblies, tail assemblies and special piano hinges for airplanes, and later I made parts for missiles at Femco. That business lasted until 1962, long after the car coolers and the gas heaters and the flatirons and the garbage disposals.

One of the main things we made at Femco was these huge piano hinges for airplanes like the C-47. Some of those hinges cost as much as $3,000 a pair. These were hinges for airplane doors that open up wide enough for trucks to come out. The larger hinges were about 18 feet long, 6 inches wide, and 4 inches deep. That means you have to cut slots out of one side of the hinge and drill a hole an eighth of an inch in diameter through the entire hinge, and you can't be off my more than $1/1{,}000$th of an inch. Otherwise, with all the vibrations in a plane while it's flying, the aerodynamics are affected. If you don't meet that tolerance of $\frac{1}{1,000}$th, the aircraft company won't accept the part. You've spent $1,000 to mill it, $300 to notch it, a few hundred dollars more to grind it, and if you're off $\frac{1}{1,000}$th of an inch, all you've got is junk. You've got to throw it away.

POLITICS FROM THE INSIDE

During the early 1930s, while I was participating in Republican politics, both in Utah and nationally, I had become acquainted with Bob Craig. Bob was a professor at the University of Southern California and was very active in Republican politics in California. Soon after I moved to Los Angeles, Bob Craig called me and asked me to go to a meeting where several people were trying to get Benjamin F. Bledsoe to resign his position as a federal judge and run for mayor of Los Angeles. They had a roundtable luncheon with about twenty-five people there and Bledsoe, a fine-looking gray-haired man who looked like he should be president.

They went around the table, and everyone said what they thought. And everyone thought Bledsoe should run for mayor. Finally they came to me. I said, "I don't think I should make any comment, I'm new here. I don't know enough about California politics."

"Well," Bledsoe said, "maybe we need an outside opinion."

So I said, "If you ask me my view on that basis, I'll tell you what I think: if I were a federal judge, I wouldn't consider running for mayor even for one minute. A federal judge is one of the top positions in the United States. It's a position for life. And compared to it, being mayor is quite a comedown, in my opinion." I sat down. And there was no applause, I can tell you that. But everyone else wanted him to run. So he resigned from the federal bench, ran for mayor, and was defeated. Then he went back to the practice of law in a firm called Hill, Morgan and Bledsoe, which was quite a prominent law firm.

About three or four years later, I needed a lawyer and I decided I would go talk to Judge Bledsoe; he was a good lawyer. I started talking about my case, and he said to me, "Haven't I met you some place before?"

And I said, "Yes, you did. I was the fellow who didn't want you to resign from the federal bench and run for mayor."

"Oh, you're that fellow from Utah. I'll tell you, I should have taken your advice. And you know something? Of all the people who were there that day, you're the first one who has walked in here to be a client."

As time went by, I got very active in Republican politics in California, just like I had been in Utah. I was precinct chairman for Los Angeles County, which had 14,000 precincts, more than any other place in the country; chairman of the speakers' bureau; and president of several Republican groups, such as the Los Angeles County Republican Assembly.

I was involved in planning strategy in many Republican races, deciding who should run, how they ought to campaign, what they ought to say, what attacks ought to be made, what positions they ought to take, and trying to coordinate the thing so they weren't all off running in different directions. It's a very hard thing to teach a candidate how to make a speech. It's practically impossible in most cases.

THE EARLY NIXON CAMPAIGNS

The era when Roosevelt was president and for a few years later was the heyday of Democratic political control of this country. Those of us who were active Republicans often had difficulty finding people to run on our ticket. One of our jobs was to go out and try to persuade somebody to run. We'd generally look for some fellow who was pretty successful in business, but we'd have a hard time convincing him that he ought to seek office. That used to be the difference between the Republican and the Democratic candidates in California and across this country. The Democrat would want the office because he could probably make more money doing that than he had before; but the Republican candidate was usually a guy who had a business of his own, and he would be independent as hell. If you did something he didn't like or if you wanted him to do something he didn't want to do, he would say, "The hell with you guys, I don't need this job, I've got my drugstore or my clothing store, and I'm going back to that."

We were going through elections where we only had half the ballot filled with Republican candidates; 1946 was one of those years when we were short on candidates. So we decided to advertise in local papers. Something like: "Position offered: good pay, short hours, little or no special skills required." Well, the ads weren't worded exactly like that, but we were advertising for candidates.

Whittier was one place where we needed a candidate for Congress that year. We ran an ad in the Whittier paper, and four or five young fellows expressed an interest. Several of us Republican leaders had a meeting at a hotel—I believe it was the William Penn—and we interviewed the applicants.

We interviewed them all, and we decided the guy in the sailor suit was the best prospect. We offered him the spot, but he said he wasn't sure he could run because he didn't have any money. I think the reason he came to the meeting was just to see what was going on, which was perfectly legitimate. In those days the Communist issue was very hot, and we thought his being in the service and being able to campaign in a uniform would be a plus. The party was looking for any political edge it could get. We talked him into running and told him we would raise some campaign money for him.

The name of the sailor was Richard Nixon.

He made a pretty nice impression, but little did anyone know that he was a champion debater. He was running against Jerry Voorhis, a very bright guy who had been in Congress for ten years and was generally considered one of the most capable members of the House. Nixon got Vorrhis to agree to debate him throughout the district. Nixon took him apart in those debates and won big. Even we were amazed. We were just hoping to fill the spot on the ballot and make a respectable showing so that people would know our party was still in business.

I am not an apologist for Richard Nixon, but there are some longstanding misapprehensions about his early days in politics. I was there, and I would like to tell the way it was. First, there was his campaign against Helen Gahagan Douglas for the U.S. Senate in 1950. All these years Nixon's enemies have talked about what a dirty campaign Nixon ran against her on the Communist issue, but here are the facts:

The Communist issue originated with Manchester Boddy, who ran against Helen Douglas in the Democratic primary. Boddy was publisher of the *Los Angeles Daily News*, which is no longer in business. He was a guy who came to Los Angeles as a hobo in the 1920s and worked his way up. It was Boddy who first compared Mrs. Douglas' voting record and that of Vito Marcantonio, who was a radical leftist Congressman from New York. During that primary, one of Boddy's supporters charged that Helen Douglas had "a consistent policy of voting along with the notorious radical, Vito Marcantonio," which "indicates that her sympathies and commitments are far to the left of what they should be for the next U.S. Senator from California." That's the way the *Los Angeles Times* reported it. And Boddy put out a fact sheet showing how often Mrs. Douglas voted with Marcantonio. That was in the Democratic primary, and it was a tactic used against Mrs. Douglas by a fellow Democrat.

When Boddy lost the primary, Murray Chotiner, who was running Nixon's campaign, took the same piece of paper Boddy had used and reprinted it on pink paper. Chotiner didn't change any of the language in Boddy's flier; he just used pink paper instead of white.

Then there was the famous Nixon slush fund back when he was in the Senate—the one that led to the Checkers speech and all. I know about that situation very well, and Nixon never initiated it. His supporters did. Nixon was never a man with money in those days. He'd been in the Navy and he was married and trying to raise a family and pay for a house, just like the rest of us. And here he was, a senator from California, and California is 3,000 miles from Washington. The senators from the east could hop on a train and be home in a few hours, but a senator from California had to fly, and it was very expensive back then.

We wanted our senator to be able to come back and meet with us and address audiences who wanted to hear him. And we felt we had no right to put an impossible burden on him. So we put in some money to pay for Nixon's airfare and hotel bills and other expenses when he came out here because he couldn't afford it.

I'm as sure as I'm alive that not a nickel of that money was ever spent for other than what it should have been spent for.

As I recall, Nixon was unhappy because he felt Eisenhower wasn't giving him enough support on that slush-fund thing, so Nixon wrote out his resignation and gave it to Murray Chotiner for him to send to Eisenhower. And Murray went out into the hall and tore it up. Tearing up that piece of paper changed the nation's history.

Murray Chotiner was under a cloud with a lot of people, but he was never under a cloud with me. I met him soon after I came to California, long before the Nixon campaigns, and he and I worked on a number of campaigns together: Earl Warren's campaigns, Bill Knowland's campaigns, Goody Knight's campaigns, Fletcher Bowron's campaign for mayor of Los Angeles, and many other races. He was sort of the brains of the Republican Party in California for many years, and Murray and I had desks across from each other at Republican headquarters. We were involved together in most of the important races in the southern end of the state. He was considered the expert. I thought Murray was the best political mechanic I ever saw, although he wasn't such a great overall strategist.

Because I had been very active in Republican affairs, having managed Eisenhower's campaign in several states in the Midwest in 1952, I was able to get in to see Eisenhower through Jim Hagerty, his press secretary, when I heard Ike was considering appointing Earl Warren Chief Justice of the U.S. Supreme Court. I had completely lost faith in Warren as a Republican so I didn't want him to be put on the court at all, much less be made Chief Justice. When I met with President Eisenhower he said to me, "I understand that you're opposed to the appointment of Earl Warren to the Supreme Court. I'd like to ask who you are for." I told him I wasn't for anybody, that I didn't have a candidate for the job, but if I were the president I would look at the chief justices of the various states or I would look at the most eminent federal judges. I told him Warren had had hardly any experience practicing law; he was a longtime politician.

Eisenhower said the court was in a state of disorganization and he needed someone who had ability as an administrator. He said he had looked in the other places I suggested and hadn't been able to find anybody he thought could do the job. I couldn't argue with that. I did say to him that if we only have nine people on the Supreme Court and they can't organize themselves, then we're in a hell of a bad way. But I had to admit that Warren was a great organizer. Eisenhower told me he had decided to appoint Warren because Warren was the best organizer he could find. Finally he said to me, "Thank you very much," and that was the end of our conversation. And Warren got the job.

A few years later, I happened to be in Colorado Springs while Eisenhower was there recuperating from his heart attack and playing golf. One Sunday morning after a hard Saturday night, I was standing there in the bar at the country club drinking a bloody mary when Eisenhower came through the door and passed me and walked a few feet past. All of a sudden he turned around and walked back to me and pointed his finger at me and said, "Aren't you the fellow who didn't want Earl Warren on the court?"

I said, "Yes, Mr. President, I was."

Ike said, "You were right." And he turned around and went on out to the golf course.

However, I was not a part of the movement to impeach Earl Warren. I don't feel you can properly impeach somebody for making judgments you don't agree with. So I thought it was a bad idea. Besides, that was a John Birch thing. When the John Birch Society first began, Robert Welch asked me to join. I told him I couldn't because, although I agreed with some of their ideas, I thought they were too drastic and I didn't think a group like that had a place in partisan politics, which is what I was interested in. So when I ran for the Senate in 1962, I had some people say they were against me because I belonged to the John Birch Society and others say they were against me because I wouldn't join. The truth is I never belonged to the Birch Society, nor had any desire to.

MY INVOLVEMENT WITH EISENHOWER

When Eisenhower was running for president I had produced a television show for the Republican Party called "What's Ike

Like?" in which we had interviews with all sorts of people, like his caddy and the guy who washed his car and the guy who shined his shoes. Because of that and my other political activities I got invited to a White House dinner early in the Eisenhower administration at which Winston Churchill was the guest of honor.

Churchill was always an idol of mine. I had done a lot of reading about him, and I knew he liked to sleep in the daytime and do most of his work at night. So, on the day of the banquet in June 1954, I got as much sleep as I could, in order to be wide awake that night. I had received my invitation about three weeks before the dinner and I spent a lot of time trying to decide what questions I should ask Churchill if I got the chance. It's hard to keep from asking a man like that a dumb question. Of course I really didn't expect to have a chance to say anything more than "Good evening, sir," and "Good-bye" at the end before I made a quick disappearance.

There was a long table in the East Room at the White House, and I was way down at the opposite end from Eisenhower and Churchill. As I recall, all sorts of important people were there, like Lewis Strauss, the head of the Atomic Energy Commission; Milton Eisenhower; Bernard Baruch, the financier; Allen Dulles, the head of the CIA; and Postmaster General Arthur Summerfield.

At a dinner like that nobody can leave before the President leaves. Along about nine o'clock or so, Eisenhower excused himself. Then, one by one, the big wheels excused themselves and there got to be a few holes at our table. A few of the men who stayed were fairly far up in years and were nodding.

Churchill was sitting at the head of the table, smoking a long cigar and drinking brandy. I could see his blue eyes up there and he was just looking for someone to talk to. It might as well be me, I thought. Almost everyone else there was having trouble staying awake.

Finally Churchill said to me, "What are you doing down there, son?" He called me "son." I was about fifty then. He said, "Come on up here and sit down." I walked around and sat down in the chair that Eisenhower had left. Mr. Churchill asked me a few things about myself. I told him I didn't know how I got invited to this dinner, that I was low on the totem pole, and that I never thought I'd have a chance to talk to him and how much I appreciated it. He started to talk. I guess he just wanted to talk to somebody and I happened to be the lucky guy. In the wee hours, we were still talking. I finally got to the point where I could ask him the question I had been thinking about for three weeks or so. It sounds silly, but I said to him, "A man of your experience and stature, how would you sum up your philosophy of life in one sentence?" He said something to the effect of "That is quite a question, but I'll have a go at it. I suppose I would say that no matter who you are, no matter how much education and how much experience you have, no matter what position you hold, the decisions you make will probably be wrong. And that goes for me, too." He went on, "You don't have to have a lot of brains to make the right decision *if you have all the facts. Where you need the brains is to get the facts on which to make the decision.*" That's some advice I've never forgotten. And that night was a memorable one for me.

I got to know Eisenhower pretty well. For a long time I didn't think he was a very good president. I didn't understand what a great president he was until after he was dead. The reason I had my doubts about him was that he was so nonpolitical, just like Earl Warren. He didn't do much to help the Republican Party, which I thought a Republican president should do. He dragged his feet on making appointments from the Republican Party for eight years. He resented the word "politics." Eisenhower had a tremendous dislike for politics and for party. When Eisenhower was elected on the Republican side, after twenty years of having Democrats in the White House, he could have replaced all the Democrats. But he wouldn't do it—not during his whole eight years.

But after Eisenhower was dead I got to thinking it over, and I finally came to the conclusion that he was one of our greatest presidents. I decided that everyone in the United States—whether they're president or a machinist or a housewife or a nurse—has a job description. I decided that a president's job description consists of two things: First, he must keep us out of war. Eisenhower ranked 100% on that count. Not only did he keep us out of war, he got us out of the Korean War that Truman had gotten us into.

Second, he must advance the cause of freedom in the United States. And I gave Eisenhower a 95% rating there. I think those are the two jobs a president must do, and everything else—like Johnson running around turning off the lights in the White House, is just so much foam on the beer. So I came to the conclusion that Eisenhower was a great president.

THE 1958 CAMPAIGN OF WILLIAM KNOWLAND

My only complaint against Eisenhower, as I've said, was that he was not political, just like Earl Warren. Between the two of them and what happened in Bill Knowland's last campaign for governor in 1958, they just about killed off the Republican Party, especially in California. By then I was up to my ears in politics. I had been active in Knowland's campaigns for the Senate in 1946 and 1952, and for a number of years whenever Knowland couldn't appear to make a speech, he would send me in his place. I made several dozen speeches for Knowland over the years.

In 1958 Knowland decided to run for governor on the right-to-work issue. Goodwin Knight, who was also a Republican, was governor then, but when Knowland decided to run for governor, Knight went after Knowland's seat in the Senate. One Sunday that July I was out in the garage of my house on Crescent Heights Boulevard—the same house I've lived in for almost forty years—working on my sports car, which was a fiberglas custom car with a Cadillac Eldorado engine and a Lincoln Continental transmission. I owned that car until shortly after Proposition 13 passed, when I gave it to a friend of mine. Anyway, about ten o'clock in the morning I got a call from Bill Knowland. He said he had to be in Indio that night to make a speech, but the President had called him and he had to do something else. He asked me if I would go out there and give his speech for him.

Indio was a long way, and it was hot as hell out there in the desert in July. I got there about four or five o'clock in the afternoon. I met Knowland's local chairman and he took me all over the town and showed me how they had put up Knowland posters in all the windows. Then he took me out to where the meeting was going to be, and there was only one guy there. At that time Knowland was majority leader of the Senate and a delegate to the United Nations, and he was going to go all the way out there to Indio and only one guy showed up. They didn't know Knowland had had to cancel out and I was coming in his place. So we took this lone guy over and got him a bottle of beer and I made a speech to him for Knowland anyway.

After that I knew Knowland was going to lose. He was running against Pat Brown, who was then attorney general. About two weeks before the election I was invited to a luncheon for Knowland at Perino's. All the top Republican brass was there. As is so at most of these political things, there came a time during the luncheon when everyone got up and said what he thought. One by one these people got up and said Knowland was going to win the election by 100,000 to 120,000 votes. When it got to me I said, "I don't think I should say anything."

Knowland said, "Why not? You've been active in this campaign."

So I said, "I'm sorry, Senator, I hate to say this, but you are not going to win the election. You're going to lose because the people in this room and a lot of others, all they've done about your campaign is talk to each other. They haven't really gone out and run a campaign for you. It's just too bad and I hate to see it, but you're going to lose." And, unfortunately, he did lose. After that there hardly was a Republican Party in California until 1966, when Ronald Reagan came along.

THE NIXON-KENNEDY CAMPAIGN

In 1960, when Nelson Rockefeller and Richard Nixon were vying for the Republican presidential nomination, one of the top people in the Rockefeller camp called me and said they were looking for delegates. They knew I was well acquainted with the West, so they asked me if I would get on a plane with them and go on a tour all over the western part of the United States. I said, "Well, you know I'm for Nixon, and I'll still be for Nixon, regardless of this trip." They said, "We know that, but nevertheless we'd like you to go with us and introduce us around." I called up

Dick in the vice-president's office in Washington and asked him what he thought I ought to do, and he said, "Why don't you go? It's all right with me."

So I went, I didn't tell Rockefeller I thought he was wasting his time because he was very unpopular in the West. I think every candidate should have a chance. But we spent about three weeks flying around the West, and I don't think Rockefeller got six delegates out of the whole trip. They picked me up in Los Angeles, and we finally finished in Salt Lake City. I offered to fly from there back to Los Angeles so they could go back to New York, but Rockefeller wouldn't hear of that. He insisted on flying me back to Los Angeles, where we had started. So they flew 1,500 miles farther than they had to. Rockefeller had his private plane, I think it was a DC-6. It was very plush. It had a conference room and a bar. And he had a very brilliant group of people with him. Rockefeller offered to pay me for my time, but I wouldn't take it.

During World War II and while Eisenhower was president, I was spending so much of my time in Washington that I maintained a residence there. Between politics and the defense industry, I was in Washington about half the time. I had a room in a nice house behind one of the House Office Buildings, and an office at Fourteenth and K Streets, about four blocks from the White House.

While Eisenhower was president I used to lunch upstairs in a VIP room at Harvey's Restaurant near the Mayflower Hotel. That was where all the politicians hung out. You couldn't get in unless you had an important sponsor. I couldn't get in there until Nixon got to be vice-president—he got me in. Jack Kennedy used to eat there often, too. I talked to him some. I thought he was a hell of a nice guy and a great storyteller. But I thought he was a smalltime senator and he'd been a smalltime congressman. He'd practically never written a bill or done much work. As far as I was concerned, Kennedy knew very little about government. But he was a charming man, an actor—a lot like Roosevelt.

I advised Nixon not to debate Kennedy, because Kennedy had charisma and Nixon didn't. I thought that Kennedy, because he had a basic lack of knowledge of government, would resort to clichés, which he did. I felt that the general public didn't know too much about government and that Nixon would know much more than Kennedy, but would still lose in a public debate because Kennedy had so much charm. Also, Nixon was the vice-president then, and I didn't think he should treat Kennedy as a political equal. I didn't think a high office holder should give his opponent a chance to debate him on an equal basis. When we were talking about whether or not to hold those debates, I told Nixon two things: "First, don't debate him. And second, if you do debate him, never say, 'I agree with Senator Kennedy.' Always say, 'I'm glad to see that the junior Senator from Massachusetts agrees with me.'" I thought Nixon won those debates. But winning the debates didn't win the election. I've always felt that without those debates Nixon would have swept the country, but he gave Kennedy his chance, and Kennedy took advantage of it.

During that 1960 election, I was asked to direct the campaigns of Republican candidates from Southern California for the state legislature. After my experience with Warren and Eisenhower, I said I would do it on one condition: that the candidate for president, which was obviously going to be Nixon, would endorse all the Republican candidates in California. They said, "You'll have to ask him." So I did. Nixon agreed to do it.

I said, "I'll have to have that in a letter."

He said, "We'll get you a letter." And he didn't do it. I saw him several times, in Washington and in Los Angeles, and he kept saying he would give me the letter. But it did not come. Finally I gave him an ultimatum: I said I would not run the show unless I got the letter. Then I got the letter.

Nixon was nominated and planned to open his campaign against Kennedy in Whittier. On the strength of his letter I had arranged to have all the Republican nominees for the legislature sit on the stage when Nixon made his first major address as a candidate for president in Whittier. None of the candidates were going to say a word. Each one would have just had a little sign on the bottom of his chair saying, "Smith for 12th Assembly District." When Nixon came out to make his speech, I wanted him to say, "I endorse all of the party's candidates here on the stage." So I got the whole thing set up. I got hold of all the candidates, which was quite a task, and got them all to agree to come to Whittier.

I thought I saw a chance to put the whole party together. They were all running on the same ticket, so why the hell—unless we had a horse thief on the ticket—shouldn't they all be there and be all for one and one for all? The Democrats do it. I wanted us to be as smart as the Democrats for once. But as usual, we weren't.

At five o'clock the afternoon of the meeting, I got a call from Bob Finch. He told me that we would have to take down all the chairs, that the top brass of the party wouldn't allow what I had arranged. I said I wouldn't take them down unless I got a direct call from Nixon. Pretty soon I got a call from Nixon. He said the Republican National Committee had made the decision and the chairs had to come off. I said, "You tell the Republican National Committee to go screw themselves. I won't be at the meeting and I don't give a damn what you do with the chairs. But I'm going to tell every candidate what you guys pulled." The chairs came off and I told all the candidates why. A little while later, I was in Washington, and I went to Nixon's office. I told him I thought I got a bad deal, and I had his letter to prove it. We got into quite a row, and finally he asked me to leave his office.

Not long after that one of the leaders from Republican national headquarters called me and said Oscar Levant had spent two hours on his national television show attacking Nixon and they wanted me to go on Levant's show and answer for Nixon. I said I wouldn't do it unless Nixon himself called me because he and I had just had a big fight. So Nixon called me. And being a good soldier, I went ahead and did it.

During the show Levant cast some aspersions on me and my candidate. So I said, "Well, I'll tell you. Just move over from that piano for a minute, and I'll demonstrate." I took one finger and played a Brahms lullaby. Then I said, "That's how I compare to you as a musician—and that's how your knowledge of politics compares to mine."

Levant was very smart. We got down close to the end of the show and Levant said, "There's one thing that puzzles me. How could Mr. Nixon attract someone like you, who obviously has a brilliant mind?" I didn't have much time to answer, but I wanted to make sure I didn't leave any time for Levant to have the last word. I had been on many television shows, and I had learned how to watch the clock while I was on the air. I'm watching that damned clock. I watch it for about 30 seconds. Then there's 15 seconds, then there's 10 seconds, and then I say, "What has Nixon got? Brains. Guts. Talent. That's all."

And we went off the air.

I was speaking four and five times a week all over the country during that campaign. I debated Jesse Unruh and Paul Ziffren in Los Angeles, Wayne Morse in Oregon, the Burtons in San Francisco, and Kefauver and I had a debate at a big meeting of blacks in Chicago. It was a hot and heavy debate, but I knew the Republicans didn't have a vote there. I said the Democrats were using the blacks as patsies, that all the things they were being promised by the Democrats they weren't going to get, that if they wanted some real help, the Democrats had been in for a long time and they had never done anything for the blacks before and I didn't think they were going to do anything for them now. They ought to give the Republicans a chance.

After the debate was over, a couple of men came over to me and said they wanted to take me to dinner. I didn't know why, and I was kind of scared. It was way down in the black district of Chicago. They took me to a gorgeous place to eat, and we had a great meal. Finally I said to them, "It puzzles me why you fellows would invite me to dinner because I know I haven't got a vote in that crowd."

They said, "The reason we invited you is because you're the only Republican who's ever come in here and told us the truth."

During the 1960 campaign between Nixon and Kennedy I was Western Regional Director for the Republican National Committee. Nixon won all but two of the eleven states I was responsible for. On December 22, 1960, six weeks after the election, a party director named J. J. Wuerthner wrote me, "The real testimony to your effectiveness is found in the election results, with both Dick Nixon and Cabot Lodge [Nixon's running mate] winning in nine out of your eleven states. As you know, Howard, that's an excellent batting record in politics." I cherish that letter to this day.

I have always believed that Nixon actually won that election, but it was stolen from him by the Daley machine in Illinois and Lyndon Johnson's bunch in Texas. I was never so incensed in my life because I had my whole heart and soul in that campaign. But after it was all over, Nixon refused to file suit to have the result overturned, even though we had evidence of voter fraud by the Democrats. He said he didn't think the country could stand having the outcome of a presidential election held up and thrown into the courts, and he walked away from it. I was never so proud of a man in my life.

MY 1962 RACE FOR THE U.S. SENATE; THEN I "RETIRE"

In 1962 I ran for the U.S. Senate because I was disenchanted with Tommy Kuchel. He took over Nixon's Senate seat when Nixon was elected vice-president. I thought Tommy Kuchel voted with the Democrats on every crucial issue, and I thought the Republican Party ought to have a *Republican* U.S. Senator. As far as I was concerned, Kuchel's voting record proved he was not a Republican. Later on he joined Pat Brown's law firm, which showed I was correct.

The U.S. Senate was the only office I ever really wanted. I never wanted to be governor or be in Congress. I could have run for Congress half a dozen times in a safe Republican district, but I wouldn't do it. It just never interested me. I thought being in Congress would drive a guy like me up the wall.

Running for the Senate was absolutely the most fascinating experience I had until Proposition 13 came along. I was on the road for eighteen months. I built myself a mobile home with a toilet, a shower, radio, and television. I even had a sound system on top, and inside I had a printing press and typesetting equipment so I could go into a town and print posters and have kids hand out hundreds of them for me. I campaigned all the little towns and cities, some 400 of them. I didn't think I could do very well in the big cities, but I thought maybe I could get the country vote and beat Kuchel that way. I just had a ball traveling around the state in my van. I slept in it every night. The house where Nixon lives now was vacant for many years, and when I was near San Clemente I used to drive my mobile home out there between the house and the ocean and sleep beside the sea.

One night I had to give a speech in a place called Eagleville, and then the next day at noon I had to be back in Los Angeles to appear on a television show. I didn't realize it when I made my schedule, but Eagleville is way up in the northeast corner of the state, near the Oregon border. I had to fly to Redding and some ladies picked me up there and we drove most of the afternoon to get to Eagleville, which is a real small town out in the middle of nowhere. There were several hundred people at this banquet. Everyone sat at long tables and on each table there were several roast pheasants and mounds of wild rice. What a fabulous night that was. Afterwards two brothers put me in their car and drove all night on these little back roads to get me to Reno in time to catch a flight to Los Angeles in the morning. I think I got about 95% of the vote in Eagleville, but there were only a few hundred people in the town.

I spent $58,000 on that campaign; $25,000 of it was my own, and as I went along people gave me the other $33,000. I never had a finance chairman or sent out a request for money, and I had hardly any organization. I thought that was a hard job until we did Proposition 13.

Murray Chotiner was sort of the generalissimo of all the Republican campaigns in California then. When I was running for the Senate as a conservative, he and Nixon wanted Kuchel to get reelected. Kuchel was minority whip in the Senate, and Chotiner and Nixon used the argument to me that that was an important position for California to have. I thought that was an absurd argument because being whip of the minority party amounted to peanuts. He didn't have any power, and on top of that he voted Democratic. Nixon endorsed Kuchel, even though it was a hard-and-fast rule in Republican politics that incumbent Republicans weren't supposed to make an endorsement in the primary.

Then Chotiner persuaded Lloyd Wright, who was past president of the American Bar Association and was a very noted anti-Communist, to enter the race. They were trying to split the conservative vote. I knew the game was to make certain that Kuchel would be renominated.

I heard that Lloyd Wright was going to file for the Senate. I had been out on the road in my mobile home for a long time and

I was making much better progress than anybody—even I—expected. I came in to Los Angeles and went to see Wright at his office downtown. This was the last day of filing. I told Wright I had heard he was going to file, and I asked him if it was true. We had a very nice chat. He said he agreed with me that Kuchel was a Democrat. But he said, "I wouldn't consider filing under any circumstances because I'm going to Europe tomorrow." I left his office, and that afternoon Wright filed for the race and Ronald Reagan changed his registration from Democratic to Republican and became his campaign manager. I never held that against Reagan; he wasn't the one who had made the deal to beat me. I knew Ronnie Reagan when he was an actor and doing commercials on television and he and George Murphy headed up the Screen Actors Guild. They got involved in a big fight over attempts by Communists to take over Hollywood. I never was close to George Murphy, and I never thought Reagan would go into politics.

I was a distant third in the 1962 Republican primary for the Senate. Kuchel won by a mile, and Wright came in second. After the election was over, I decided to get out of both politics and business. By then I had several thousand employees, and I was one of the largest industrial employers in Southern California. It was a terrific strain. I had a huge payroll and a lot of problems. It got to be very hard to hire people who were good at their jobs because most people didn't seem to care any longer. A lot of my friends who owned their own businesses and were about the same age I was were dropping dead, and I found myself spending a great deal of time going to their funerals. I felt if I didn't get out, I would probably die in the saddle at my office. It was just too much for one man. So I sold all my companies—Erla, Femco, and Jarvis Manufacturing—to some investors from Chicago. They later relocated my companies in the Midwest.

I was well-to-do, with about $750,000 to my name, and almost sixty. I had a trimaran with a five-room house in the middle built in Taiwan. I was going to have it shipped to the Bahamas and go spend the rest of my life on it, enjoying myself. I had earned it.

Then I got mixed up in taxes and never went. My boat is under charter in the Bahamas to this day. I've seen it, but I've never been on it.

CHAPTER NINE

Here's What We
Must Do

THE VICTORY OF 13 proved to me, at least, that, by God, something can be done. Practically the only social-political development that I see that has happened in the last fifty years that is a turn in the right direction for the United States is Proposition 13, when at last the people took it upon themselves to reverse a trend toward disaster. I think everything else for fifty years has been a downhill trend. Everything is a big word. But generally speaking, the country has been going downhill. Sure, putting a man on the moon was a tremendous scientific feat. But it doesn't overcome the fact that we've got 40 million people out there who are functionally illiterate. Yes, we've made progress from a technological standpoint. But what kind of social and political progress have we really made? Progress to me is the welfare of the public, the enlightenment of individuals, and an increase in the atmosphere of freedom. And by those standards we haven't made any progress at all for fifty years.

But the victory of 13 in California and the passage of similar measures in many other states since June 6, 1978, has persuaded

me that America can still be saved, because the people are still
eager to save it *and can do it themselves*. These developments
have certainly restored my optimism. And as I view the America
of 1979, I see plenty to be optimistic about. America still has
more assets than any other nation in the world. We still have more
material wealth, more freedom and more educational opportunity
than any other country does.

If we fail as a nation, it will be only because we have grown
ignorant and permitted our own mistakes to create opportunities
for other nations to take advantage of. But success or failure begins
at home. I hope one thing this book and 13 will make more clear
is that politicians reflect the voters. If our public officials are not
worthy of our trust, it is ultimately our own fault, for it is we who
are responsible for them, not they for us. If we are indifferent,
our public officials will be indifferent. It is we who in a democracy
must set the patterns for the elected officials to follow. Real leadership must come from the private citizens of America.

We average Americans must create the climate in which leadership develops. Only when the American people exercise their
combined will with determined action and unrelenting energy will
America be saved from its own destruction. We as a people must
continue responding as we responded on 13.

Here are some of my suggestions for improving this country
and restoring it to the greatness it was born to:

1. ELIMINATE ALL PROPERTY TAXES

I would like to see property taxes cut out entirely, not just in
California, but in every state that now has such a tax. I hope 13
will start us in that direction. Let me repeat: property taxes are
inherently unfair because they have little or no relation to the
property owner's ability to pay. Income taxes are fairer than property taxes because they are related to ability to pay. I believe that
sales taxes are the fairest of all, if they don't apply to food and
medicine. When I'm paying the sales tax, I have to pay only as
much as I decide I can afford; otherwise, I don't buy the item.
I've got some control over my money. And sales taxes are easier
and cheaper to collect.

In short, while total tax levels should be reduced, the property tax burden should be shifted to income, sales, and other forms of taxes.

2. ENCOURAGE MORE PUBLIC PARTICIPATION IN THE PUBLIC BUSINESS

The Declaration of Independence says:

> We hold these Truths to be self-evident, that all Men are created equal, that they are endowed by their Creator with certain unalienable Rights, that among these are Life, Liberty, and the Pursuit of Happiness—That to secure these Rights, Governments are instituted among Men, deriving their just Powers from the Consent of the Governed, that whenever any Form of Government becomes destructive of these Ends, it is the Right of the People to alter or to abolish it.

Our job is to make these truths *more* self-evident.

The authors of the Declaration had a complaint about bureaucrats, even back in those days. They blamed the King of England because "He has erected a Multitude of new Offices, and sent hither Swarms of Officers to harass our People, and eat out their Substance."

And in their timeless and deathless words they held the King responsible "For imposing Taxes on us without our Consent."

Two hundred and three years have passed since those words were written. And I have lived for seventy-six years, most of them observing and participating in politics and government, and I still haven't come across any words that state the truth any better than those words drafted by Thomas Jefferson and his fellow patriots.

"Life, Liberty, and the Pursuit of Happiness"—not "Life, Liberty, and Welfare or Food Stamps." "Governments derive their just Powers from the Consent of the Governed." When government stops serving the proper ends, "It is the Right of the People to alter it." No more "Swarms of Officers, eating out their Substance" on the hard-earned money of the taxpayers, feeding at the public trough. And, as almost every school child knows, "No taxation without representation." In a very real sense, the American Revolution was the first American tax revolt. Proposition 13 simply followed in that hallowed tradition.

Unfortunately, we've gotten into a situation in the last half century or so—I trace it back to the election of Franklin Roosevelt and the beginning of the New Deal—where government power no longer comes from the consent of the governed. Government power today comes from the ignorance of the governed, whom the politicians and bureaucrats have set out to discourage from participating in the political process, except for voting, and the people in power would be just as happy if the people they rule didn't even bother to vote. By excluding the masses of the people, those in government have succeeded in transferring government power to the consent of the politicians.

In a dramatic moment during the Watergate hearings, Gordon Strachan, a young aide to Bob Haldeman, told the Senate Watergate Committee and millions of people who were watching the hearings on television that his advice to other young people who were considering a career in politics was to stay out of politics and go into something else. I think Strachan was undoubtedly under emotional strain when he said that. He had to have something to strike back at. I think it's a real shame that they got those young guys involved in the whole mess.

I want to stress the fact that I think Gordon Strachan was wrong in his advice to young people. This is a political country, a self-governing people, not a dictatorship, and if everybody stays out, things will only get worse—not better. The trouble is, participation in the political process has deteriorated to the point that there's really no such thing as a political party in this country any more. There's no Democratic Party and there's no Republican Party. In the Republican Party, only about ½ of 1% are active in politics, and in the Democratic party only about 1% are involved. Most of the elections in the country these days are nothing more than a contest between the Republican Women's Clubs and the AFL-CIO.

In selling Proposition 13, we had to talk people out of that well-entrenched idea that they couldn't do anything, that they had only one vote each and it didn't count for anything. There is a very dangerous trend in this country: people become disgusted with politics, so they drop out of the political parties. Unfortunately, the next step is for those people to drop out of the political process altogether; they don't even bother to vote. On 13 there were 5.6 million registered Democrats in California, and 68% of them voted. There were 3.5 million Republicans, and 75% of them voted. But out of the 750,000 registered voters who declined to state a party, only 50% voted. And on top of that, there were another 5 million people in California who were eligible to vote, but who didn't even bother to register. Those are the ones we have to reach—the ones who have given up on the political process. We have to get them back into it, so that our country will become a better place.

I don't have a brief for either the Democratic or Republican party, but if you have a free country without political parties, there's no place that you can lay the responsibility for bad government. You've got to lay it on individual politicians, but they're so many of them that that doesn't do any good. Britain has the vote of confidence. But here we have fixed terms. I guess fixed terms are better, but the politicians don't have to keep selling their ideas to the people, except every two or four or six years.

We need to have a situation where the people can say the Democratic Party is responsible for this disaster or the Republican Party is responsible for that disaster. *We must have a place to put responsibility for our political decisions.* People say political parties are machines and they're not any good. To some extent, that is true. But generally speaking, for a country of this size, if you have two strong political parties you've got accountability. I like it when the president has a very narrow margin in Congress and the Senate from his own party. But just a very narrow one, so you don't have a bulldozer effect the way we've had for all these years with one party in such an overwhelming majority.

I don't like the controlling party in government to have such numbers that they can absolutely negate the minority. I don't want a monopoly in this country for the Democrats or the Republicans. Because then in effect you have a one-party system, the way they do in totalitarian states. A monopoly is bad, whether it's in the oil business or the wheat business or the government business, except that it's ten times worse if it's in the government business. The political balance between the two parties should be close enough so that if the President and his party have a program, by God, they ought to be able to sell it to a majority of the people. And if they can't sell it to a majority of the people, no matter what party they're in, then that program should go down the drain. I'm satisfied that if we have two strong parties in the United States, it will benefit all the people, the whole country.

3. ONLY THE KNOWLEDGE THAT THE PEOPLE CARE WILL KEEP THE POLITICIANS HONEST

Proud as I am of Proposition 13, it disturbed me in one sense. Our overwhelming victory showed that people have contempt for government. It's unfortunate that the politicians have forced the people to feel that way. I think the people would like to trust their government; I know I would like to. I think people dislike having to feel contempt for their government. I think they would like it much better if they were able to look at government with a smile and say, "These people are doing what I want them to do." And I hope 13 will start things in that direction, will help return government to something we can all be proud of.

The problem is that we don't really have representative government today. Is anybody going to tell me that the people in Congress and the state legislatures and on the city councils and the school boards *really* represent the people of the United States? No way. If they did, we wouldn't have gotten almost 4.5 million votes for 13 and received so many more votes than the candidates for governor did.

The only way we can have truly representative government and be able to take pride in our government is to have a better caliber of people to serve in office. If one man can run General Motors or Union Oil, then one man should be able to run the country, and we ought to be able to find people who can do a good job in all the elective offices—from the school board and the board of supervisors all the way up to the top offices.

Unfortunately, we usually seem to elect people to office without the ability to do the job. We have a low grade of people who get elected to public office. They have big mouths and big stomachs, but they also have very small IQs. You get some two-bit politician who's lucky enough to put together a coalition of a few special-interest groups, who has some hocus-pocus program, and can raise enough money, and before you know it, he gets himself elected.

I'm sorry to have to say that once a politician gets into office, he becomes a member of another nation, another club, another society. His feeling after he gets elected seems to be, "The job of our society is to exploit the people in that society I used to belong to before I got here." That's what politics has degenerated into. After the politician gets into office his interests become entirely different from the interests of the people he's supposed to represent. So he leaves John Doakes, the average voter, out to fend for himself. The name of the game for politicians is "Double-cross the Boob." And the boobs are all of us on the outside. John Q. Public must control the Government, or the Government will control John Q. Public.

And so, in spite of what Gordon Strachan said when he was down, we must attract a better class of people into politics. There always have been—and there still are—a few politicians who have the idea that they're supposed to vote their consciences, regardless of what their constituents think. I have a lot of respect for a guy who stands up and votes against what his own best interests are, if he has the guts to do it and he thinks he's right.

During the past twenty or thirty years, the best way to be elected or reelected is not to take a stand on anything. That has turned out to be a very successful formula for election. As Sam Rayburn, the former Speaker of the House of Representatives, once said, "In order to get along, you have to go along." Going along, or compromising yourself all the time, means in effect that you can't make any hard decisions; you make only the easy ones.

The more people who take an interest in our political system, the greater the pool of talent to draw from when we choose our leaders, and the more responsive our leaders will be to our wishes. I hope we will elect the kind of people to office who will serve our interests, instead of their own. At the same time, I want the leaders to have the freedom and the courage to say to us once in a while, "I know what you want, but I know more about this than you do. I'm going to vote against your desires and against my own best political interests in order to do what I think is right. I'm going to try to convince you that I am right, but if I fail, I'm not afraid to take the consequences and have you vote me out of office." Those are the type of people we need in office.

4. CURTAIL THE POWER OF POLITICIANS BY LIMITING THE NUMBER OF GOVERNMENT EMPLOYEES

Politicians are elected to do what the people pay them to do: to represent the will of the people and serve the best interests of the country. Unfortunately, we've gotten into a situation in this country where the number-one objective of most politicians is to get a lot of people to work for them. By using that scheme, they can increase their chances to be reelected. They don't look at the real layers on layers of fat in the bureaucracy. The politicians need those mules in their offices and out there in the other branches of government to be working for them in order to increase their own power.

Waste and inefficiency in government happens because the guy working for government has neither an investment to protect nor any responsibility to anything but holding onto his job. Civil service is an organization where you do nothing, you think nothing, you innovate nothing, you make sure you don't rock the boat. The only thing you're there for is to retire and get a pension. There's really no incentive to do anything. There are some exceptions all along the line, but generally it's a lush life in government.

An even bigger problem than the size of the bureaucracy in all the executive branches of government is the size of legislative staffs. The 535 members of the Senate and the House of Representatives have about 17,000 employees on their own staffs and their committee staffs. Each of the two senators from California—Cranston and Hayakawa—spends more than $1 million a year on staff and office expenses. In fact, by mid-1978, after he had been in office just a little more than a year, Hayakawa had 76 people on his staff and the highest payroll in the Senate. And in California, the 80 members of the Assembly spent almost $25 million to staff and run their offices in 1977. That's just too much.

One solution is to cut the size of the legislative staffs. I think there should be a limit on the number of employees a legislator can have. A senator used to have two or three people on his staff; now he has twenty or thirty times that many. It's because government is sticking its nose in too many places where it shouldn't be. We have to begin by cutting off their money, which will limit the number of people on their staffs and force them to do what they should be doing, and no more.

Having huge legislative staffs means that the staff members become more powerful than the guy they work for. He can't keep track of all they're doing. He has to take their word for everything, including how he should vote. He hires experts. Then he figures he has to take their advice on how to vote because they know more than he does. So we're being run by nonelected people— people we've never heard of and can't hold accountable.

On top of that, we have a number of people on the public payroll whose only job is to try to make the public payroll larger. The counties and the cities have lobbyists in the state capitals, and the counties, the cities and the states all have their own lobbyists in Washington. And each one of these lobbyists has one major task: to get as much money for the place he represents as he can. The successful government lobbyist is the one who cons the federal or state government into giving his state or city or county the most money. You've got representatives of fifty states and thousands of cities and counties acting like pigs at a trough. The net effect is that you need more food than you would if you didn't have all those lobbyists. That costs the taxpayers a lot of money.

Of course the Federal Government encourages all this. They've got a racket where they'll say to California, "We have this program here to breed butterflies with carrots. We'll give you $10 million to come up with a hybrid of a butterfly and a carrot. But you've got to put up $10 million, too. Now, if you don't do it, some other state will, and they'll get this $10 million we have." It never occurs to them that they shouldn't spend the $10 million; it's just a question of who is going to be the first lucky customer to get it. And all this is just a promotion to not only steal the money from the taxpayers for useless things, but to obtain more power over people. We must put an end to this fraudulent and costly cycle.

5. FOUR CRUCIAL WORDS: "GOVERNMENT MUST BE LIMITED"

About two hundred years ago, Thomas Paine said, "Government, even at its best, is but a necessary evil; in its worst state, an intolerable one." More recently, Woodrow Wilson declared, "Liberty has never come from the government. The history of liberty is the history of the limitation of governmental power, not the increase of it."

Those are two quotes that summarize the meaning of Proposition 13—an effort to reestablish the basic principle of free government: "Government must be limited." Those four words tell the whole story; if government is not limited, tyranny follows.

Government's proper role is to do what people cannot do for themselves: no more, and no less. We must stop asking more than that from our elected officials. By the same token, our office holders, along with the bureaucrats, must stop trying to provide more services than are needed, to stop attempting to do for people what they can already do for themselves. I am not advocating that we allow anyone who is truly poor to go without the essentials of life, such as food, clothing, shelter, and medical care. But we must insist that those who can take care of themselves *do* take care of themselves, instead of permitting them to live off the taxpayers.

I think the best thing that ever happened to me was something I didn't appreciate at all at the time—when my father refused to sign the note for me to buy that newspaper back in Magna. He just said flat out, "I've got four other kids, I'm not going to sign your note." And I thought to myself, "How cruel he is. He could sign the note. He's good for the money." But he was smarter than I was. He knew that if he forced me to rely on myself, I'd do it on my own and amount to something. And I want to tell you, I appreciated that when I got old enough to have an ounce of brains. I think if my old man had signed that note, I wouldn't be what I am today.

Maybe the best way to define what I believe in is as a Republican, a mainstream Republican, at least as I understand that term. A guy who doesn't want to spend more money than you take in, who wants to cut the government down to the size it ought to be, who wants to stop using public funds for the reelection of office holders, who wants to make sure that the programs that get enacted are productive and not destructive to the country, who wants to try to improve the attitude of the people of the United States, who wants to have a strong national defense, superior to any other country, but who wants to keep us out of war unless it's absolutely necessary for the defense of the country.

6. A DRASTIC OVERHAUL
OF OUR PUBLIC SCHOOLS

Next, I hope that Proposition 13 will result in a regeneration of our schools. This country was built on a statement: "Know the truth, and the truth shall set you free." I believe that and I always try to tell the truth outspokenly, whether my audience wants to hear it or not. I tell some people, "I'm sorry to say this, but when you know the truth, I think it will make you sick."

I believe that the school system is at the bottom of much that is wrong with this country. They no longer teach the principles of liberty and freedom. I think that unless we can rectify this, it will eventually obliterate freedom in this country.

In my view, the educational system in this country went wrong twenty-five or thirty years ago under the philosophy of Dr. Benjamin Spock, the philosophy of permissiveness. The schools taught the children their interpretations of Dr. Spock's philosophies, which told the kids they can do their own thing, they don't have to work, they don't have to assume any responsibility. Because if they don't want to take care of themselves the country has the resources to take on the obligation of providing them with bread and butter and shoes and surfboards and whatever else they want.

And so the kids grow up under the effects of this national disease of permissiveness, learning that thrift is bad, work is for the dummies, and everybody has the inalienable right to do his or her own thing. When you inculcate that kind of idea into people who really don't know any better, you are creating a terminal cancer on the civilization of the United States. It is shocking to read that about half of the youngster who graduate from high school are functionally illiterate. You can't expect DuPont or IBM or Times-Mirror or CBS to want to hire people that are functionally illiterate and start them at minimum wages that are dictated by the government and the unions. That would bankrupt the companies that hired them. That's what the school system's doing.

What can we do about the failings of the school system? I think the first step is to get them back into teaching the basics, like reading, writing, arithmetic, American history, and civics. Let the schools teach the youngsters of this country how the government works and what freedom really means and the difference between freedom and a dictatorship and the difference between right and wrong.

Proposition 13 will generate pressure for better schools because it will force the schools, just like every other part of government, to cut out the frills and get back to the necessities. It will take away the power of the school boards to raise all the money they want. It will create a hell of a lot of resistance in the legislature to vote blindly for whatever the schools want. It will force the schools to cut their curricula. I got the shock of my life when I found out there are about 150 different courses available in kindergarten through twelfth grade in the Los Angeles Unified School District. I don't think you *can* teach 150 different subjects. They should be forced to reduce their curricula to just a few subjects so that they can teach those courses properly. As it is, with them teaching far too many courses in the schools, nobody can teach them properly, nobody understands them and nobody learns that much from them.

During the 13 campaign the California Teachers Association put out a bulletin warning what would happen if 13 passed. The CTA said that among the cuts 13 would cause would be community services, meals for needy pupils, child development centers, summer schools, regional occupation centers, and adult education programs.

What do any of those have to do with educating children? Take summer schools, for instance. They're nothing more than a baby-sitting program. Most of them got shut down after Proposition 13 won, and I couldn't have been more pleased. If the parents don't want to do their own baby-sitting, they should hire baby-sitters with their own money, instead of forcing the taxpayers to pay for the huge bill.

We don't need programs in the schools like driver education—which the insurance companies say are totally worthless; finger-painting, and ethnic studies. If the kids are interested enough to study their own cultures, they'll do it on their own. I'm not just talking about black studies and Indian studies and Latino studies. I would be just as opposed to courses in white studies.

During the campaign, the *Anaheim Bulletin* reported that a community college down there actually offered a course in surfing. One boy who enrolled in the course found out that the instructor was apparently making money off the students on the side by steering them to his friends, who would sell surfboards to the students. This kid who had enrolled in the course was so turned off that he didn't go to any classes. Then he received his report card, and guess what his grade was in surfing? An A—that's what. "A certified surfer in the eyes of the state," as the May 27, 1978 *Bulletin* put it. There's no reason in God's green world why colleges should be teaching things like surfing. There are plenty of private surfboarding schools around for those who want to learn how to surf and can afford it.

Even Proposition 13 did not wake up some school officials, such as those on the Los Angeles City School Board—at least it didn't wake them up immediately. Two weeks after 13 passed, the school board appropriated $5,000 to purchase twenty bicycles—at $250 apiece!—to give to students in a pilot program so they could pedal to San Diego. The school board also provided in its 1978–1979 post-13 budget for the hiring of six piano tuners at a cost of $100,241, not to mention four brass and percussion instrument technicians at an annual cost of $68,820. Perhaps they got the message later on; better late than never.

The teachers and the school administrators and the thousands of elected board members around the state put up a tremendous fuss during the 13 campaign. What they didn't say was that there was never any chance the schools were going to be shut down; state law required the schools to be open at least 175 days a year. What they didn't say was that whether 13 won or lost, the schools would still be in pretty good financial shape. Out of the $17 billion state budget that was adopted after 13 passed, $3.6 billion went to public education up to twelfth grade, and another $2.1 billion went to state colleges and universities, for a total of $5.7 billion, or more than a third of the 1978–79 state budget. *Tax Revolt Digest*, the bureaucratic mouthpiece, admitted in its December 1978 issue that: "Overall, schools received funding equal to 98.6% of their 1977–78 funding [after Proposition 13]. Stated another way, school funding is about 90% of the 1978–79 budgets" that the schools had wanted, due to the state bailout after Proposition 13.

Another thing the school apologists didn't say during the 13 campaign—or before or afterward—was that private schools are a lot more efficient than the California public schools are. According to state figures, the average yearly cost of educating a student in 1978 was $1,300 in the public schools, grades kindergarten through twelfth, and $6,000 per student at the University of California. But more than a million students were enrolled in private schools at an average cost of $600 per student per year in the elementary and high school grades and $2,000 a year at private colleges. That tells a lot about the monumental waste that takes place in public schools—at the taxpayers' expense.

So 13 must and should force a total reevaluation of the public school system in California, and a similar reevaluation on a nationwide basis would be very beneficial.

Actually, if I had my way, I would go a lot further than that. If I had the power, I would issue an executive order requiring that beginning next September, all the public schools would be closed for a year. In that year while the schools were shut down I would hope that parents could get acquainted with their kids. And we could clean out the deadwood and the moochers and the grifters and the grafters and the phonies in the school districts.

The only reason I came to this possibly radical conclusion is that if a patient is dying and the only chance you've got to save his life is a major operation, you've got to take that chance, even though it may cost the patient's life. He may still die. But if you don't operate, he's surely going to die. And as far as I'm concerned, the great part of the educational system in this country is a terminal cancer on the United States. So what do you do? You either let the country die with the present school systems or you make a radical operation in the hope that you just might save the school systems and the country.

If I could close down the schools for a year, I wouldn't do a thing for a few months. I'd let the disaster get big. Because you will never be able to revamp the schools if you do it piecemeal or program by program by program. I may be criticized severely for saying this, but I have yet to see anybody in education come up with an idea that's any better. Everybody in education and politics would be forced to take a long, long look at the school systems during that year, and so would the parents. When the Japanese took Java and shut off our supply of latex, we invented synthetic rubber. If OPEC shuts down our oil supply, we'll be forced to find an alternative like shale oil, or something else. We never move, and I guess it's a disease of this country or perhaps just a quirk of human nature—until there's a hurricane approaching. The operation is not the most pleasant thing in the world, but that's the situation as I see it in education.

I know my proposal to shut down the schools for a year is a radical one, and I know I will be criticized for it. But if I'm wrong, we'll just lose a year. If my critics are wrong, we might lose the country.

7. REAL SECURITY FOR THE ELDERLY TO REPLACE THE SOCIAL SECURITY SYSTEM

I hope 13's victory will encourage everybody to take a hard look at all taxes, particularly the Social Security tax. FDR proclaimed that Social Security was going to provide a golden age for every American over sixty-five. I was there when Roosevelt signed the Social Security Act in Washington in 1935. Money for old-age pensions was going to be raised from a payroll tax levied on both employees and employers.

Social Security has always been a fake. It has led millions of trusting workers to believe it was going to provide for them in their sunset years, and all it provides half the time is beans and water. Anyone with an ounce of brains and a five-cent pencil should have been able to foresee what was going to happen.

I could see that Social Security was not actuarially sound at all and that we were going to have a huge mess with it. And that's what has happened. The poor people get cheated on the money they paid into the Social Security system, and they can't get it out until it's no good to them. A kid who is working and paying Social Security tax isn't going to get one nickel of his own money back. He's paying for someone who has already retired. The guy who is paying the tax now has to depend on someone who is now four years old to make sure that he'll get something later on. That's because the Government uses the money it gets today for Social Security to pay for other things, and then it has to scrape together enough money later on to pay for each worker as he retires. If Social Security is going to work at all—and I have my doubts about it—it must be on a pay-as-you-go basis, so that each worker pays for himself, not for some guy thirty or forty years older than he is. Otherwise, the whole thing is going to fall apart sooner or later, just like the giant house of cards, the huge pyramid scheme it is.

Because I was self-employed I was able to put the money that other people had deducted from their pay for Social Security taxes into a bank account of my own. With all the money I put in and the interest on my money, I wound up with $900 a month, while the poor guy on Social Security gets about $300.

President Carter signed a law in 1977 that provided for new and much higher Social Security withholding tax rates. The new rates will result in employees and employers paying $227 billion between now and 1988. That's more than the entire federal budget for 1971, which was $211 billion. It's unbelievable.

The Los Angeles Apartment Association advertises in the paper for apartment managers every day of the year, and if we get three answers a month, we're lucky. Retired people rightfully do not want to work, because for every nickel they make, they lose one in Social Security payments. The only way you can get them to work is to pay them in cash and not record it—but this would be illegal.

A false sense of security accounts for a lot of cowardice. When a guy depends on his $300 a month, even if he's unhappy about it, there's not much he dares to say. The government's got him in a position where that's all he's got. If he opens his mouth against it, he won't even get that much. So they really have him by the short hairs. They've got him herded into a corral, like cattle in the stockyards. He knows that if he causes any trouble, it's going to get a lot worse. If the cattle in the stockyard all ran together, they could break down the fence and get out of there. But they're too frightened to do it.

It's exactly the same thing with Social Security. By the time people retire and find out how bad off they are, they're scared to death to try to do anything about it. And so I hope that what we accomplished in 13 will give all these people who are being played for boobs by the Government the guts to stand up and fight back. With a concerted effort, we can force the Government to pay the current crop of retirees enough money to live decently, and then put future generations on a true pay-as-you-go basis.

Besides that, if we can stop inflation through 13 and now our major program, the American Tax Reduction Movement, we'll help everyone, especially elderly people who live on fixed incomes, to be better off. The main thing, though, is to find a way to assure the elderly of a comfortable standard of living; not lavish, just comfortable. And cutting taxes and inflation is the first step.

8. FOREIGN POLICY:
A RETURN TO OUR POSITION AS NO. 1

When it comes to foreign affairs, I'm a conservative. I don't follow the John Birch line, but I agree with them about the United Nations. I want us out of the United Nations, and I want the United Nations out of our country. I felt the same way about the League of Nations. I was on the side of Walsh and Borah and Vandenburg when they tore the League of Nations to shreds. It has been sixty years, and I remember those debates like they were yesterday.

To me, politics is like war, and vice versa. There are only two results: one is total victory, and the other is total defeat. If you get 10 million votes in an election and the other side gets 10 million and one, you're totally defeated. There's no such thing as a moral victory. If one guy gets one more vote, he doesn't get just a little more power than the other guy, he gets all the power.

So it is in war—either victory or defeat. We should have applied that in our overseas wars in the past thirty years, but we haven't. Do you think the Green Bay Packers under Vince Lombardi didn't care if they came in first or second or last? The object in life is to win. In the end you're going to lose, everybody does. But while you're alive, the object is to win. However, in defending the country, a lot of people say we don't have to be first. I don't buy that at all.

It bothers me that we've been squandering our resources all over the world for many years, ever since the end of World War II. I was never very happy for us to transfer our technology and our scientific advances to industrial countries like Japan that compete with us. I don't think when we pour money into other countries it does us any particular good. I don't think it makes any friends for us.

In terms of foreign aid, I think the proof of the pudding was when Kennedy went down to South America and said he was going to give them something like $12 billion through the Alliance for Progress. Of course, he got roaring ovations everywhere he went. So we gave them the $12 billion. That's *12,000 million dollars*. Then we found out the housing we had given them had all disappeared. They burned it for firewood and they still slept under their cars. Then they said, "If you don't give us another $12 billion, by God, we'll hate your guts." And they hate us to this day.

I think we should put our own house in order; but I don't think that we should tell any other government how to run their country. We shouldn't prop up other governments with our money and our military might. I think we're obligated to make the United States the most productive, the most powerful, and the most secure nation in the world. The other countries should fend for themselves, just as we do. It's a tough world. And if we are to survive and prosper, we must be tough. We must look out for ourselves first.

SOME FINAL OBSERVATIONS

In the end, I have to ask myself the same question a lot of people have asked me: Why did I do it? I'm not sure I know the answer. I thought that because of my political experience and my legal knowledge and my knowledge of taxes and the fact that I had some money, I might be able to help the people who were losing their homes because they couldn't make the tax payments. If there's a chance you can accomplish something like that, I think you have an obligation to try.

I expect to keep on trying to improve the national condition with the American Tax Reduction Movement. Proposition 13 proved that the people were not numb anymore. The people decided to force the elected officials to stop playing politics and do what was right for the people of the United States. The people told the politicians and the bureaucrats to start being statesmen instead of opportunists. They told the politicians to stop thinking of themselves first and start thinking of us. They told the politicians we want leaders who will make the hard and the proper decisions, instead of being yes men for the public employee unions.

Proposition 13 proved that perennial losers can be ultimate winners if they never quit fighting. It proved that hope for America is alive and strong, and the days of the arrogant, cynical politicians are on the wane.

For all of these reasons I am carrying the concept of Proposition 13 to every state in the union through my tax reduction movement. The ringing acceptance of this great crusade has motivated people in every state to march and fight in the cause of guaranteeing liberty and freedom of choice for every American citizen.

My vision and prediction is that, sparked by Proposition 13, we will rededicate and reinforce the cause of freedom and the free enterprise system in the United States; we can and will control inflation, restore the value of our dollar and end our dependence on foreign sources of energy; and we will regain our position of moral and spiritual leader of the free world.

I am convinced that all of this can be done and will be done. The word is "Work," and the motto is "Charge."

INDEX